629.43 Caprara, Giovanni.
C
    Space satellites

10/87   24.00

629.43 Caprara, Giovanni.
C
    Space satellites

10/87   24.00

DATE	BORROWER'S NAME	
DEC 26 '87	Shawn Winter	
JAN 9 '88	Renew	

SPACE
SATELLITES

GIOVANNI CAPRARA

SPACE SATELLITES

Every civil and military satellite of the world since 1957

Illustrations by Amedeo Gigli

Portland House
New York

This © edition
published by Portland House,
distributed by Crown Publishers, Inc.,
225 Park Avenue South,
New York, New York 10003

Conceived by Enzo Angelucci

Created by Adriano Zannino
Editorial assistant Serenella Genoese Zerbi
Editor: Maria Luisa Ficarra, Victoria Lee
Black and white drawings: Egidio Imperi,
Valeria Matricardi, Roberto Rubino
Translated from the Italian by John Gilbert and Valerie Palmer

ISBN 0-517-61776-5

Color separation SEBI srl., Milan
Typesetting Tipocrom srl., Rome

Printed in Italy by SAGDOS S.p.A., Milan

The Publisher would like to thank NASA, ESA, CNES,
Selenia Spazio, and the space companies for kindly
supplying textual and photographic material.

CONTENTS

Introduction

This book brings together the most up-to-date and reliable
information concerning the satellites so far launched into Earth
orbit by various nations or by international consortiums, such as
Intelsat, of several countries. They include satellites for Earth
and ocean resources, for meteorology, for telecommunications,
for navigation, and for the science of space and our own planet.
In addition there are military satellites, these being condensed
into tabular form.
Three particular aspects of method and coverage need to be
mentioned.
Firstly, in preparing this encyclopedia, the principal criterion
I have adopted is that of chronology. The satellites are listed,
section by section, in order of launch, and this automatically
reflects the international development in technology.
Secondly, in the case of series of satellites of the same kind, as
with the three types of Soviet Molniya telecommunications
satellites, I have described the initial launching of the three
respective types.
Thirdly, I have not included manned spacecraft.
This is the first attempt at describing, on an international basis,
all types of unmanned satellites sent into orbit around the Earth
since October 4, 1957. Naturally, some accounts, notably those
relating to Soviet or Chinese satellites, are briefer than others;
the scarcity of information given out by these countries prevents
more detailed appraisal.
Obviously, given the enormous number of satellites involved, the
odd ones may have been omitted. Pleading human fallibility, I
shall be grateful to any one who takes the trouble to bring it to
my attention.
In conclusion, I would like to offer my thanks to my wife
Daniela of all the patience she has shown, and to Gianluigi who
is as yet unaware either of time or space.

GIOVANNI CAPRARA

Earth and ocean resources satellites

In the early 1970s, thanks to the experience gained with meteorological satellites, both in the USA and in the USSR, technology in Earth observation took another step forward. The objective, by periodic overflying of the whole planet from a polar orbit, was to study the geological features of land surfaces and their vegetation, as well as the vast expanses of ocean. It was recognized that a detailed survey of land and sea from an altitude far higher than was possible from any aircraft, affording a much fuller global view, could furnish valuable information for national economic purposes.

In 1972, therefore, NASA paved the way, with Landsat-1, for a new space activity: remote sensing.

This entailed the collection of solar radiation reflected from land surfaces (passive system) or of radiation artificially emitted and reflected from land surfaces. To achieve this, the remote sensing satellites were provided with sensors capable of picking up such forms of radiation and of using them to reconstruct an image of the area reflecting them. Naturally, not all materials reflect in the same manner: a desert will reflect radiation of a certain wavelength and a forest will send back a different wavelength. So it was necessary to utilize sensors capable of responding in diverse bands of the electromagnetic spectrum in order to formulate different maps according to conditions.

Among the optical sensors devised were the Multispectral Scanner Subsystem (MSS), the Return Beam Vidicon (RBV), the Thematic Mapper and the High Resolution Visible (HRV). The technological advance, as manifested in the development of all these instruments, was particularly marked in three specific areas.

The first related to spatial resolution, whereby the satellite gradually came to distinguish ever smaller details of ground surface, ranging from 80m (260ft) with the MSS sensor to 10m (32.5ft) with the HRV sensor.

The second concerned spectral resolution, namely the satellite's capacity to identify increasingly smaller differences among the material features of the areas overflown, ranging from the four spectral bands and 64 signal levels of the MSS to the seven bands and 256 levels of the Thematic Mapper.

The third applied to the optics of the sensor, the means of compensating errors and the scanning systems. There was a notable advance from the earliest complex electromagnetic forms of apparatus with oscillating mirrors to the later systems of electronic scanning with CCD (Charge Coupled Device) sensors.

The other type of sensor used for remote sensing was the microwave sensor. These included the Synthetic Aperture Radar (SAR), the Radar Altimeter (RA) and the Microwave Scanning Radiometer (MSR). In this case the instrument itself sent a belt of radiation down to the ground which was subsequently collected after being reflected back.

In practice every surface element detected by the sensors was transformed into

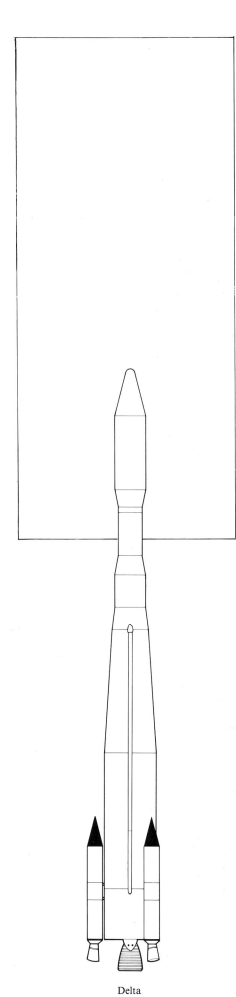

a digital electric signal which was then transmitted to Earth. Here too, the improvement of sensors and electronic equipment carried by the satellites made possible the increase of the transmission rate from 15 million bits per second (Landsat-1) to 85 million bits per second (Landsat-5); the higher the number of bits received, the more detailed, naturally, the potential reconstructed image.

The work accomplished by the remote sensing satellites was complemented by what was also done on the ground. The computers at ground stations collected and treated all the data received from the satellites and transformed this mass of information into images. These were presented in false colors which helped to identify particular aspects of the photographed surfaces. Thus the success of the work accomplished in orbit depended in large measure on the technological development of computers, ranging from the general purpose machines used in the early 1970s, fairly restricted in scope, to the more modern parallel processors now being developed. The individual processors of the latter type of computer can concentrate on portions of images, and the results are then integrated to produce the final, definitive image. This increases considerably both the speed of processing and the quantity of bits processed.

The United States initiated two major research programs to demonstrate the value of remote sensing. The first was called LACIE, from the initials of Large Area Crop Inventory Experiment, and lasted from 1974 to 1978, being sponsored jointly by NASA, the Department of Agriculture and the National Oceanic and Atmospheric Administration. In addition to justifying the technique, the LACIE program aimed to show that a more speedy and more accurate forecast of global harvests could be achieved. The inventory covered virtually the entire planet. In addition to United States territory, the investigation was extended, among others, to the Soviet Union, Australia, China, India, Brazil and Argentina.

The LACIE program was followed in the USA, from 1980 on, by the AGRISTARS program, after the initials of Agriculture and Resources Inventory Surveys Through Aerospace Remote Sensing. AGRISTARS was originally devised to cover six years but soon ran into considerable financing difficulties.

After years of experimenting, remote sensing is nowadays regarded as a fully developed form of technology for profitable use in the management of Earth resources; it is an activity which includes the administration of urban land, the production and health control of agricultural crops, and the identification of mineral deposits. Remote sensing is thus destined to become, after telecommunications, the second most important activity in space.

Delta

LANDSAT-1 /-2 (USA-1972)

Landsat-1 was the first satellite launched by NASA for the study of Earth resources (remote sensing), and originally bore the initials ERTS-1, Earth Resources Technology Satellite. The main body of the satellite was based on the structure of the Nimbus meteorological satellite; it was 3.04m (10ft) high, diameter 1.52m (5ft), and weighed 891kg (1,960lb). Two panels of solar cells, each measuring 1.2×2.4m (4×8ft), provided the requisite electrical energy. Landsat-1, which was three-axis stabilized, was equipped with two sensors, the Multispectral Scanner Subsystem (MSS) and the Return Beam Vidicon (RBV). The MSS, built by the Hughes Aircraft Company, was an optical-mechanical system which sensed radiation in the green, red, infrared and near-infrared spectral bands, with wavelengths from a minimum of 0.5 microns to a maximum of 1.1 microns. The surface observed by the instrument was a continuous strip of 185km (115mi), i.e. 34,225sq km (13,225sq mi), and scanning was done by a mirror that oscillated thirteen times a second. The images received had a resolution of 80m (260ft). The RBV television system

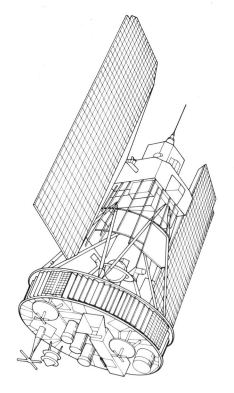

Landsat-1

comprised three 4,125-line cameras, built by RCA's Astro Electronics Division. It took photographs with a resolution of 70-80m (227.5-260ft) in the green, red, infrared and near-infrared wavebands (from a minimum of 0.475 microns to a maximum of 0.830 microns) over precisely the same area as that covered by the MSS. The satellite also carried a Data Collection System (DCS) for gathering data transmitted by remote ground stations, used to integrate the information provided by the images. Two wide-band video recorders, each with a recording time of 30 minutes, stored the pictures when the satellite was out of range of the receiving stations. The images were reconstructed on the ground in false colors, based on transmitted black and white photographs. Landsat-2, weighing 953kg (2,096lb), was essentially the same as the first but also carried a computer with a 4,096-word memory, and weighing 14kg (31lb), very advanced for that time. It could carry out 55 commands from the various stations, and could thus control independently all the operations performed by the satellite throughout 24 hours, even when it could not be "seen" by the ground stations. Landsat-1 and -2 were built by the General Electric Space Division. Management of the satellite in orbit was carried out by the Goddard Space Flight Center of NASA.

Launching and orbital data - Landsat-1 was launched from Vandenberg July 23, 1972 by a Delta rocket and was taken out of service January 16, 1978. The two recorders were damaged and ceased to function in August 1972 and July 1974, as did the mechanism for controlling position. Altogether the satellite transmitted over 300,000 pictures of the Earth. Its circular, sun-synchronous, near-polar orbit was 903-921km (561-572mi) high, with a period of 103 minutes, inclined at 99° to the equator. The satellite overflew the same point of the planet every eighteen days. Landsat-2 was launched January 22, 1975 also from Vandenberg. Sent into the same type of orbit, it was nevertheless synchronized with the first so that the two active satellites were able to scan a single point of the planet every nine days instead of eighteen days. The two recorders on Landsat-2 also broke down (January 1977 and May 1981), and there were problems, too, with the stabilizing system. Landsat-2 was deactivated in November 1979 and reactivated in June 1980. It was finally shut down in February 1982.

LANDSAT-3 (USA-1978)

The third Landsat satellite was substantially the same as the other two except for some variations to the sensors. Its weight was 960kg (2,116lb). There were alterations to the Return Beam Vidicon (RBV) system, which had only two cameras instead of three. Both worked in the wavelength between 0.505 and 0.750 microns. Furthermore, the dimension of the scene produced by the RBV was only a quarter of that supplied by the previous system, so that four images were need-

ed to cover the same 185km (115mi) swath of the Multispectral Scanner Subsystem (MSS). The resolution was improved, 26-40m (84.5-130ft), depending on the exposure time. In addition to the four previous wavebands, the MSS had a fifth, the thermal band, with a wavelength of 10.4-12.6 microns. The resolution of the images taken in the four traditional bands remained at 80m (260ft) whereas in the fifth band it was 240m (780ft). There was no change, however, to the Data Collection System (DCS) of the preceding satellites, and this collected data from a thousand or so remote automatic ground stations. Prime contractor for Landsat-3 was the General Electric Space Division, and the mission was managed by the Goddard Space Flight Center of NASA.

Launching and orbital data - Landsat-3 was launched March 5, 1978 from Vandenberg polygon by a Delta 2910 rocket. The circular, sun-synchronous orbit was 900×918km (561×570mi) high, inclined at 99° to the equator. The period of rotation was 103 minutes.
One of the onboard recorders failed in June 1979, and there were problems, too, with the MSS, particularly with the thermal waveband, which had trouble soon after the launch. In October 1981 the RBV system also broke down. The satellite was taken out of service in September 1983.

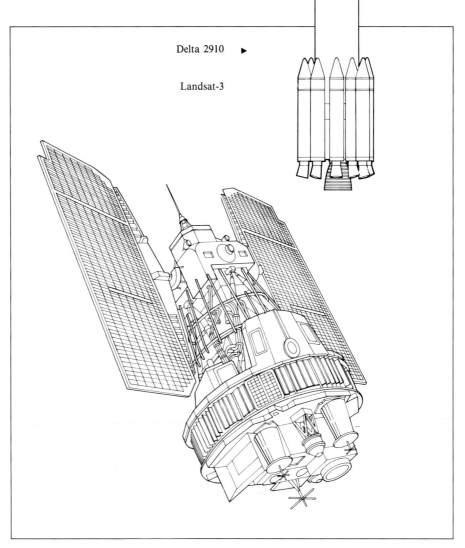

Delta 2910 ▶

Landsat-3

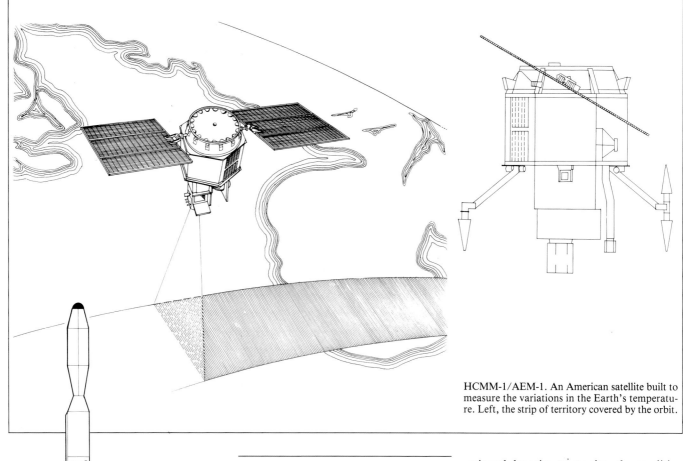

HCMM-1/AEM-1. An American satellite built to measure the variations in the Earth's temperature. Left, the strip of territory covered by the orbit.

Scout

HCMM/AEM-1 (USA-1978)

This was the first satellite built for measuring Earth temperature variations. HCMM (Heat Capacity Mapping Mission) was also known as AEM-1 (Applications Explorer Mission). The satellite was capable of taking measurements at medium latitudes in sample areas situated in the USA, western Europe and Australia; it recorded the minimum temperature and, eleven hours later, the maximum temperature. The main section of the HCMM satellite was in the form of a six-sided prism with a maximum width at the base of 63.5cm (24.75in) and a total height, including the antennae, of 162cm (63.2in). Made up of two modules, one for attitude control, data processing, communications, power and remote control systems, the other for the research instruments, the overall weight was 134kg (295lb). Three-axis stabilized, it was equipped with two panels of solar cells for recharging the batteries supplying the requisite energy. The satellite carried a two-channel radiometer capable of taking pictures in the visible and near-infrared bands (0.5-1.1 microns) by day, and in the infrared band (10.5-12.5 microns) during the night. It collected data from the surface strip it overflew, 700km (435mi) wide, with a resolution of 500m (1,625ft) in the visible waveband and 600m (1,950ft) in the near infrared. Precision in the collected temperature data was around 0.5°C. The information gathered on night and day variations of surface temperature made it possible to distinguish different types of rock, to pinpoint mineral deposits, to monitor the condition of vegetation by determining plant transpiration, and even to forecast the quantity of water generated by melting snow. Temperature differences were dependent upon the properties of the upper layers of the soil. The HCMM data was correlated with that of the other Earth's resources satellites, Landsat and Seasat. The Goddard Space Flight Center of NASA was responsible for the designing, production and testing of the satellites, as well as the handling of all collected data. Boeing Aerospace built the base module and ITT the instrument module.

Launching and orbital data - HCMM was launched April 26, 1978 from the Vandenberg air base by a Scout rocket. The circumpolar orbit was 560 × 641km (348 × 398mi) high, orbital period 97 minutes and inclination 97.6° to the equator. The satellite's group of batteries deteriorated eight months after the launch but this did not prevent it from transmitting a large amount of data up to September 30, 1980, when the satellite ceased to operate.

SEASAT-1 (USA-1978)

Seasat was the first American oceanographic satellite, designed to study and scan the world's oceans. It thus assembled information on winds, surface temperatures, currents, wave height, ice conditions, ocean topography and storm activity along coasts. Seasat was built in the form of two modu-

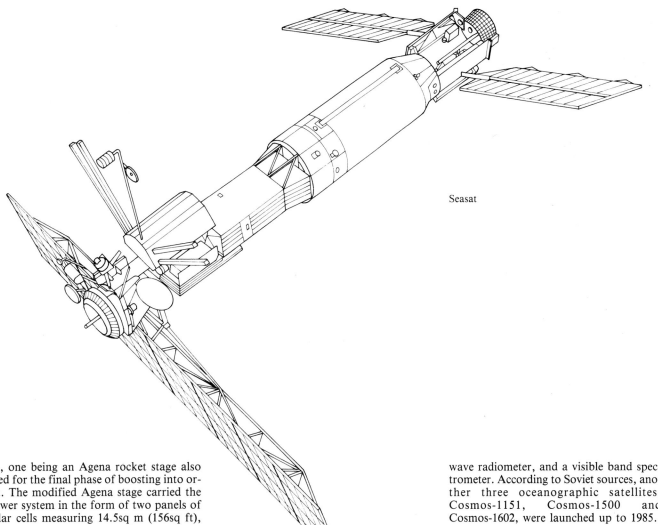

Seasat

les, one being an Agena rocket stage also used for the final phase of boosting into orbit. The modified Agena stage carried the power system in the form of two panels of solar cells measuring 14.5sq m (156sq ft), and producing 1,000 watts. The second module, forming the lower part of the satellite, accomodated the sensors and the five observation instruments, including the large synthetic aperture radar antenna, 10.7m (34.75ft) long and 2.1m (6.8ft) wide. The satellite was altogether 21m (68.25ft) high, the central section measuring 1.5m (5ft) across, and the total weight was 2.3 tons. The five instruments comprised a radar altimeter which measured with an accuracy of 10cm (4in) variations in the curvature of the oceans and the effect of gravitational variations on their topography, i.e. the tides; a microwave scatterometer, measuring with an accuracy of 2m (6.5ft) per second the velocity and direction of the winds; a scanning multichannel microwave radiometer to measure the water surface temperature with an accuracy of 1°C, wind velocity and ice cover, and to furnish corrective data on the satellite's radar according to the atmospheric water content; a visible and infrared radiometer taking photographs with a resolution of 5km (3mi) and assembling data to temperature with an accuracy of 2°C; and a synthetic aperture radar to provide high-resolution images of the ocean waves in clear or cloudy weather conditions, by night or day. The resolution of the synthetic aperture radar was 25m (81.25ft) over a 100km (62mi) observation strip. Seasat-1 was designed and built by Lockheed Missile and Space Company, Inc.

Launching and orbital data - Seasat-1 was launched June 27, 1978 into a circumpolar orbit 776 × 800km (482 × 497mi), inclined at 108° to the equator. The satellite encircled the Earth 14 times a day and scanned 95 percent of the ocean surface every 36 hours. On October 9, 1978, after 106 days of successful functioning, Seasat-1 interrupted communications as a result of a short-circuit of the power system installed in the Agena module.

COSMOS-1076 (USSR-1979)

The first Soviet satellite officially designed for exclusive study of the oceans. It provided information in the visible, infrared and microwave bands. Among the instruments on board were a multispectral scanner (MSU-M) with a visual field of 1,930km (1,200mi) and four spectral bands (0.5-1.0 microns), a radar, a three-channel microwave radiometer, and a visible band spectrometer. According to Soviet sources, another three oceanographic satellites, Cosmos-1151, Cosmos-1500 and Cosmos-1602, were launched up to 1985.

Launching and orbital data - Cosmos-1076 was launched February 12, 1979 into a near-circular polar orbit inclined at 82.53° to the equator. The orbital height recorded on the first day was 637-666km (396-414mi).

BHASKARA-1 /-2 (INDIA-1979)

During the late 1970s India built a satellite for studying Earth resources over the Indian subcontinent. The satellite, with experimental features, was called Bhaskara (originally SEO after the initials of Satellite for Earth Observation) and had the shape of a near-spherical, 26-sided polyhedron, its solar cells providing 47 watts. The total height was 1.19m (3.86ft), the maximum diameter 1.55m (5ft), and the weight 444kg (977lb). On board were two telecameras taking pictures in the visible (0.6 micron) and near-infrared (0.8 micron) bands. They served to gather information relating to hydrology, geology and forests. A second instrument carried by Bhaskara was a microwave radiometer operating in two frequencies (19 and 22 GHz), used for observing ocean surface conditions. The satellite's attitude control was maintained by a cold gas propulsion system (vertical and horizontal microjet). The second satellite, Bhaskara-2, was essential-

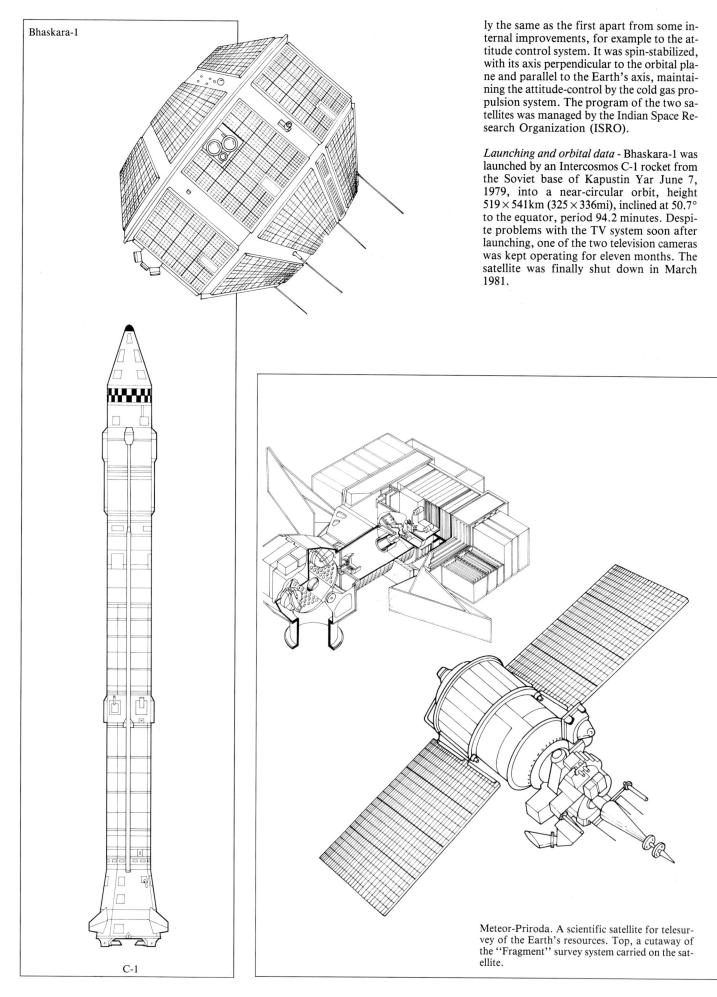

Bhaskara-1

C-1

ly the same as the first apart from some internal improvements, for example to the attitude control system. It was spin-stabilized, with its axis perpendicular to the orbital plane and parallel to the Earth's axis, maintaining the attitude-control by the cold gas propulsion system. The program of the two satellites was managed by the Indian Space Research Organization (ISRO).

Launching and orbital data - Bhaskara-1 was launched by an Intercosmos C-1 rocket from the Soviet base of Kapustin Yar June 7, 1979, into a near-circular orbit, height 519 × 541km (325 × 336mi), inclined at 50.7° to the equator, period 94.2 minutes. Despite problems with the TV system soon after launching, one of the two television cameras was kept operating for eleven months. The satellite was finally shut down in March 1981.

Meteor-Priroda. A scientific satellite for telesurvey of the Earth's resources. Top, a cutaway of the "Fragment" survey system carried on the satellite.

Bhaskara-2 was also launched from Kapustin Yar by an Intercosmos C-1 rocket November 20, 1981, and went into virtually the same orbit, with an altitude of 541×557km (336×346mi), inclined at 50.6° to the equator, period 95.3 minutes.

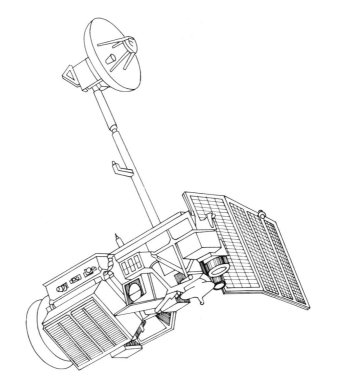

Landsat-5

METEOR-PRIRODA-1 (USSR-1981)

The Soviet Union officially launched its first satellite devoted exclusively to Earth resources in 1981, but the Meteor-Priroda (Priroda means «nature») program had already been started in 1974; from then on experimental remote sensing instruments were sent up in the Cosmos or Meteor-1 satellites, which were meteorological in scope. This space activity was intensified in 1978, and

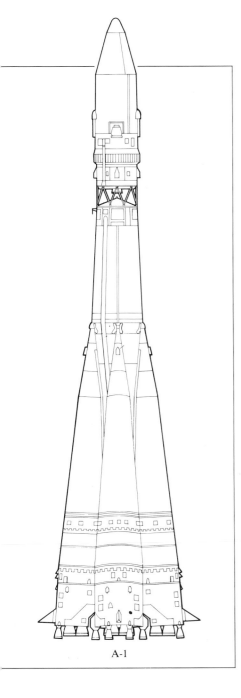

A-1

in 1980 a Meteor-1 (the thirtieth of the series) was sent into orbit, furnished with a remote sensing section weighing 600kg (1,320lb). In 1981 came the first satellite wholly devoted to Earth observation, known as Meteor-Priroda. This employed the basic structure of the Meteor-1 satellites, being three-axis stabilized and using an electric propulsion (steady-state plasma) for the attitude control system. Experimental apparatus in the earlier satellites had included two multispectral television systems (MRTVK) with mechanical scanners. The first (MSU-M) had four channels covering as many spectral bands with wavelengths ranging from 0.5 to 1.1 microns, an area of 1,930km (1.200mi) and a resolution of 1×1.7km (0.6×1.05mi). The second (MSU-S) had two TV channels (0.5-7 microns), a coverage of 1,380km (857mi) and a resolution of 0.24km (0.15mi). The data was recorded and transmitted to the ground stations overflown by the satellite. In 1980 three other types of scanner were tested: MSU-SK, with four channels, a coverage of 600km (373mi) and wavelengths of 0.5-1.0 microns; MSU-E, with three channels, a coverage of 28km (17.4mi) and wavelengths of 0.5-0.8 microns; and a third scanner called «Fragment», with eight channels, a coverage of 85km (52.8mi) and wavelengths of 0.4-2.4 microns. All three systems were carried by Meteor-Priroda in 1981. During the early 1980s it was established (according to a memo presented to the congress of the International Astronautical Federation of Stockholm in 1985 by J.A. Dyemardian and other members of the remote sensing research center and of the State Committee for Science and Technology) that the Earth resources satellites had high- and medium-resolution multispectral scanners with the following characteristics: MSU-V, capable of scanning an area 180-200km (112-124mi) wide, with a spectral resolution of 30-50m (97.5-162.5ft) in the visible waveband, eight spectral bands and a cycle covering the entire planet every

7-8 days; MSU-S, with a coverage of 600km (373mi), a resolution in the visible waveband of 150-200m (93-124ft), six spectral bands and a cycle of Earth coverage every 2-3 days.

Launching and orbital data - Meteor-Priroda-1 was launched July 10, 1981 by an A-1 rocket from Baikonur-Tyuratam into circumpolar, sun-synchronous orbit, at a height of 650km (404mi), inclined at 98° to the equator. These orbital parameters remained unchanged in the case of the other satellites devoted to the study of Earth resources.
The preceding year, June 18, 1980, saw the launch of Meteor-1, from Baikonur-Tyuratam into a polar orbit 561-630km (348-391mi) high, inclined at 98° to the equator. This Meteor weighed 3,475kg.

LANDSAT-4 /-5 (USA-1982)

Landsat-4 and -5 represented the second generation of American remote sensing satellites. They were designed with a standard module that could be used by other satellites; this was known as Multimission Modular Spacecraft and it provided four subsystems: power, attitude control, communications and data processing, and propulsion. The same standard module was utilized, for example, for the Solar Maximum Mission astronomical satellites. The two satellites possessed the same characteristics and each, with antenna and solar cell panel extended, measured 4m (13ft) long, 2m (6.5ft) wide and 3.7m (12ft) high. The launch weight was 1,941kg (4,270lb), and the electrical power available at the start of the mission was 990 watts. The two sensors carried were the Multispectral Scanner Subsystem (MSS) and the Thematic Mapper (TM). The MSS was the same type as had been used in the previous Landsat-1 and -2 satellites, with four spectral bands and a picture resolution of 80m (260ft). The TM scanned radiation reflected from the Earth's surface in seven spectral bands. The first five and the seventh (respectively 0.76-0.9, 0.63-0.69, 0.52-0.6, 0.45-0.52, 1.55-1.75, and 2.08-2.35 microns) provided improved resolution compared with what had gone before, i.e. 30m (97.5ft); the sixth band (10.4-12.5 microns), however, had a resolution of 120m (390ft). The TM produced data at the more increased rate of 85 megabits per second, against that of the MSS, which was only 15 megabits per second. Landsat-4 and -5 did not carry recorders on board because they transmitted data directly to Earth via the TDRSS satellite.

Launching and orbital data - Landsat-4 was launched July 16, 1982, from Vandenberg by a Delta 3920 rocket. Set into a circumpolar orbit at a height of 689 × 696km (428 × 433mi), it was capable of observing the whole planet in sixteen days, two less than its predecessors. On February 15, 1983, seven months after the launch, transmission of data from the Thematic Mapper ceased, due to a failure of the X-band transmittor. A second failure to the electrical power system subsequently reduced by a half the satellite's available energy.
Landsat-5 was launched, also from Vandenberg and by a Delta 3920 rocket, March 1, 1984; its orbit, too, was circumpolar, height 705km (438mi), inclination to equator 98.2°.

Toward the end of the 1970s France decided to launch a remote sensing satellite known as SPOT, from the initials of Satellite Probatoire de l'Observation de la Terre. Sweden and Belgium also took part in the program. The satellite's functions were to study the use of land, to investigate renewable resources (agriculture and forests) as well as mineral and oil exploration, and to draw up maps. SPOT consisted of a central square-based body, each side 2m (6.5ft). It comprised two parts, one, a standard module accommodating all the service systems (attitude control, feeding, telemetry and telecommunications, and handling of onboard activities), the second, a payload module. Instruments installed were two telescopes, 2.5m (8.125ft) long and each weighing 250kg (550lb), which formed the High Resolution Visible (HRV) system. Operating in the visible and infrared bands, it provided panchromatic (black and white) images in the 0.51-0.75 micron spectral band, with a resolution of 10m (32.5ft), and multispectral (color) pictures in three narrow spectral bands — 0.50-0.59, 0.61-0.68 and 0.79-0.89 microns — with a resolution of 20 × 20m (65 × 65ft). In both cases the width of the swath observed was 60km (37mi). The image taken through the telescope in a line crosswise to the satellite's direction was immediately collected by 6,000 photodiodes which transformed the light signal into digital signals. The HRV system's transmission rate was 25 megabits per second. The satellite, weighing 1,830kg (4,026lb), was furnished with a panel of solar cells 15.60m (50.7ft) long, producing 1,800 watts; energy was stored in four nickel-cadmium batteries. SPOT was provided with an information system controlling all the satellite's activities. In the event of anything going wrong, the system pinpointed it in order to prevent the trouble spreading. In such a contingency the onboard computer was programed to effect a reconfiguration. SPOT was designed by the

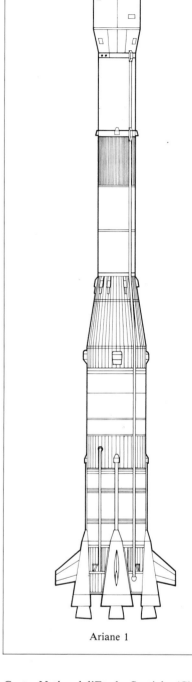

Ariane 1

Centre National d'Etudes Spatiales (CNES), the principal contractors being Matra, which also built the HRV system, and Alcatel-Thomson Espace.

Launching and orbital data - SPOT-1 was launched February 22, 1986 by an Ariane 1 rocket from the test site in French Guiana. The Swedish Viking satellite was launched by the same carrier rocket. SPOT-1 went into a sun-synchronous, near-polar orbit with a perigee of 818km (508mi) and an apogee of 833km (518mi), inclination to the equator 98.7°.

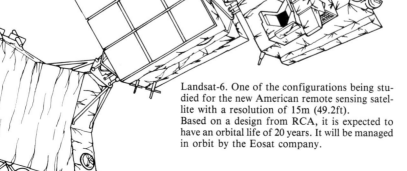

Landsat-6. One of the configurations being studied for the new American remote sensing satellite with a resolution of 15m (49.2ft).
Based on a design from RCA, it is expected to have an orbital life of 20 years. It will be managed in orbit by the Eosat company.

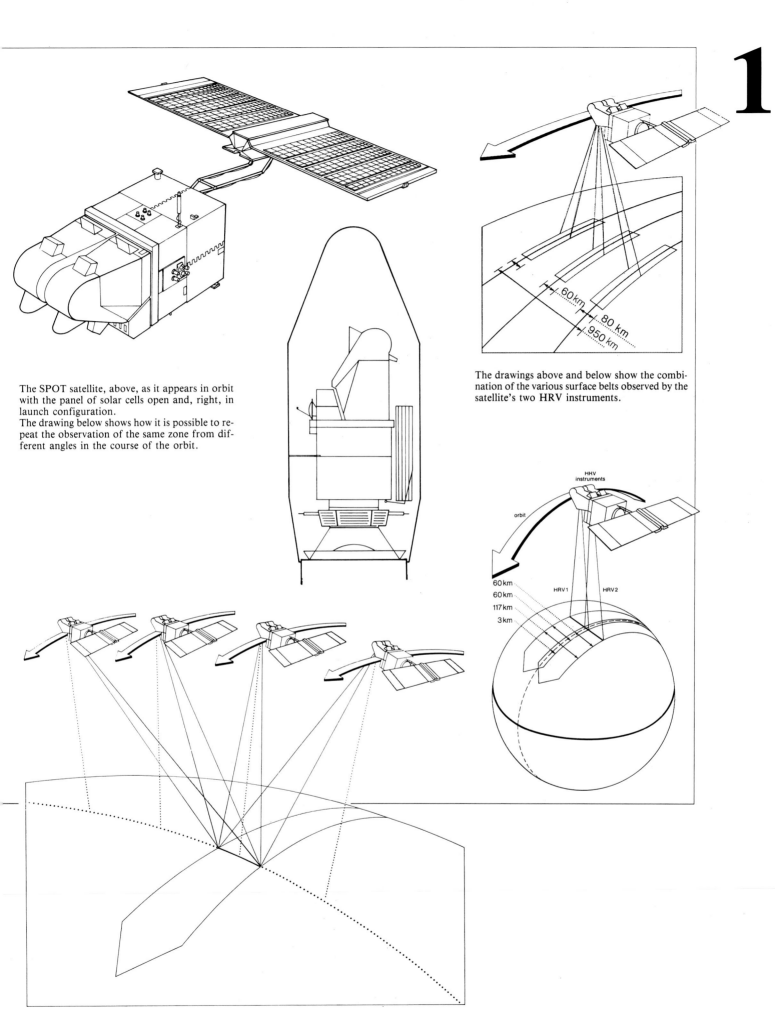

The SPOT satellite, above, as it appears in orbit with the panel of solar cells open and, right, in launch configuration.
The drawing below shows how it is possible to repeat the observation of the same zone from different angles in the course of the orbit.

The drawings above and below show the combination of the various surface belts observed by the satellite's two HRV instruments.

60 km
80 km
950 km

HRV instruments

orbit

60 km
60 km
117 km
3 km

HRV 1   HRV 2

MOS-1, standing for Marine Observations Satellite, is the first Japanese Earth-observation satellite and has been in development since 1980. Its primary objective is to scan the oceans with three instruments. MOS-1 is equipped with the Multispectrum Electronic Self-Scanning Radiometer (MESSR), which gathers land and ocean data over a strip 100km (62mi) wide, with a resolution of 50m (162.5ft), utilizing four spectral bands (0.51-1.1 microns). A second instrument is the Visible and Thermal Infrared Radiometer (VTIR) for collecting information on clouds, water surface temperature, etc. over a swath 1,500km (932mi) wide, with a resolution of 900m (2,925ft) in the visible wavelength (one spectral band) and of 2,700m (8,775ft) in the infrared (three spectral bands). The third instrument is the Microwave Scanning Radiometer (MSR), collecting data on sea ice, snowfall and water vapor at the ocean surface and in the atmosphere. Its resolution is 23km (14mi) in the 31 GHz band, or 32km (20mi) in the 24 GHz band. For land research, MOS-1 will be used for studying geological and energy resources, for land survey and for preparing crop inventories. The satellite is planned to have a technical lifespan of two years, and will weigh 740kg (1,628lb). Prime contractor for the program is the NEC Corporation. It will be managed in orbit by the National Space Development Agency (NASDA).

Launching and orbital data - MOS-1 is to be launched in 1987 by a N-2 rocket from the Tanegashima Space Center on the island of Tanegashima. It will go into circular, sun-synchronous orbit at a height of 900km (559mi).

In 1982 the European Space Agency was authorized by its constituent nations to go ahead with the ERS program (European Remote Sensing Satellite). The aim was to build a satellite for long-range scanning of land, ocean and coastal regions with instruments possessing all-weather capability. The satellite uses as its service module the same basic structure as for the French SPOT satellite, also designed for remote sensing. It contains the systems for attitude control, telemetry and telecommunications, and for

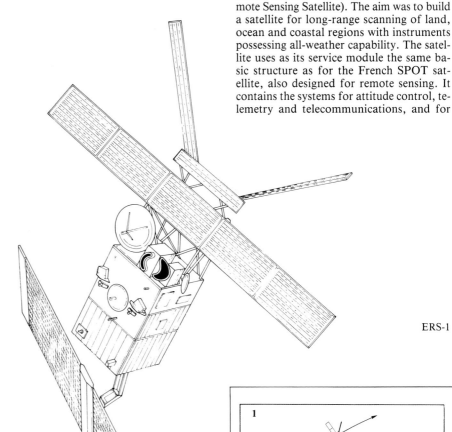

ERS-1

ERS-1. The satellite designed by the European Space Agency (ESA) to study the Earth's resources. The diagrams 1, 2 and 3 show survey techniques along the orbit, the strip of territory observed and the resolution permitted by the instruments on board. The diagram 4 shows the radar altimeter; the diagram 5 the laser reflector which will permit the accurate determination of the satellite altitude by the use of laser ranging stations.

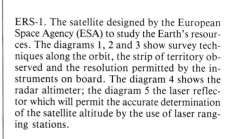

MOS-1

handling the satellite by computer. A panel of solar cells 11.7m (38ft) long and 2.4m (7.8ft) wide provides the necessary power, to a maximum of 2,600 watts as required for the payload. Three-axis stabilized, ERS-1 has a total weight of 2,160kg (4,752lb) and is 11.8m (38.35ft) high, the central section measuring $2 \times 2 \times 3.5$m ($6.5 \times 6.5 \times 11.5$ft). There are three principal instruments. The first is a Synthetic Aperture Radar (SAR) equipped with an antenna 10m (32.5ft) long and 1m (3.25ft) wide, for scanning the surface of an overflown strip 80km (50mi) wide, in any weather conditions, with a resolution of either 100×100m (325×325ft) or 30×30m (97.5×97.5ft). The same SAR can be used as a scatterometer for measuring the direction and dimensions of waves over a distance of 100-1,000m (325-3,250ft) with a tolerance either way of 25 percent. The SAR has been built by Marconi, Dornier and Ericsson. The second instrument is a scatterometer for measuring the direction and speed of surface winds within a velocity range of 4-24m (13-78ft) per second, with a tolerance either way of 2m (6.50ft) per second. It has been built by Dornier and Ericsson. The third instrument is a radar altimeter built by Selenia Spazio, which measures the distance between satellite and ocean surface, determining the height of the waves within a range of 1-20m (3.25-65ft) and with a tolerance of 0.5m (1.625ft). The same radar can also provide information on currents and wind speed, and on the topography of ice, defining type and distribution. ERS-1 which can transmit to Earth 100 mbit per second has a laser reflector that gives an improved definition of the satellite's altitude from stations in charge of following it. Prime contractor of the program is the German Dornier company.

Launching and orbital data - ERS-1 will be launched by a rocket of the Ariane family from the French Guiana site in 1989. It will go into circular, sun-synchronous orbit, height 675km (419mi), inclination to equator 98.10°. The satellite will overfly the same area every three days.

JERS-1

1

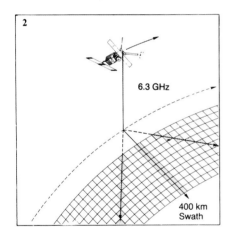

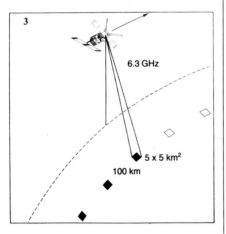

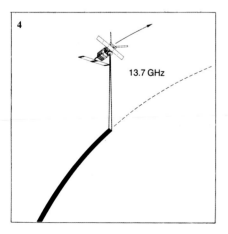

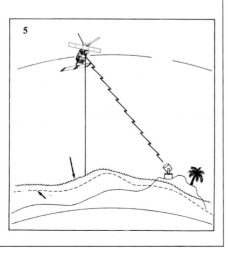

JERS-1 (JAPAN-1991)

Research on the Japan Earth Resources Satellite (JERS-1) began in Japan in 1980 as part of the NASDA program, while the development of the sensors was backed by the Ministry of International Trade and Industry (MITI). The main objective was to construct a synthetic aperture radar with optical sensor for use in all-weather conditions. The synthetic aperture radar will monitor the global environment, including natural resources, agricultural crops, forests and fish populations over a strip 75km (47mi) wide, with a resolution of 25m (81.25ft). The second instrument is a Visible and Near-Infrared Radiometer (VNIR) for gathering data in four bands of the spectrum (0.45-0.95 microns), with a resolution of 25m (81.25ft) over a 150m (487.5ft) swath. Other observations by the satellite will concern fire prevention and coastal survey. JERS-1 will weigh 1.5 ton and its projected technical lifespan is two years.

Launching and orbital data - JERS-1 is to be launched in 1991 by a H-1 rocket from the Tanegashima Space Center into circular, sun-synchronous orbit, height 570km (354mi).

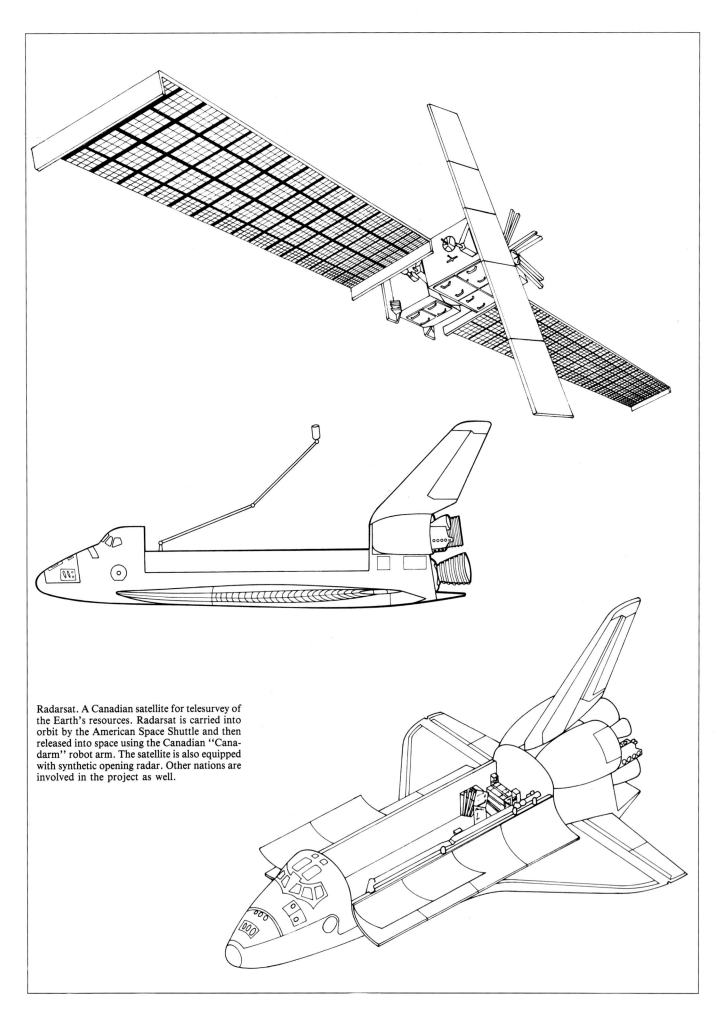

Radarsat. A Canadian satellite for telesurvey of the Earth's resources. Radarsat is carried into orbit by the American Space Shuttle and then released into space using the Canadian "Cana-darm" robot arm. The satellite is also equipped with synthetic opening radar. Other nations are involved in the project as well.

RADARSAT (CANADA-1991)

In 1985 Canada launched a program for building a remote sensing satellite, inviting foreign collaboration. The satellite's main instrument is a synthetic aperture radar developed by Spar Aerospace with Canadian Marconi and Canadian Astronautics. The radar observations will serve especially to monitor ice distribution to assist navigation in the Northwest Passage and to protect the oil platforms. The other instruments projected are an interchangeable multispectral sensor to scan a strip 400km (248mi) wide with a resolution of 30m (97.5ft), an electrical-optical sensor developed by the German MBB company for daytime monitoring of the ground, and an Advanced Very High Resolution Radiometer supplied by the American NOAA, for measuring temperatures and cloud distribution. The satellite will be formed of two modules, a bus containing the services (propulsion, attitude control, transmission systems, etc.), and a second part accommodating the remote sensing payload. Power will be provided by two panels of solar cells, with a span of 42m (136.5ft), producing 5.5. kilowatts until the end of the satellite's estimated life of five years. It is envisaged that the satellite will be serviced in orbit by the American Space Shuttle; in the course of maintainance further instruments can be installed. The project is managed by the Canadian Center for Remote Sensing, an agency of the Canada Department of Energy, Mines and Resources.

Launching and orbital data - Radarsat is programed to be launched by the American Shuttle in 1991. Its orbit will be polar, sun-synchronous, at a height of 1,000km (621mi).

TOPEX (USA-FRANCE-1991)

The Ocean Topography Experiment satellite (TOPEX), given the additional name of Poseidon by France, stems from a joint Franco-American program initiated by the Centre National d'Etudes Spatiales (CNES) and the Jet Propulsion Laboratory (JPL). Its purpose is to furnish a detailed topographic map of 90 percent of world oceans so as to determine the general circulation of the oceans and its variations, marine conditions, height of waves, wind velocities and ice distribution. Oceanic altimetry will be carried out by three types of instruments used at the same time: two radar altimeters for measuring, with an accuracy of 2cm (0.78in), the distance between the satellite and the ocean surface every 20km (12.4mi) along the trajectory; a microwave radiometer for correcting the variations induced by the atmosphere; and two systems of radiolocation for determining the height of the satellite. One of the two radar altimeters will be American, operating in two frequencies (Ku, C), the other French, in a single frequency (Ku). Of the two radiolocation systems, one, again, will be the American Tranet, precision 14cm (5.46in), the other the French Doris, precision 10cm (3.9in). The satellite will have a technical lifespan of three years, capable of being prolonged to five.

Launching and orbital data - TOPEX-Poseidon will be launched in 1991 from the test site in French Guiana by an Ariane rocket. The circular orbit will be 1,334km (829mi), inclined at 63.13° to the equator.

1

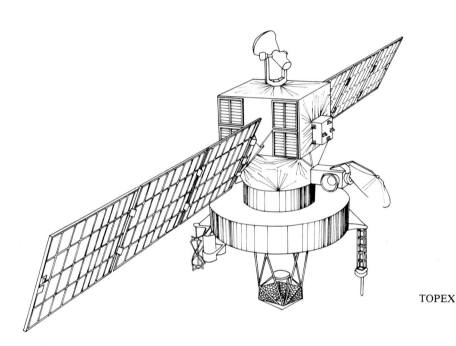

TOPEX

2

Meteorological satellites

The first practical field of application for satellites was that of meteorology. From orbit, thanks to the wide-ranging view afforded, it became possible to observe cloud formations and movements. Tiros-1, launched by the USA in 1960, proved the worth of such a satellite and of the data it collected.

Satellites have transformed meteorology, which has become a more scientific and less empirical activity, developing into a discipline which attracts an ever-growing number of researchers.

The fundamental problem of meteorology is to assemble environmental data from every corner of the planet, in the oceans as well as on land. So long as some areas remain to be discovered, there is no possibility of studying general climatic evolution because this results from the interaction of diverse environmental situations on land, at different latitudes, or at the ocean surface.

Satellite instruments have, to a large extent, fulfilled requirements which up to the late 1960s could not be satisfied because there were still many areas on Earth where climatic monitoring apparatus could not be installed.

Thanks to satellites in geostationary orbit at a height of 36,000km (22,370mi), it has also become possible to keep 30% of the Earth constantly under observation, and to photograph almost the whole planet using three satellites in geostationary orbit with a manual separation of 120°, using the infrared spectrum at night and the visible waveband by day. In addition to that from the information and pictures assembled, data can be obtained on the paths of cloud formations, on temperatures at the surface and in the different layers of the atmosphere, on atmospheric water content and on wind velocity — all essential factors for defining climatic phenomena.

The satellites used for this work are essentially of two types: some are sent into a near-polar orbit at a height of about 900km (550mi), so that as the planet rotates they can successively observe all parts of the Earth; others are placed in geostationary orbit at an altitude of around 36,000km (22,370mi), so as always to view the same "side" of the Earth, the rotation patterns of both being synchronized, and thus appearing from a ground station to be permanently fixed at the same point in the sky.

Meteorological studies are controlled at international level by the World Meteorological Organization (WMO). The use of satellites has made it possible to create a world meteorological service (Global Data Processing System) operating at international, regional and national levels. Internationally, the three World Meteorological Centers are located in Washington, Moscow and Melbourne, Australia. Regional centers exist in strategic areas such as the Caribbean and Central America. Finally, the National Meteorological Centers are concerned with the gathering and utilization of local information, within national boundaries. All three groups are closely interlinked, combining to provide a global system of meteorological information.

In 1978 the World Meteorological Organization and the International Council of Scientific Unions jointly launched the biggest meteorological research program ever undertaken. The principal aim of this Global Atmospheric Research Program (GARP) was to investigate and assemble a wealth of data relating to the Earth's atmosphere, and to develop and test appropriate instruments in order to increase the global knowledge in this field.

In addition to more than one hundred ground stations, meteo-research oriented ships, platforms and automatic aircraft, ten satellites were used in this ambitious project, six from the USA, two from the USSR, one from Japan and one from Europe. The program lasted 11 months, ending in November 1979, and all data was distributed for processing to 22 centers throughout the world.

The result of combining satellites with ground computers capable of handling the immense quantity of collected data has been an increase in scientific knowledge concerning the evolution of meteorological phenomena; it has also made it possible to extend the weather forecasting period to about seven days, albeit with variations of reliability, such information being used for general purposes and specifically for farming, transport, tourism, etc. The satellite-computer combination has also made it possible to predict the course of violent phenomena such as hurricanes and tornadoes, thus saving many lives.

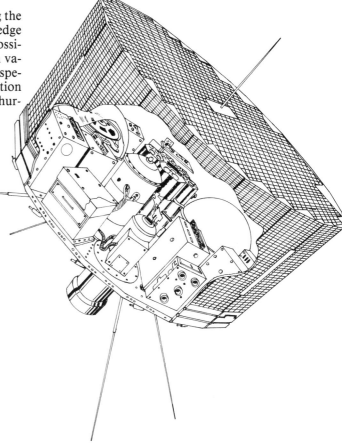

TIROS-1/-10 (USA-1960)

The United States launched its first meteorological satellite in 1960. Tiros-1 was in the form of a squat, many-sided cylinder, diameter 106.7cm (42in), height 42.3cm (16.75in). Tiros stood for Television and Infrared Observation Satellite, and over five years ten experimental satellites bearing this name were launched, all of the same shape, their weight varying, according to the instruments carried, from 122 to 135kg (269 to 298lb). All were spin-stabilized, rotating around their vertical axis. The outside of each satellite, apart from the base, was covered by 9,200 solar cells which provided the electrical energy for recharging the nickel-cadmium batteries. The instruments of the first eight Tiros satellites were mounted on the base platform and their observation lenses protruded from the bottom of the vehicle. The axis of rotation, however, was not constantly related to the Earth's axis, so that the instruments could only observe the Earth's atmosphere for one-third of the orbital period. The last two Tiros satellites, on the other hand, had the rotational axis perpendicular to the plane of the orbit and thus they resembled a wheel rolling around the Earth. The two television cameras were no longer installed on the base of the satellite but on the rim, 180° apart, and so sent back about three times as many pictures. The main Tiros instruments were two compact telecameras (vidicon) of 1.27cm (0.5in), one with a wide-angle lens covering an area of 2,000sq km (772sq mi), the other with a narrow-angle lens covering 190sq km (73 sq mi), and two infrared radiometers of low and medium resolution. There were no ra-

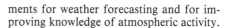

Tiros-1

diometers on Tiros-1,-5,-6,-8,-9 and-10. The telecameras were used for photographing cloud distribution and the radiometers for determining the temperature and altitude of clouds. Each camera was furnished with a video recorder which stored data relating to 32 photographs. The cameras operated when the satellite was traveling in the period illuminated by the Sun and photographic transmission occurred when the space vehicle was within range of the receiving stations on the ground. Tiros-8, launched in 1963, showed a notable advance on the earlier models with its two telecameras, one of which was equipped with Automatic Picture Transmission (APT). This allowed immediate transmission of images, which could be picked up at once by stations installed inexpensively in the countries over which the satellite passed. Thus the application of the meteorological images taken by the satellite was much extended, with APT data received by 871 known stations in 123 countries. The Tiros satellites, built by RCA Astro-Electronics, proved the value of space instruments for weather forecasting and for improving knowledge of atmospheric activity.

Launching and orbital data - Tiros-1 was launched April 1, 1960 into an orbit 693km (430mi) high at the perigee and 750km (466mi) at the apogee. Inclination to equator 48.3°; orbital period 99.2 minutes. The orbital height of the first eight Tiros satellites was about the same, around 800km (500mi), but for Tiros-5,-6,-7 and-8 the orbital inclination was higher, 58.2° to the equator, thus enabling more pictures to be taken at higher latitudes. The orbital features of the last two Tiros satellites showed a marked change. Tiros-9, launched on January 22, 1965, was sent into a near-polar orbit inclined at 96.4° to the equator, with a perigee of 806km (501mi) and an apogee of 967km (601mi). Tiros-10 was launched July 2, 1965 into an orbit inclined at 98.6°, perigee 848 km (527mi), apogee 957km (594mi). All launchings were from Cape Canaveral by Delta rockets, except for Tiros-1, which used the Thor - Able II.

23

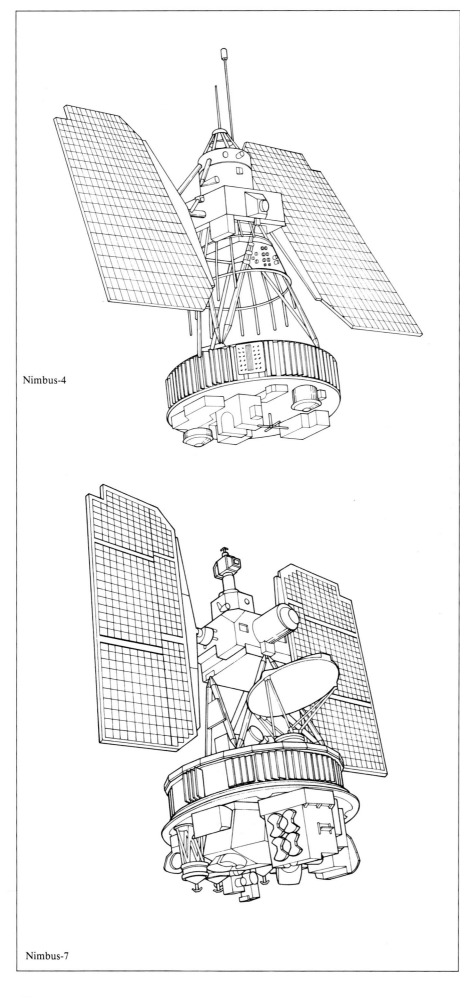

Nimbus-4

Nimbus-7

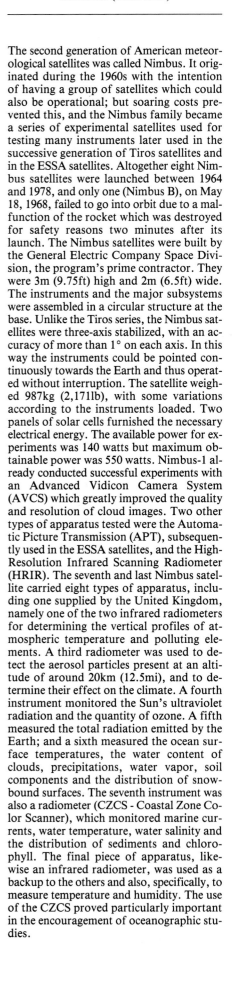

The second generation of American meteorological satellites was called Nimbus. It originated during the 1960s with the intention of having a group of satellites which could also be operational; but soaring costs prevented this, and the Nimbus family became a series of experimental satellites used for testing many instruments later used in the successive generation of Tiros satellites and in the ESSA satellites. Altogether eight Nimbus satellites were launched between 1964 and 1978, and only one (Nimbus B), on May 18, 1968, failed to go into orbit due to a malfunction of the rocket which was destroyed for safety reasons two minutes after its launch. The Nimbus satellites were built by the General Electric Company Space Division, the program's prime contractor. They were 3m (9.75ft) high and 2m (6.5ft) wide. The instruments and the major subsystems were assembled in a circular structure at the base. Unlike the Tiros series, the Nimbus satellites were three-axis stabilized, with an accuracy of more than 1° on each axis. In this way the instruments could be pointed continuously towards the Earth and thus operated without interruption. The satellite weighed 987kg (2,171lb), with some variations according to the instruments loaded. Two panels of solar cells furnished the necessary electrical energy. The available power for experiments was 140 watts but maximum obtainable power was 550 watts. Nimbus-1 already conducted successful experiments with an Advanced Vidicon Camera System (AVCS) which greatly improved the quality and resolution of cloud images. Two other types of apparatus tested were the Automatic Picture Transmission (APT), subsequently used in the ESSA satellites, and the High-Resolution Infrared Scanning Radiometer (HRIR). The seventh and last Nimbus satellite carried eight types of apparatus, including one supplied by the United Kingdom, namely one of the two infrared radiometers for determining the vertical profiles of atmospheric temperature and polluting elements. A third radiometer was used to detect the aerosol particles present at an altitude of around 20km (12.5mi), and to determine their effect on the climate. A fourth instrument monitored the Sun's ultraviolet radiation and the quantity of ozone. A fifth measured the total radiation emitted by the Earth; and a sixth measured the ocean surface temperatures, the water content of clouds, precipitations, water vapor, soil components and the distribution of snowbound surfaces. The seventh instrument was also a radiometer (CZCS - Coastal Zone Color Scanner), which monitored marine currents, water temperature, water salinity and the distribution of sediments and chlorophyll. The final piece of apparatus, likewise an infrared radiometer, was used as a backup to the others and also, specifically, to measure temperature and humidity. The use of the CZCS proved particularly important in the encouragement of oceanographic studies.

Launching and orbital data - Nimbus-1 was launched August 28, 1964 from Vandenberg with a Thor Agena B rocket into a near-polar orbit inclined at 98.7° to the equator, with a perigee of 1,103km (685mi) and an apogee of 1,179km (732mi).
Nimbus-3 (1969),-4 (1970),-5 (1972) and -6 (1975) went into virtually the same orbits. Nimbus-7 launched October 24, 1978 from Vandenberg by a Delta rocket, had an orbit of 943km (586mi) at the perigee and 953km (592mi) at the apogee, with an inclination of 99.3° and a period of 104.1 minutes.

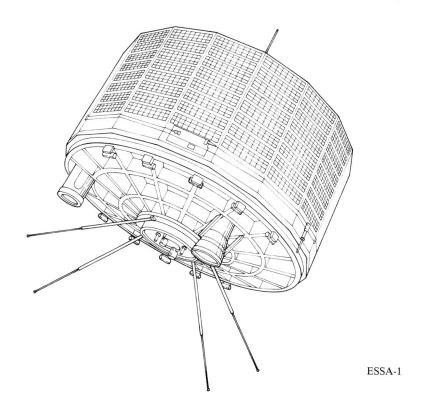

ESSA-1

ESSA (USA-1966)

In 1966, with the launching of ESSA-1, weighing 138kg (304lb), the United States created the first operational satellite system for meteorology. The system was operated by the National Satellite Center (NESC) of the Environmental Science Services Administration (ESSA) belonging to the Department of Commerce. The system was based on the use of improved Tiros satellites known as Tiros Operational Satellite (TOS). The name was altered to ESSA once the satellite had reached its final orbit. Altogether nine ESSA satellites were launched within four years. ESSA-1 was identical to Tiros-9; thus its structure was a kind of faceted wheel, diameter 106.7 cm (42in), thickness 42.3cm (16.7in), with a flight configuration like that of Tiros-9 and with the monitoring instruments arranged around the satellite's rim. All the ESSA satellites retained the same form of structure but varied the onboard apparatus. Those with odd numbers (-1, -3, -5, -7 and -9) were equipped with the Advanced Vidicon Camera System (AVCS), namely a television system that took global photographs of the planet, storing them in the onboard recorder and then transmitting them to the Command and Data Acquisition (CDA) stations of the Department of Commerce on Wallops Island in Virginia and at Fairbanks, Alaska. From here data and pictures were relayed to the National Environmental Satellite Service at Suitland, Maryland to be processed and distributed to weather forecasting stations in the United States and elsewhere. The even-numbered ESSA satellites (-2, -4, -6 and -8), however, were provided with the Automatic Picture Transmission (APT) television system, transmitting pictures directly to the stations situated in the countries overflown by the satellite. It was planned that two satellites should operate simultaneously in orbit, one with the AVCS and the other with the APT system. Each satellite was capable of providing global coverage with 144-156 images every 24 hours. The ESSA satellites were built by RCA Astro-Electronics.

Launching and orbital data - ESSA-1 was launched from Cape Canaveral February 3, 1966 by a Delta rocket. It was sent into a sun-synchronous, near-polar orbit, inclination to equator 97.9°, perigee 702km (436mi), apogee 845km (525mi), period 100.4 minutes.

ESSA-2 (launched from Cape Canaveral February 28, 1966) went into a higher orbit, perigee 1,356km (842mi), apogee 1,408km (875mi), inclination 101°, period 113.6 minutes. Subsequently the other ESSA satellites launched from Vandenberg (ESSA-3 in 1966, ESSA-4, -5 and -6 in 1967, ESSA-7 and -8 in 1968, and ESSA-9 in 1969) maintained the same orbital height of about 1,400km (870mi). The last, ESSA-9, launched from Cape Canaveral February 26, 1969, varied slightly, with an apogee of 1,508km (937mi) and a perigee of 1,427km (886mi).

COSMOS-METEOR (USSR-1967)

The Soviet Union initiated the Meteor program for weather satellites in 1967, giving it the name Cosmos. First to be launched was Cosmos-122, testing the entire system, which left June 25, 1966. The Cosmos-144, cylindrical in shape, had the following presumed dimensions: diameter 1.5m (5ft), height 5m (16ft), weight around 2,000kg (4,400lb). The satellites had three-axis stabilization and two panels of solar cells per-

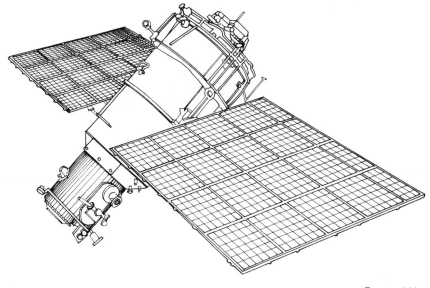

Cosmos-144

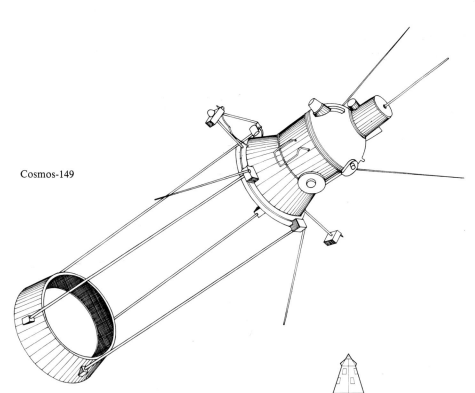

Cosmos-149

solar cells, and the lower one accommodated the scientific instrumentation. The total weight was about 2,000kg (4,400lb). The principal instruments of Meteor-1 were the same as those tested by preceding vehicles of the Cosmos-Meteor series. An addition in 1971 was an automatic apparatus for distributing pictures compatible with receivers in use in the West. It was planned that there should always be two operative satellites in orbit, combining their observations. Data was transmitted to the three headquarters of the Hydrometeorological Service, situated in Moscow, Novosibirsk (Siberia) and Khabarovsk. Altogether 30 Meteor-1 satellites were launched between 1969 and 1980.

Launching and orbital data - Meteor-1 was launched March 26, 1969 from Plesetsk by an A-2 rocket into a near-polar orbit, inclined at 81.2° to the equator; perigee 633km (393mi), apogee 687km (427mi). After 1977 Meteor-1 satellites were also launched from the Baikonur-Tyuratam range, with orbital inclinations of up to 98°. The thirtieth Meteor-1 was launched June 18, 1980.

ITOS-A to -H/NOAA-1 to -5 (USA-1970)

From 1970 the United States put into orbit the second generation of operative meteorological satellites known as ITOS after the Improved Tiros Operational System. Launching of the ITOS satellites coincided with the founding of the new National Oceanic and Atmospheric Administration (NOAA) which absorbed the preceding Environmental Science Service Administration (ESSA). The meteorological satellites were given the initials NOAA once they had reached orbit. The ITOS satellites were three-axis stabilized, constantly directed toward the Earth, with a central section 1.22m (4ft) high and 1.09m (3.5ft) across. The three panels of solar cells in the upper portion, when deployed, had a span of 4.26m (14ft). ITOS-1 (also known as Tiros-M), weighing 309kg (680lb), simultaneously fulfilled the functions of the pair of ESSA satellites previously launched; for this purpose it was equipped both with the Automatic Picture Transmission (APT) system for instantaneous transmission of images, and with the Advanced Vidicon Camera System (AVCS), which stored the pictures taken. But ITOS-1 also made use, for the first time in an operational capacity, of a two-channel radiometer (SR-Scanning Radiometer) which simultaneously recorded and transmitted the collected data in real time. The instrument worked continuously night and day. In this manner a single ITOS was capable of observing the whole planet in 12 hours instead of 24 hours as previously with the ESSA satellites. In addition to these three instruments, ITOS-1 carried a Solar Proton Monitor (SPM) for measuring the flux of protons emitted by the Sun, and a Flat Plate Radiometer (FPR) for measuring atmospheric heat. Following ITOS-1, which was experimental, ITOS-A/NOAA-1, identical to the former, was wholly operational. In 1972

manently pointed toward the Sun. Instruments carried on board comprised two television cameras for daytime observation of a surface strip 1,000km (621mi) wide, with a resolution of 1.25km (0.75mi); an infrared TV camera operating between 8-12 microns in the spectral band, with a resolution of 15km (9.25mi) and four instruments for measuring the radiation emitted by the Earth in three wavelengths (0.3-3, 3-30 and 8-12 microns) along a swath 2,500km (1,553mi) wide. The Cosmos satellites of the Meteor series were able, during a single orbit, to monitor one eighth of the surface of the globe and to measure 20 percent of emitted radiation. The data was memorized aboard the satellite and then transmitted to Earth when overflying the receiving stations.

Launching and orbital data - Cosmos-144 was launched February 28, 1967 from the Plesetsk test range by an A-2 rocket. The near-polar orbit was inclined at 81.2° to the equator, with a perigee of 574km (356mi) and an apogee of 644km (400mi). Among other Cosmos satellites subsequently launched and with similar orbital characteristics were Cosmos-156 (1967), Cosmos-184 (1967), Cosmos-206 (1968) and Cosmos-226 (1968).

METEOR-1 (USSR-1969)

The satellites of the Meteor-1 series had the shape of a cylinder about 5m (16ft) high and 1.5m (5ft) in diameter. The body of the satellite was divided into two separate modules: the upper one contained the satellite's control systems and two attached panels of

A-2

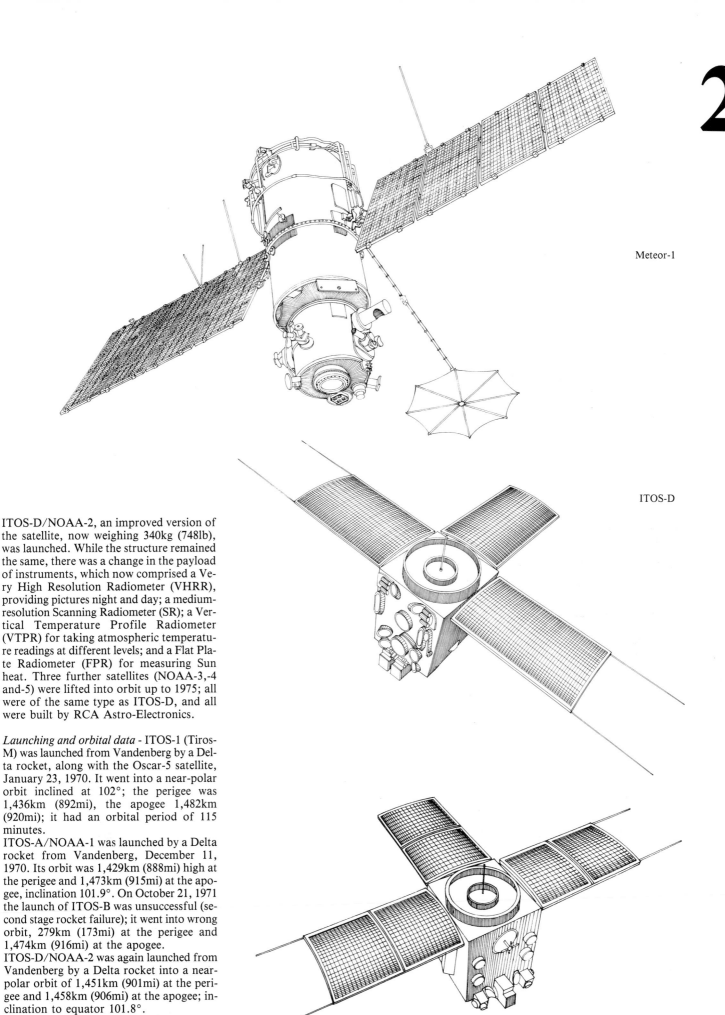

2

Meteor-1

ITOS-D

ITOS-D/NOAA-2, an improved version of
the satellite, now weighing 340kg (748lb),
was launched. While the structure remained
the same, there was a change in the payload
of instruments, which now comprised a Very High Resolution Radiometer (VHRR),
providing pictures night and day; a medium-
resolution Scanning Radiometer (SR); a Vertical Temperature Profile Radiometer
(VTPR) for taking atmospheric temperature readings at different levels; and a Flat Plate Radiometer (FPR) for measuring Sun
heat. Three further satellites (NOAA-3,-4
and-5) were lifted into orbit up to 1975; all
were of the same type as ITOS-D, and all
were built by RCA Astro-Electronics.

Launching and orbital data - ITOS-1 (Tiros-
M) was launched from Vandenberg by a Delta rocket, along with the Oscar-5 satellite,
January 23, 1970. It went into a near-polar
orbit inclined at 102°; the perigee was
1,436km (892mi), the apogee 1,482km
(920mi); it had an orbital period of 115
minutes.
ITOS-A/NOAA-1 was launched by a Delta
rocket from Vandenberg, December 11,
1970. Its orbit was 1,429km (888mi) high at
the perigee and 1,473km (915mi) at the apogee, inclination 101.9°. On October 21, 1971
the launch of ITOS-B was unsuccessful (second stage rocket failure); it went into wrong
orbit, 279km (173mi) at the perigee and
1,474km (916mi) at the apogee.
ITOS-D/NOAA-2 was again launched from
Vandenberg by a Delta rocket into a near-
polar orbit of 1,451km (901mi) at the perigee and 1,458km (906mi) at the apogee; inclination to equator 101.8°.
On July 16, 1971 the launch of ITOS-E was

ITOS-1

a disaster, with the failure of the second stage of the rocket. After that, and with the same orbital features, came the launchings of ITOS-F/NOAA-3 (November 6, 1973), ITOS-G/NOAA-4 (November 15, 1974) and ITOS-H/NOAA-5 (July 29, 1976) which ceased functioning on July 16, 1979, concluding the ITOS/NOAA series.

EOLE FR-2 (FRANCE-1971)

This small French satellite, 71cm (28in) in diameter, 58cm (28in) high and weighing 82.5kg (182lb), was the first applicational satellite launched by the Centre National d'Etudes Spatiales (CNES). Its task was to gather data regarding atmospheric pressure and temperature as monitored by 500 stratospheric balloons cruising at a height of 12,000m (39,000ft). The satellite made contact with each balloon, located it, received and stored the data with subsequent transmission to Earth. The structure, the antennae and the systems for heat regulation, stabilization and energy provision were furnished by the Aérospatiale company.

Launching and orbital data - EOLE FR-2 was launched from Vandenberg August 16, 1971 with an American Scout rocket. Its orbit, inclined at 50° to the equator, had a perigee of 677km (420mi) and an apogee of 908km (564mi).

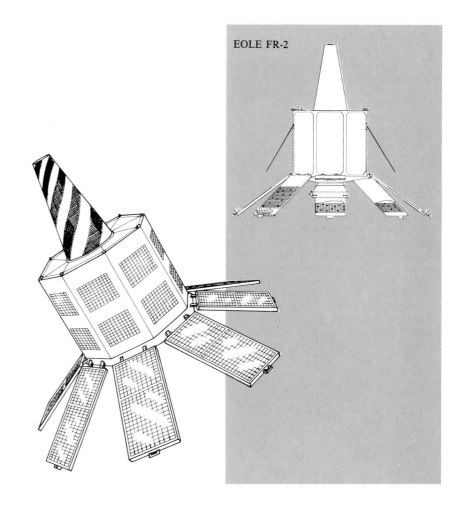

EOLE FR-2

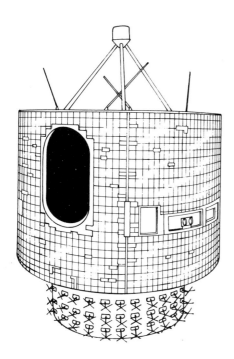

SMS-GOES

SMS-1/-2/ GOES-1/-3 (USA-1974)

After the testing of several meteorological instruments aboard the ATS-1 and ATS-3 satellites in geostationary orbit, the first American geostationary meteorological satellite was launched in 1974. Named Synchronous Meteorological Satellite (SMS) and, after the second launch, Geostationary Operational Environmental Satellite (GOES), it was cylindrical in form with a diameter of 1.9m (6ft) and a height of 2.3m (7.5ft). Its weight in orbit was 243kg (535lb) and it was spin-stabilized. Recharging two nickel-cadmium batteries were 15,000 solar cells around the satellite's rim. The principal onboard instrument was the Visible Infrared Spin Scan Radiometer (VISSR), with two spectral bands, capable of taking pictures in the infrared and visible bands both by day and night. The radiometer used a single optical mechanism, namely a telescope with an aperture of 4.06cm (1.5in), and it produced an image of the entire hemisphere every 20 minutes. This was digitalized and transmitted at the rate of 28 million bits per second to the NOAA center on Wallops Island, Virginia. Here the images were stored and processed so as to be retransmitted to the satellite, which in turn distributed them at a lower speed of 1.75 million bits per second by means of the Weather Facsimile (WEFAX)

system. They could likewise be received by minor stations. The radiometer also recorded the surface temperature of the oceans. Other instruments aboard the satellite were a Data Collection System (DCS), gathering information from some 1,500 observing stations all over the world, and a Space Environment Monitor (SEM) for surveying solar activity, measuring the X-rays, the energy of emitted protons and electrons, and the magnetic field. The SMS/GOES satellites were built by Philco Ford; they also provided support for the international research program of GARP (Global Atmospheric Research Program).

Launching and orbital data - SMS-1 was launched May 17, 1974 from Cape Canaveral by a Delta rocket into equatorial, geosynchronous orbit at a height of 35,830km (22,260mi). SMS-2 was launched February 6, 1975, GOES-1 October 16, 1975, GOES-2 June 16, 1977, and GOES-3 June 16, 1978.

METEOR-2 (USSR-1975)

Meteor-2 used the same basic structure as the Meteor-1 satellite but carried new and improved instruments. The three-axis stabilization used a more accurate attitude and aiming control system. The power supplied by the panels of solar cells was also increased, and a computerized system for the control of the sensors was installed. The instrumentation accounted for 30 percent of the total weight. Differences in comparison with Meteor-1 were the following: better quality of TV pictures in respect to resolution, visual range and information content; the application of television sensors for global and local images, with data recorded for an entire orbit; the use of infrared digital equipment to take temperatures at sea surface level and at varying heights, thus producing a vertical profile of temperatures up to an altitude of 40km (25mi); the use of sensors for measuring the intensity of radiation emitted by the Earth; and the application of two independent radio links for transmitting to Earth the global observation data accumulated during each orbit in the frequency range of 460-470 MHz and also sending the pictures directly to local stations in the 137-138 MHz frequency range. Meteor-2 was thus able to furnish twice-daily information on cloud distribution and snow cover, with images in the visible and infrared bands; twice-daily global data on temperature distribution, cloud heights and ocean surface temperatures; twice-daily information on the intensity of Earth-emitted radiation; and three times-daily TV images to local stations, by means of a system analogous to that used in American satellites.

The Meteor-2 system forecasted the simultaneous operation in orbit of two or three satellites.

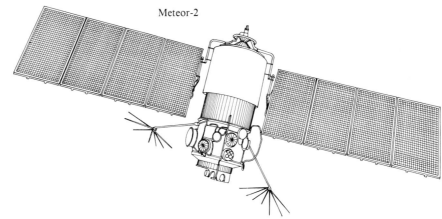
Meteor-2

Launching and orbital data - The first Meteor-2 satellite was launched July 11, 1975 from Plesetsk by an A-1 rocket. The near-polar orbit was inclined at 81.3° to the equator; perigee 858km (533mi) and apogee 891km (554mi); period 102 minutes.

METEOSAT (EUROPE-1977)

In 1972 the eight European member countries of the European Space Research Organization (ESRO), which later became the European Space Agency (ESA), initiated the program for the development of two preoperational meteorological satellites to be put in geostationary orbit. Meteosat was cylindrical in form with a diameter of 2.10m (6.8ft), a height of 3.20m (10.4ft) and an orbital weight of 300kg (660lb). Six panels of solar cells on the rim provided power of 250 watts. The satellite was spin-stabilized (100 rotations per minute), its axis perpendicular to the orbital plane. The satellite was furnished with a high-resolution radiometer ta-

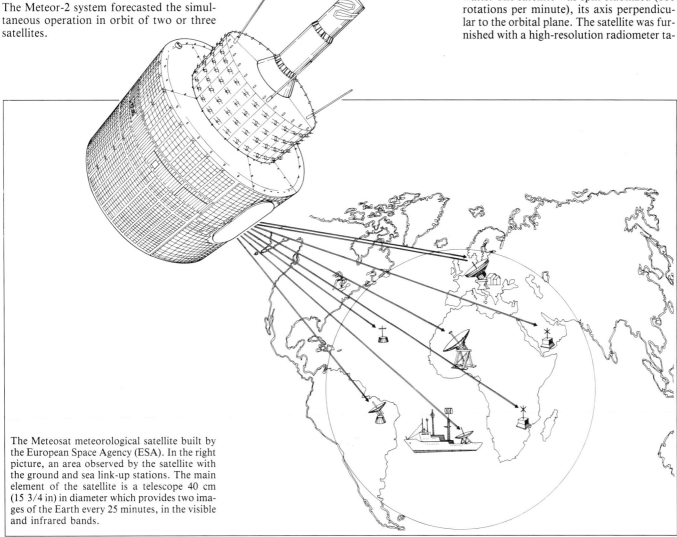

The Meteosat meteorological satellite built by the European Space Agency (ESA). In the right picture, an area observed by the satellite with the ground and sea link-up stations. The main element of the satellite is a telescope 40 cm (15 3/4 in) in diameter which provides two images of the Earth every 25 minutes, in the visible and infrared bands.

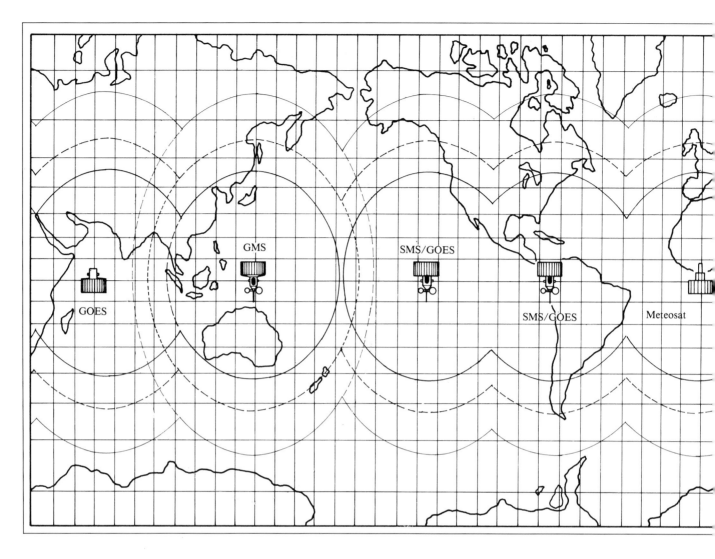

king pictures in three spectral bands; the visible (0.4-1.1 microns) with a resolution of 2.5km (1.5mi); the thermal infrared (10.5-12.5 microns) with a resolution of 5km (3mi); and the water vapor (5.7-7.1 microns) with a resolution of 5km (3mi). The radiometer was an electrical-optical appliance, the main element of which was a Ritchey Chrétien telescope of 40cm (15.6in) diameter. It was capable of providing two images of the Earth in the visible and infrared wavebands every 25 minutes. The data was transmitted at the rate of 166,000 bits per second. Meteosat also carried a Weather Facsimile (WE-FAX) image and data distribution system as well as a second system for gathering various types of data from automatic or semiautomatic, fixed or mobile stations situated both on land and at sea. From the basic data gathered by the radiometer, it was also possible to deduce the sea surface temperatures, the direction of cloud movement, cloud summit temperature and altitude, and the humidity of the upper troposphere. Prime contractor for the building of the satellite was the French company Aérospatiale. Management in orbit was effected by the ESA center at Darmstadt near Frankfurt, West Germany. In addition to the first two Meteosat, in 1987 Meteosat P2 derived from an engineering model of the other two is to be launched. In 1983 the multinational organization Eumetsat was formed in Geneva; it

was responsible for the launching of the last two Meteosat-type satellites named European Meteosat Operational (MOP). Compared with the earlier ones they carried an improved system of data transmission, with a channel operating in the water vapor spectrum, in parallel with the other visible and infrared bands, plus a series of other general improvements. Meteosat-1 formed part of the Global Atmospheric Research Program (GARP) of the World Meteorological Organization (WMO).

Launching and orbital data - Meteosat-1 was launched November 23, 1977 from Cape Canaveral by a Delta 2914 rocket into a geostationary equatorial orbit, altitude 35,692km (22,175mi). On November 24, 1979 a failure on board the satellite put the radiometer out of service and from then on Meteosat-1 was used only for gathering data. Meteosat-2 was launched June 19, 1981 from the test site in French Guiana with the European Ariane rocket and placed in an equatorial geostationary orbit 35,797km (22,240mi) high. The Indian Apple satellite for telecommunications was launched together with Meteosat-2. Launching of Meteosat P2 is scheduled for 1987. The three operational MOP satellites of the Eumetsat organization are due to be launched in 1987, 1988 and 1990.

GMS/HIMAWARI (JAPAN-1977)

The Japanese GMS satellites, from the initials of Geostationary Meteorological Satellite, were launched as a program of the National Space Development Agency (NASDA). The GMS satellite was cylindrical in shape with a diameter of 2.15m (7ft) and a total height of 3.45m (11.2ft); weight in orbit was 290kg (638lb). The satellite was spin-stabilized but the antenna was mounted on a counter-rotating system. The solar cells on the rim, supplying 225 watts, were constructed by the Japanese Sharp Corporation. The principal instrument on the GMS satellites was the Visible Infrared Spin Scan Radiometer (VISSR), built in the USA by the Santa Barbara Research Center, with four channels in the visible spectrum (0.5-0.75 microns) and one in the infrared (10.5-12.5 microns). The images provided had a resolution of 1.25km (0.77mi) in the visible and 5km (3mi) in the infrared band. The second instrument on the satellite was the Space Environment Monitor (SEM), designed and built by the Nippon Electric Company, to study the effects of the Sun's activity on the system of Earth telecommunications. In addition there was a device for collecting data from Earth stations and a distribution system for images pretreated by the Data Pro-

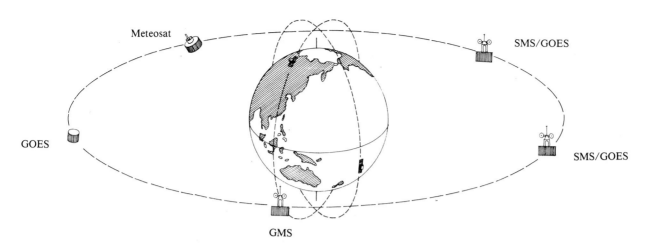

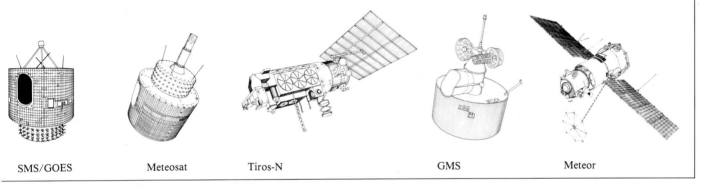

SMS/GOES   Meteosat   Tiros-N   GMS   Meteor

The position of the satellites involved in the international GARP program (Global Atmospheric Research Program): three American GOES; the European Meteosat; the Japanese GMS sent into geostationary orbit at an altitude of 36,000 km (22,369 mi); the American Tiros-N and Soviet Meteor which are positioned in a polar orbit at an altitude of about 900 km (560 mi). The left diagram shows the areas covered by the satellites of the GARP program in equatorial orbit. Above, general view with all satellites used and their respective positions.

cessing Center of the Japan Meteorological Agency which, together with NASDA, managed the satellite in orbit. The satellites were built by the American Hughes Aircraft Company in collaboration with the Japanese NEC.

Launching and orbital data - GMS/Himawari-1 was launched July 14, 1977 from Cape Canaveral with a Delta rocket into a geostationary equatorial orbit at an altitude of 35,779km (22,230mi).

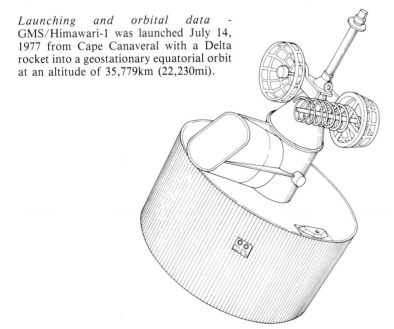

GMS/Himawari

GMS/Himawari-2 was launched August 11, 1981 from the Tanegashima Space Center in Japan with a Japanese N-2 rocket. GMS-Himawari-3 was also launched from Tanegashima by a N-2 rocket into geostationary orbit on August 3, 1984. The satellites were positioned over Australia at longitude 140°E to monitor Japan and the entire eastern Pacific.

TIROS-N/NOAA-6 to -9 (USA-1978)

This was the third generation of American meteorological satellites in near-polar orbit. The first of the new series, called Tiros-N, was experimental but was also used for operational activities. The central section of the satellite was 3.71m (12ft) long, diameter 1.88m (6.1ft). The total length, together with the extended panel of solar cells supplying 1,260 watts, was 6.50m (21.1ft). The weight in orbit was 744kg (16.37lb), 231kg (508lb) of which was represented by the payload. The main instrument on board in the whole series was the Advanced Very High Resolution Radiometer (AVHRR), furnishing pictures and data in real time both by day and night. The radiometer had four channels with a wavelength range of 0.55 to 11.5 microns, taking pictures in the visible and in-

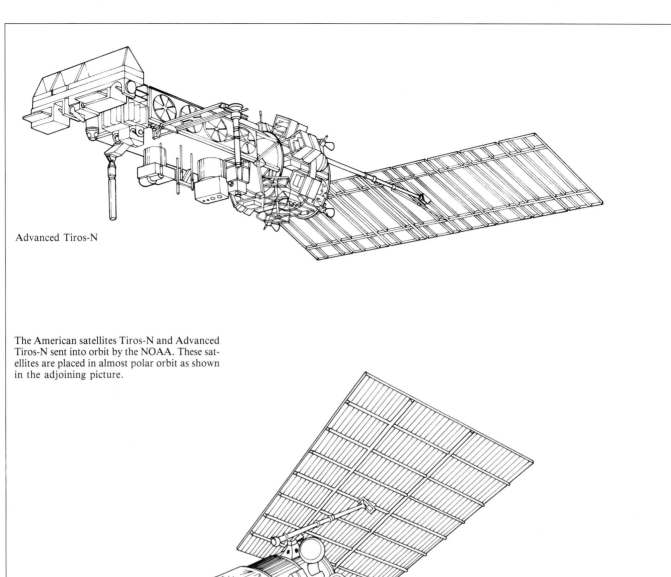

Advanced Tiros-N

The American satellites Tiros-N and Advanced
Tiros-N sent into orbit by the NOAA. These satellites are placed in almost polar orbit as shown
in the adjoining picture.

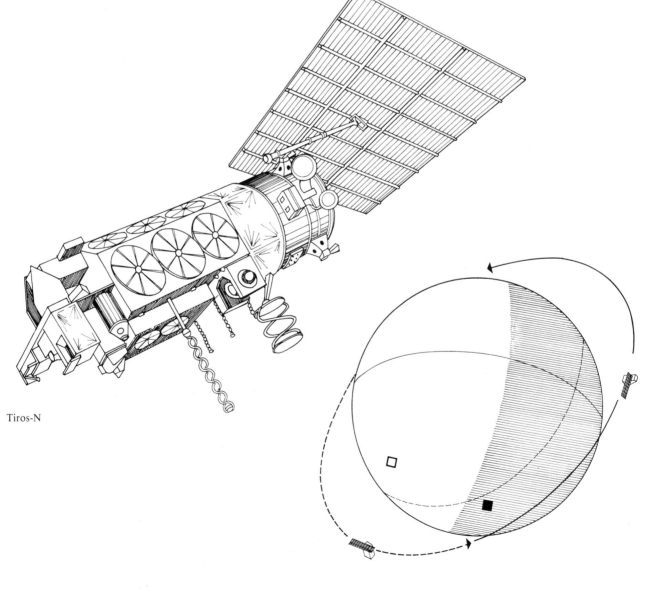

Tiros-N

frared bands of cloud distribution. Furthermore it measured sea surface temperatures, identifying snow and ice. Resolution varied from 1-4km according to the type of photograph. NOAA-7 was also provided with a fifth channel (11.5-12.5 microns), like-wise devoted to gathering data on surface water temperatures. Tiros-N carried in addition a group of three instruments (HIRS/2, SSU and MSU) collectively called TOVS from the initials of Tiros Operational Vertical Sounder. This provided profiles of atmospheric temperature from sea level up to 250km (155mi), and of water vapor and ozone contents. Another assembly of three instruments, the Space Environmental Monitor (SEM) monitored the characteristics of the atomic particles emitted by the Sun, so measuring the density of the flux of protons, electrons and other particles deriving from the planet. This information has been used during manned space flights and by high-altitude planes, and for determining the consequences caused during long-distance transmissions. Finally, Tiros-N was equipped with the Data Collection System (DCS), gathering data transmitted by fixed and mobile stations concerning temperatures, pressures, altitudes, snow deposits, speed of the station itself, etc. The position of the transmitting station could be determined, by means of Doppler effect techniques, with an accuracy of 3-5km (2.3mi). In addition to Tiros-N, the NOAA-6 and NOAA-7 satellites were launched with the same features on board. The NOAA-8 satellite showed improvements to both structure and instrumentation, and was therefore called Advanced Tiros-N. Its orbital weight was 1,014kg (2,231lb), including 367kg (807lb) of payload instruments; the central section was longer, 4.19m (13.6ft), and the overall length was increased to 7.47m (24.25ft). The solar cell panel was also improved, now furnishing more energy (1,470 watts). In addition to the instruments carried on the previous satellites, the NOAA-8 was provided with a Search and Rescue System (SAR) receiving data from an Emergency Locator Transmitter (ELT) and from an Emergency Indicating Radio Beacon (EPIRB) carried aboard ships or airplanes. In the event of an air crash or a shipwreck, a signal sent automatically to the satellite was retransmitted to ground stations which processed the information in order to identify the spot from which the signal came in order to organize a rescue. The SAR system formed part of a program initiated jointly by the USA, Canada, France and the USSR. The last nation participated in the program by launching COSPAS satellites provided with the same rescue system. The Tiros-N were the first satellites to be completely digital. An onboard computer processed the data prior to its transmission at the rate of 1.3 million bits per second. The NOAA-9 satellite also carried an Earth Radiation Budget Experiment (ERBE) apparatus, consisting of two radiometers for measuring Earth-emitted radiation. The NOAA program envisages the launching of six more satellites of the Tiros-N series between 1986 and 1990. They are built by RCA Astro-Electronics.

Launching and orbital data - Tiros-N was launched from Vandenberg October 13, 1978 by a Delta rocket into a near-polar orbit inclined at 98.9°; perigee 943km (586mi) and apogee 953km (592mi). The same orbital features applied to NOAA-6 (June 27, 1979), NOAA-7 (June 23, 1981), NOAA-8 (March 28, 1983) and NOAA-9 (December 12, 1984).

BHASKARA-1/-2 (INDIA-1979)

Indian experimental satellite carrying instruments for the study of Earth resources (remote sensing) as well as for meteorology. The meteorological objectives of the Bhaskara program related to the collection of data about the quantity of water vapor in the atmosphere above the oceans surrounding the Indian subcontinent.

Launching and orbital data - Bhaskara-1 was launched June 7, 1979 and Bhaskara-2 November 20, 1981. (See Bhaskara in chapter on Earth resources satellites.)

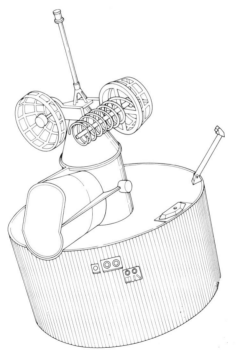

GOES-4

GOES-4 to -6 and -G/-H (USA-1980)

GOES-4 introduced a second family of GOES satellites built by Hughes Aircraft In-

ternational, and it showed notable improvements. The shape was still cylindrical with a diameter of 2.16m (7ft), height 3.5m (11.4ft). It was spin-stabilized and had an orbital weight of 396kg (871lb). Modifications compared with previous GOES satellites included the replacement of the VISSR radiometer by a Visible Infrared Spin Scan Radiometer Atmospheric Sounder (VAS) with greater capabilities. In practical terms this was a VISSR radiometer with the additional capability of gathering data concerning atmospheric features such as water vapor and carbon dioxide content, and temperature. The other new element was the group of antennae mounted on a despun platform thus improving the transmission of collected data to ground stations.

Launching and orbital data - GOES-4 was launched September 9, 1980 from Cape Canaveral by a Delta 3914 rocket into a geosynchronous equatorial orbit 35,802km (22,244mi) high. GOES-5 was launched May 22, 1981 and GOES-6 April 22, 1983. Two other satellites (GOES-G, H) belonging to the GOES family built by Hughes are also due to be launched.

INSAT (INDIA-1983)

INSAT (Indian National Satellite) was built by Ford Aerospace for telecommunications and meteorology, on contract to the Indian government. Weight 1,089kg (2,396lb), total length 19.4m (63ft) with the arm of the solar sail and the panel of solar cells extended. In addition to apparatus for telecommunications, it carried a system for collecting environmental data from 110 automatic ground stations and a Very High Resolution Radiometer taking pictures every half-hour in the visible waveband (0.55-0.75 microns), with a resolution of 2.75km (1.7mi), and in the infrared waveband (10.5-12.5 microns), with a resolution of 11km (6.8mi). The data were transmitted at the rate of 400 Kbit per second to the Meteorological Data Utilization Center in New Delhi.

Launching and orbital data - INSAT-A was launched by a Delta rocket April 10, 1982 from Cape Canaveral but a failure of the attitude control system rendered it completely useless. INSAT-B was carried into orbit by the *Challenger* Space Shuttle (eighth mission) on August 30, 1983. Its perigee motor PAM-D took it into equatorial geostationary orbit 35,797km (22,240mi) high, positioned at longitude 74°E.

ERBS (USA-1984)

The Earth Radiation Budget Satellite (ERBS) was launched as part of the Earth Radiation Budget Experiment Program (ERBE) in order to measure the radiation emitted by the Earth. The satellite weighed 2,304kg (5,069lb) and was 1.6m (5.2ft) long

ERBS

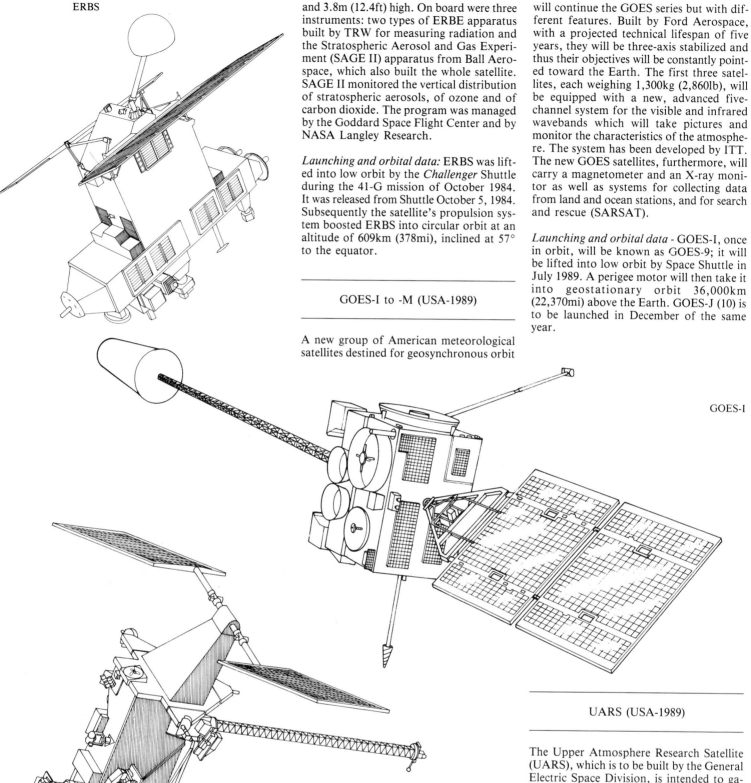

and 3.8m (12.4ft) high. On board were three instruments: two types of ERBE apparatus built by TRW for measuring radiation and the Stratospheric Aerosol and Gas Experiment (SAGE II) apparatus from Ball Aerospace, which also built the whole satellite. SAGE II monitored the vertical distribution of stratospheric aerosols, of ozone and of carbon dioxide. The program was managed by the Goddard Space Flight Center and by NASA Langley Research.

Launching and orbital data: ERBS was lifted into low orbit by the *Challenger* Shuttle during the 41-G mission of October 1984. It was released from Shuttle October 5, 1984. Subsequently the satellite's propulsion system boosted ERBS into circular orbit at an altitude of 609km (378mi), inclined at 57° to the equator.

GOES-I to -M (USA-1989)

A new group of American meteorological satellites destined for geosynchronous orbit will continue the GOES series but with different features. Built by Ford Aerospace, with a projected technical lifespan of five years, they will be three-axis stabilized and thus their objectives will be constantly pointed toward the Earth. The first three satellites, each weighing 1,300kg (2,860lb), will be equipped with a new, advanced five-channel system for the visible and infrared wavebands which will take pictures and monitor the characteristics of the atmosphere. The system has been developed by ITT. The new GOES satellites, furthermore, will carry a magnetometer and an X-ray monitor as well as systems for collecting data from land and ocean stations, and for search and rescue (SARSAT).

Launching and orbital data - GOES-I, once in orbit, will be known as GOES-9; it will be lifted into low orbit by Space Shuttle in July 1989. A perigee motor will then take it into geostationary orbit 36,000km (22,370mi) above the Earth. GOES-J (10) is to be launched in December of the same year.

GOES-I

UARS (USA-1989)

The Upper Atmosphere Research Satellite (UARS), which is to be built by the General Electric Space Division, is intended to gather global data for studying the physical processes in the stratosphere, mesosphere and low thermosphere. The satellite, which will carry ten scientific instruments for this purpose, will weigh 6,795kg (14,950lb). The program is being managed by the Goddard Space Flight Center of NASA.

Launching and orbital data - UARS will be lifted into low orbit in the course of a mission in 1989. Using its own propulsive system, it will then go into higher orbit at an altitude of 600km (373mi), inclined at 57° to the equator.

UARS

3

Navigational satellites

Satellites for navigation were developed especially for use by submarines in the event of their needing to launch missiles against enemy objectives. For such submarines it would be essential to know their exact position in order to deploy the rockets they carried with utmost effectiveness and precision. But naval surface ships likewise require navigational systems which can pinpoint their position as accurately as possible. For many years special satellites have been employed for this purpose; the race for a reliable orbital system of navigation was initiated by the United States in 1959 and was followed a few years later by the Soviet Union. The opening stages of these programs were far from easy and many satellites were launched unsuccessfully; but within years new technology was perfected and since then space vehicles of this nature, very small and, in comparative terms, not greatly complicated, have proved extremely successful. As a result decisions were taken to extend their use rapidly to the civil sector (the USA in 1967 and the USSR in 1978) in order to exploit the economic benefits. Routes, for example, could be better planned by such methods, with a great saving in time and fuel.

Satellites for navigation are nowadays used for both these purposes although the military needs obviously take precedence, as the highest measures of precision are required for defensive strategies.

The earliest satellites used by the USA were those of the Transit series and over the years these underwent a number of significant improvements. These satellites traveled in a near polar orbit fairly close to the Earth, only some 1,000km (621mi) high. The major disturbance to which they were subjected was due to the solar wind, causing incorrect positioning in space. Gradually, however, this trouble was brought under control, guaranteeing them high reliability in performance and a long operative life.

The Soviet Cosmos-1000 satellites had similar features, including those relating to orbit.

Toward the end of the 1970s there was a notable technological advance when the USA launched its new Navstar-GPS satellites. The Transit satellites carried out a survey every 90-110 minutes; although satisfactory for fast-moving ships, this was clearly inadequate for aircraft. Navstar-GPS was capable of providing virtually instantaneous determination of position for any moving object on land, sea or in the air, including inner space, with a precision of only 10m (33ft). The working orbit was higher, around 19,000km (11,630mi). This system is used mainly by the three armed services, and even soldiers on foot patrol can be provided with a simple instrument which, via satellite, will indicate their position. Aircraft also benefit from the system which can even estimate their speed with a tolerance of 0.1m (0.33ft) per second.

The USSR has had a satellite with similar general characteristics since 1982. Known as Glonass, it is also used in the civil sector.

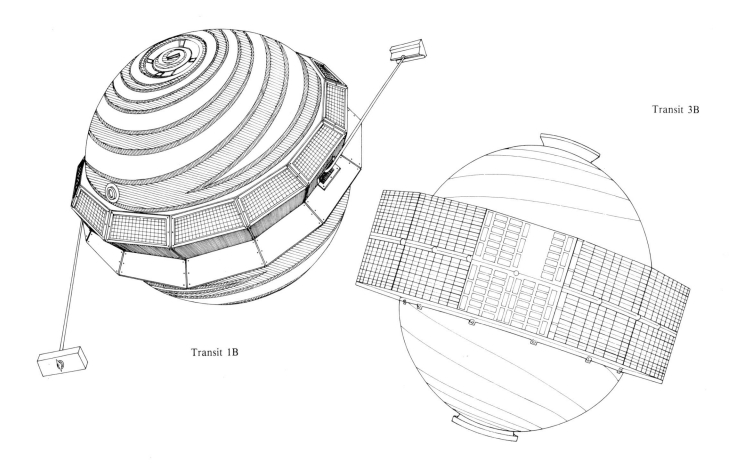

Transit 3B

Transit 1B

TRANSIT/OSCAR (USA-1959)

The first navigational satellite, Transit 1A, was spherical in shape with a diameter of 0.9m (2.95ft) and a weight of 120kg (264lb), much of which consisted of the chemical batteries it carried. It was also provided with a few solar cells. The satellite was equipped with two stable oscillators and two double-frequency transmitters (162/216MHz and 54/324MHz). It was designed by Johns Hopkins University for the US Navy as a navigational aid to submarines and surface vessels, and it was managed by the Naval Astronautics Group at Point Mogu, California. The Transit satellites were sometimes also given the name OSCAR (not to be confused with the Oscar satellites for radio hams). The Transit satellites were planned to have an average life of three months and from 1960 were also furnished with an electronic clock; in addition they had a memory containing data transmitted every 12 hours relating to the satellite's position. Making use of the Doppler effect, surface ships or submarines receiving signals and thus knowing the position of the satellite, could establish their position during navigation. Some Transit were launched together with other satellites: Transit 3B left with LOFTI. Transit 4A and 4B were cylindrical in shape and were the first satellites to be furnished with a nuclear power source, a Supplementary Nuclear Power (SNAP), radioisotope generator. The

Transit system became operational in December 1962 with the launch of Transit 5A1, but the mission failed because of a faulty onboard receiver. The launch of Transit 5BN3 on April 22, 1964 was a failure, and the kilogram of plutonium-238 from the radioisotope reactor on board was dispersed into the atmosphere, causing an international incident. The subsequent Transit 5C therefore reverted to using panels of solar cells. The operational satellites from Transit 5 onward had a central body in the form of an octagonal prism, 0.38m (1.25ft) high, with a diameter of 0.51m (1.67ft), and a weight of 61kg (134lb). After 1967 the Transit system was also applied to civil navigation and the satellites were given the further name of Navsat (Naval Navigation Satellite). In order to calculate position with even greater precision, three satellites were employed simultaneously, being placed in different orbital planes, and maximum error around 500m (1,640ft). The minimum number of operational satellites required by the Transit system was six, but even so the interval between successive bearings was 90-110 minutes. After many early unsuccessful launchings, the system soon became operational, with 99.9 per cent reliability. The Transit satellites were made by RCA Astro-Electronics.

Launching and orbital data - The first Transit was launched September 17, 1959 but did not reach orbit because of the rocket's third-stage ignition failure. Transit 1B, launched

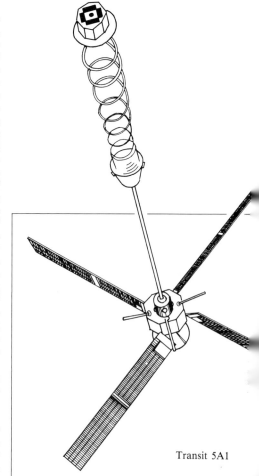

Transit 5A1

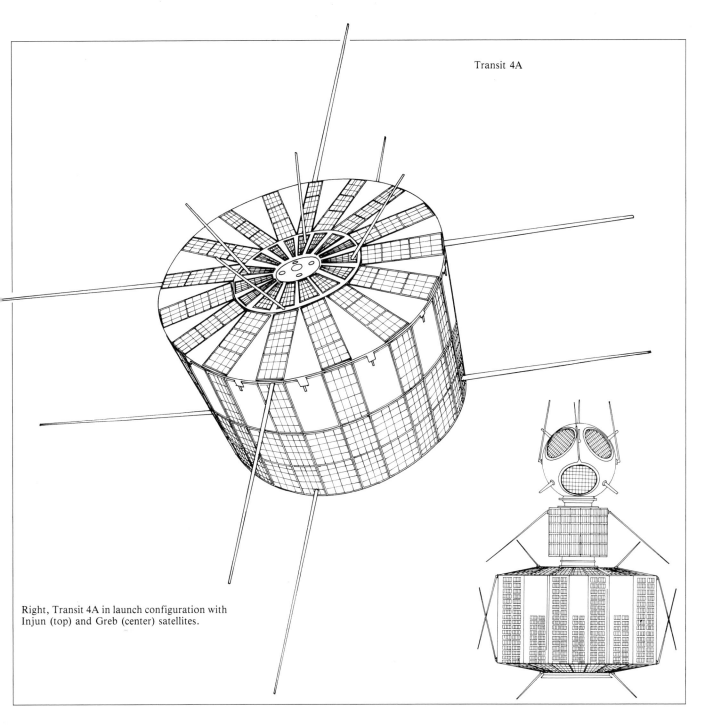

Transit 4A

Right, Transit 4A in launch configuration with
Injun (top) and Greb (center) satellites.

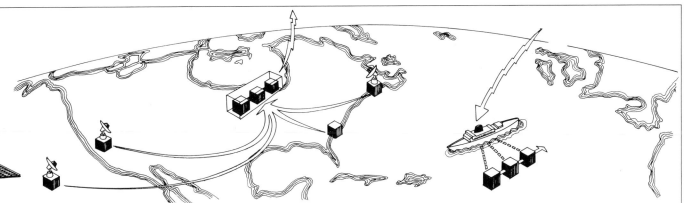

Transit. These are the most widely used American civil and military navigational satellites and the first examples were launched at the beginning
of the space era, back in 1959. According to the Transit system, the satellite transmits its position along the orbit; this is picked up by the Earth
stations, transmitted to the satellite and continuously updated. By knowing these data and measuring the time taken to receive them and the variation in frequency caused by the satellite's movements, one can establish
his position. Fixing the bearing is more precise if three satellites are used.

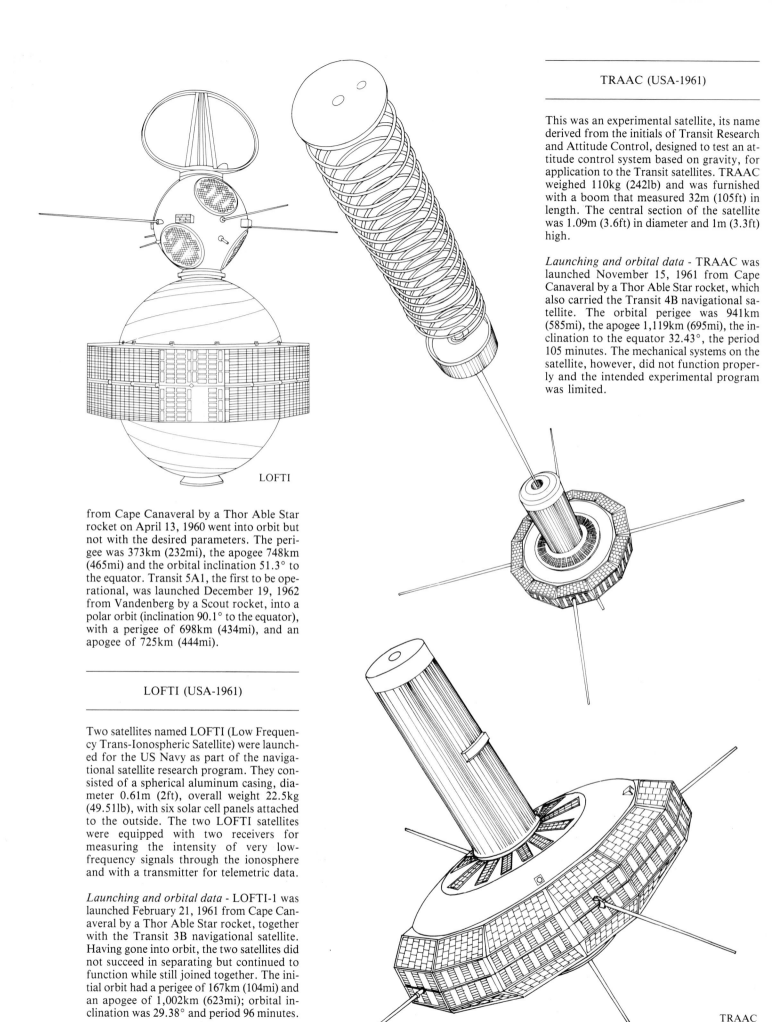

LOFTI

from Cape Canaveral by a Thor Able Star
rocket on April 13, 1960 went into orbit but
not with the desired parameters. The perigee was 373km (232mi), the apogee 748km
(465mi) and the orbital inclination 51.3° to
the equator. Transit 5A1, the first to be operational, was launched December 19, 1962
from Vandenberg by a Scout rocket, into a
polar orbit (inclination 90.1° to the equator),
with a perigee of 698km (434mi), and an
apogee of 725km (444mi).

LOFTI (USA-1961)

Two satellites named LOFTI (Low Frequency Trans-Ionospheric Satellite) were launched for the US Navy as part of the navigational satellite research program. They consisted of a spherical aluminum casing, diameter 0.61m (2ft), overall weight 22.5kg
(49.5lb), with six solar cell panels attached
to the outside. The two LOFTI satellites
were equipped with two receivers for
measuring the intensity of very low-
frequency signals through the ionosphere
and with a transmitter for telemetric data.

Launching and orbital data - LOFTI-1 was
launched February 21, 1961 from Cape Canaveral by a Thor Able Star rocket, together
with the Transit 3B navigational satellite.
Having gone into orbit, the two satellites did
not succeed in separating but continued to
function while still joined together. The initial orbit had a perigee of 167km (104mi) and
an apogee of 1,002km (623mi); orbital inclination was 29.38° and period 96 minutes.

TRAAC (USA-1961)

This was an experimental satellite, its name
derived from the initials of Transit Research
and Attitude Control, designed to test an attitude control system based on gravity, for
application to the Transit satellites. TRAAC
weighed 110kg (242lb) and was furnished
with a boom that measured 32m (105ft) in
length. The central section of the satellite
was 1.09m (3.6ft) in diameter and 1m (3.3ft)
high.

Launching and orbital data - TRAAC was
launched November 15, 1961 from Cape
Canaveral by a Thor Able Star rocket, which
also carried the Transit 4B navigational satellite. The orbital perigee was 941km
(585mi), the apogee 1,119km (695mi), the inclination to the equator 32.43°, the period
105 minutes. The mechanical systems on the
satellite, however, did not function properly and the intended experimental program
was limited.

TRAAC

3

SECOR/TOPO (USA-1964)

The SECOR (Sequential Collation of Range) satellites were built by the Cubic Corporation for the US Army for purposes of navigation and position-finding. They were shaped like a small box, measuring 0.36×0.28×0.23m (1.2×0.9×0.75ft), and they weighed 18kg (39.68lb). Two ITT solid-state transponders retransmitted signals sent in from four positions, three of them known and the fourth determined by the satellite. A SECOR satellite launched as part of a program initiated by the Topographic Laboratory of the US Army Engineers, known as TOPO, was designed for tests of triangulation for navigational purposes.

Launching and orbital data - From 1964 to 1969 13 SECOR satellites were launched. The first was sent up on January 11, 1964 from Vandenberg by a TAT-Agena D rocket together with the GGSE-1 and Solrad-7A satellites. The orbit, inclined at 69.9° to the equator, had a perigee height of 904km (562mi) and an apogee of 933km (580mi). TOPO-1 was launched April 8, 1970 from Vandenberg by a Thor AD/Agena D rocket which sent it into an orbit 1,064km (661mi) high at the perigee and 1,111km (680mi) at the apogee, with an orbital inclination to the equator of 99.7°.

TIMATION-NTS (USA-1967)

The Timation (Time Navigation) satellites were an improvement upon the preceding Transit satellites and were the outcome of a US Navy program. The shape was a box of 0.81×0.41×0.20m (2.65×1.35×0.65ft). The weight was 38kg (83.61lb). The new feature was the use of high-precision quartz clock for more accurate measurements based upon a "three-dimensional navigation" technique. The third Timation satellite was renamed Navigation Technology Satellite (NTS-1) because it also embodied the results of a parallel program of Transit improvement carried out by the US Air Force, known as System 621B. The first NTS launched in 1974 had the shape of an octagonal prism 0.56m (1.84ft) high and 1.22m (4ft) across. The weight was 293kg (645lb). In addition to two quartz clocks, NTS-1 tested two rubidium vapor atomic clocks and operated at two different frequencies (335MHz and 1,580MHz) in order to improve accuracy. NTS-2, launched in 1977, also tested a caesium atomic clock.

Launching and orbital data - Timation-1 was launched May 31, 1967 from Vandenberg by a Thor Agena D rocket in the course of a multiple launch of nine satellites. The orbit was higher than that of the Transit satellites, with a perigee of 915km (569mi) and an apogee of 925km (575mi). Orbital inclination to the equator was 70°. NTS-1 was launched July 14, 1974 from Vandenberg by an Atlas F rocket and was sent into a much higher

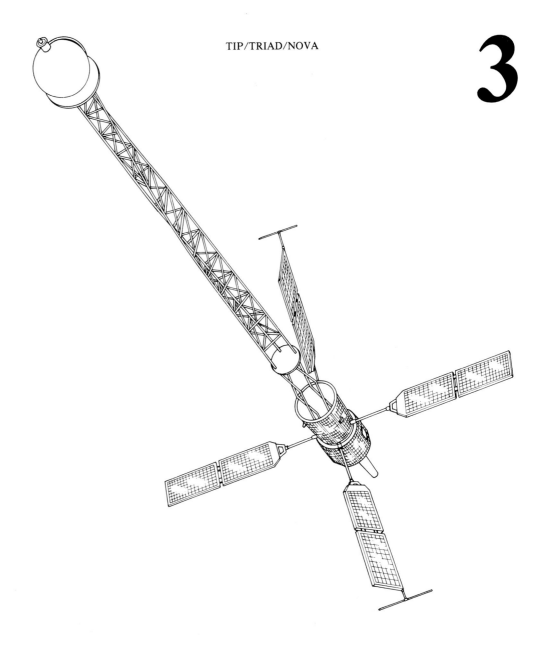

and almost circular orbit, with a perigee of 13,445km (8,355mi) and an apogee of 13,767km (8,555mi), inclined at 125° to the equator. Solar wind pressure on the panels of solar cells caused disturbances to the orbit.

TIP/TRIAD/NOVA (USA-1972)

With a view to improving still further the Transit system, and as an adjunct to the Timation program, the US Navy also tested the TIP (Transit Improvement Program); the ensuing stage of this program was the production version of the TIP, known as the NOVA satellite. The TIP satellites had a cylindrical body with a diameter of 0.61m (2ft), a height of 0.51m (1.67ft) and a weight of 94kg (207lb); improvements to it included a new position-finding system called DISCOS (Disturbance Compensation System) which was designed to maintain position in orbit by correcting disturbances caused by solar wind and atmospheric resistan-

ce. In addition, the first TIP satellite launched, known as TRIAD, was equipped with a new nuclear generator, the RTG (Radioisotope Thermal Generator), as source of power. TIP-2, however, reverted to using solar generators. Subsequent improvements included an onboard computer, electronics with better resistance to radiation and a system for correcting the clock's errors of frequency with a command from the ground. In 1981 standard production of the TIP satellites commenced, now called NOVA, and still powered by four panels of solar cells. Weighing 166kg (365lb), they required a few adjustments to position, transmitted from the ground, and for stabilization in orbit made use of a boom 7.5m (24.6ft) long, some what shorter than the one previously employed in some Transit satellites. The NOVA series of satellites were likewise produced by RCA Astro-Electronics.

Launching and orbital data - TIP/TRIAD-1 was launched September 2, 1972 from Vandenberg by a Scout rocket. It was sent into polar orbit, inclined 90.14° to the equator, with a perigee of 716km (445mi) and an apo-

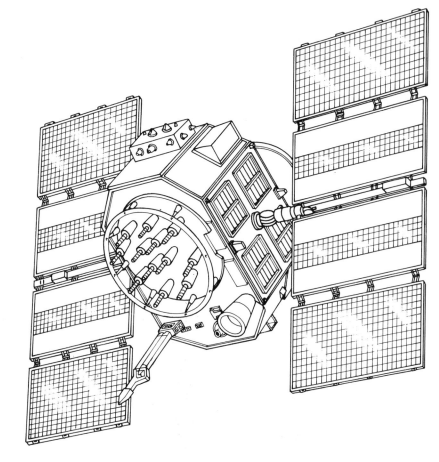

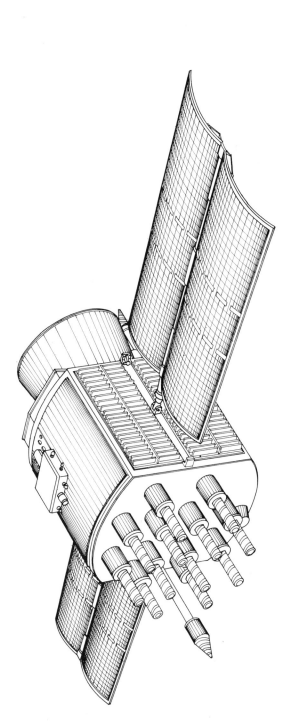

Navstar/Block 1

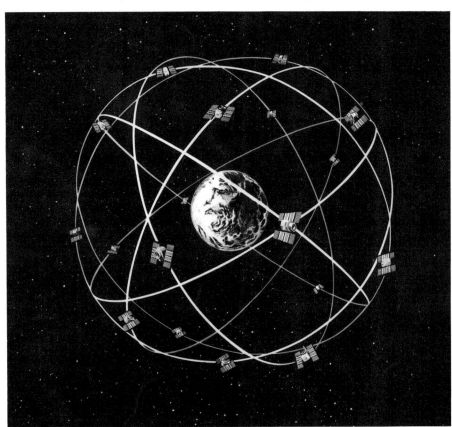

NAVSTAR-GPS. An American navigational satellite for civil and military use. The system em-
ploys a "constellation" of 18 (as in the picture)
or 24 orbiting satellites to give a margin of error
in position finding in the second case of 10 m
(32.80 ft).

gee of 863km (536mi).
The first NOVA satellite was launched May 15, 1981 from Vandenberg by a Scout rocket into an orbit with a perigee height of 1,170km (727mi) and an apogee of 1,187km (737mi).

TRANSAT (USA-1977)

This was a Transit satellite furnished with instruments for testing Satrack receivers for a US Navy program.

Launching and orbital data - Transat was launched October 28, 1977 from Vandenberg by a Scout rocket. The orbital perigee was 1,062km (660mi) and the apogee 1,101km (684mi); the inclination 90° to the equator.

NAVSTAR/GPS (USA-1978)

The decision to test the Global Positioning System (GPS) was taken in 1973, its purpose being to provide the defense and civil authorities with a means of determining position with even greater accuracy. Like Transit, Navstar (standing for Navigation System Using Timing and Ranging) operated in two frequencies. At 1,575.42 MHz, the only frequency available for civilian use, four Navstar satellites in orbit could fix position (latitude, longitude and altitude) with a margin of error of 30m (98ft). The second frequency of 1,227.6 MHz, reserved for military purposes, could, on the other hand, attain an accuracy of 16m (52.5ft) with 18 satellites in orbit, or 10m (33ft) with 24 satellites in orbit. Furthermore, speed could be determined with a tolerance of 0.1m per second and the exact time to 100 billionths of a second. Navstar satellites used atomic clocks: each carried three rubidium and one caesium clock, likely to lose or gain only one second in 36,000 years.
The Navstar satellites, three-axis stabilized, were built in two series. The first, called Block 1, weighed 455kg (1,000lb) in orbit, the panel of solar cells furnishing power of 400 watts. They had a working life of five years. From 1982 a second series (Block 2) began to be produced, the weight going up to 787kg (1,731lb) and the shape, too, being altered. The two panels of solar cells were replaced by larger ones capable of providing power of 700 watts. The Block 2 satellites had an increased working life of seven and a half years and they could also be carried into orbit with the Space Shuttle.
Navstar satellites, built by Rockwell International, were also furnished with a sensor for detecting nuclear explosions.

Launching and orbital data - The eighteen Navstar satellites that represented the entire system were sent into different orbital planes. Navstar 1 was launched February 22, 1978 from Vandenberg by an Atlas F rocket. Its orbit, inclined 63° to the equator, had a

perigee height of 20,095km (12,487mi) and an apogee of 20,308km (12,619mi). This was, in fact, the orbit fixed for all the Navstar satellites, the period being 12 hours.

COSMOS-1000/TSIKADA (USSR-1978)

Cosmos-1000 (also called Tsikada) was the first officially recognized Soviet navigation satellite. To be accurate, it was the first declared to be designed for civil navigation, others having previously been produced for military purposes.
The very first satellite launched for navigation was Cosmos-192, on November 23, 1967, and this was followed by dozens of others, divided into four generations, each of them distinguished by an ever increasing capacity. The series was comparable in performance to the American Transit satellites. The system was considered operational after 1971 with the functioning in orbit of Cosmos-385, -422 and -465. These satellites were cylindrical in shape, with a diameter of 2m (6.6ft) and a height which was originally 1.4m (4.6ft) but was then increased, in advanced models, to 2m (6.6ft.) A kind of trellised tower, comprising various systems, was attached to the base of the cylinder. The satellites transmitted in VHF and UHF on two close frequencies of 150 and 400 MHz; and each was given an identity number so that there could be no confusion of signals. In orbit the system located position with a precision of 80-100m (262-328ft). The three satellites Cosmos-1383, -1447 and -1574 were also equipped with a supplementary system for research and salvage missions within the scope of the international Cospas-Sarsat program.

Launching and orbital data - The first generation provided for three satellites placed in orbit on three planes 120° apart. The second generation, commencing with Cosmos-514 (launched August 16, 1972),

called for three satellites on orbital planes 60° from one another. The third generation, from Cosmos-700 onward, required six satellites on four orbital planes 30° apart. The fourth generation used four satellites on four planes 45° from one another. The orbits were almost circular at a height of 1,000km (621mi), the inclination to the equator being 83° and the orbital period about 105 minutes. Almost all satellites were launched from the Plesetsk base by C-1 rockets. Cosmos-1000 was launched March 31, 1978 from Plesetsk into a near-circular orbit with a height of 965-1,012km (599-629mi) and an inclination of 82.93°. Cosmos-1383 was launched June 29, 1982; Cosmos-1447 March 24, 1983; Cosmos-1574 June 21, 1984.

GLONASS (USSR-1982)

Cosmos-1413, -1414 and -1415 were the new Soviet navigation satellites launched in October 1982. The USSR gave official notice of this to the International Communications Union, declaring that they were part of a Global Navigation Satellite System (Glonass). According to the Soviet authorities, this system made it possible to fix the position of civil aircraft, merchant ships and fishing vessels, as well as military vehicles, having the same characteristics as the American Navstar-GPS series. Weight and dimensions were similar to those of the previous navigation satellites (Cosmos-1000 type). Transmissions were on frequencies of 1.2-1.6 GHz.

Launching and orbital data - The first three Glonass satellites were launched by a single D-1-E-e rocket on October 12, 1982 from Baikonur-Tyuratam and sent into an almost circular orbit at an altitude of 19,000km (11,806mi), inclined at 64.8° to the equator; period 12 hours. The Glonass satellites were in groups of six on orbital planes 120° apart.

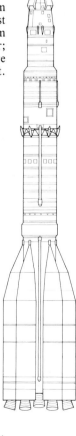

D-1-E

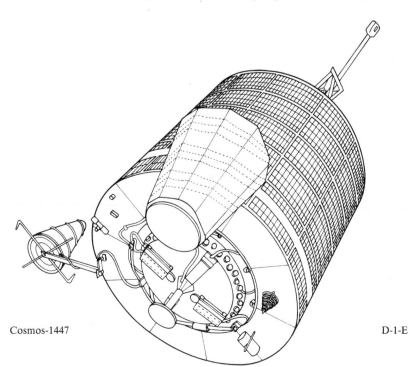

Cosmos-1447

INTO SPACE

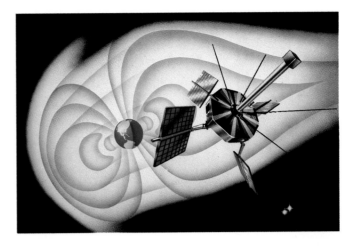

Explorer-12

Launched in 1961, the Explorer-12 has been used to increase knowledge of Van Allen belts and to carry out a series of measurements of the Earth's magnetic field. Formed by an octagonal platform with a protruding magnetometer, it was equipped with four panels of solar cells.
The illustration shows it against the complex Earth's magnetic field vizualized.

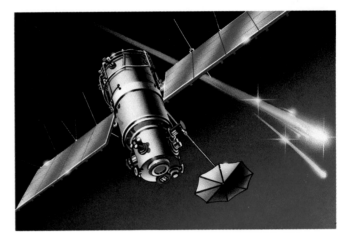

Meteor

The picture shows a first generation Meteor, meteorological satellite launched by the Soviet Union and operational since 1969. In the background, a meteorite is entering the upper strate of the Earth's atmosphere.

Esro

ESA satellites in polar orbit launched in 1968 and 1969 to study the polar ionosphere, the phenomena known as the northern lights (*aurora borealis*) and to measure the flow of solar protons and electrons.

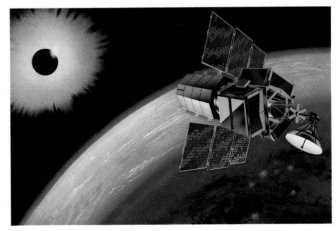

SMM (Solar Maximum Mission)

At an altitude of 500km (310mi), it is constantly turned toward the Sun.´
It was repaired by *Challenger*'s astronauts in April 1984 and is shown here during a solar eclipse.

a.gigli

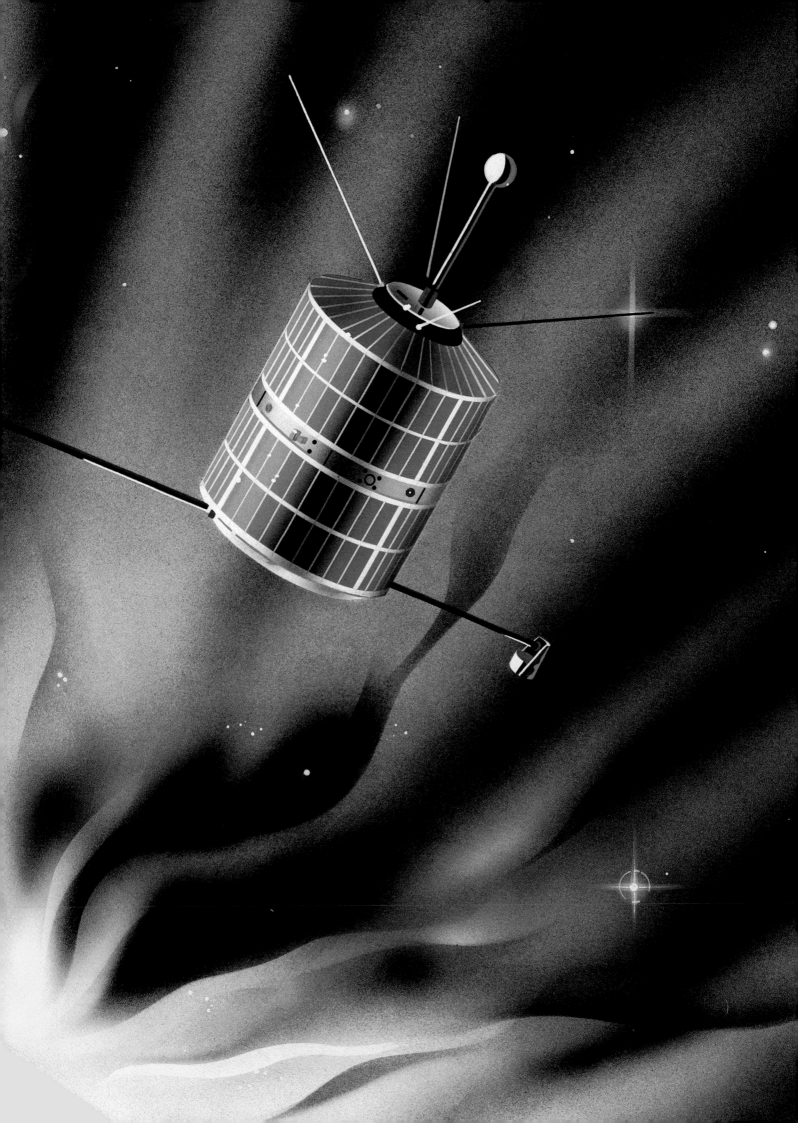

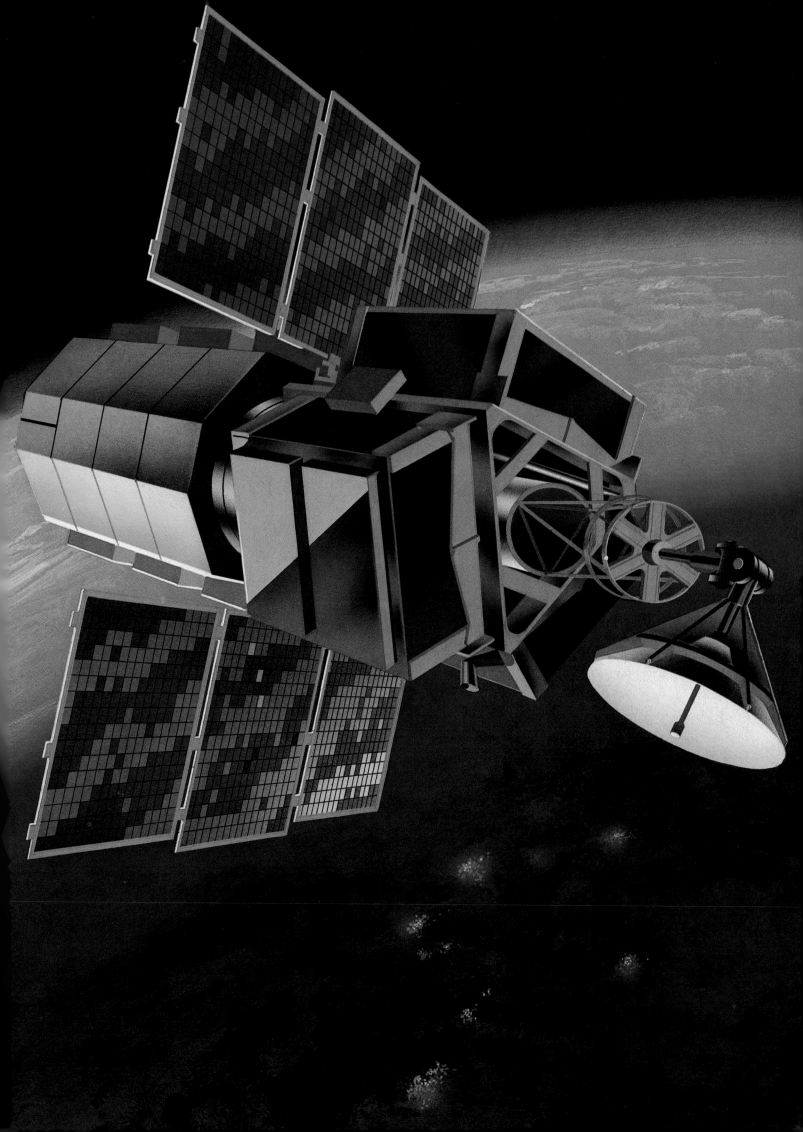

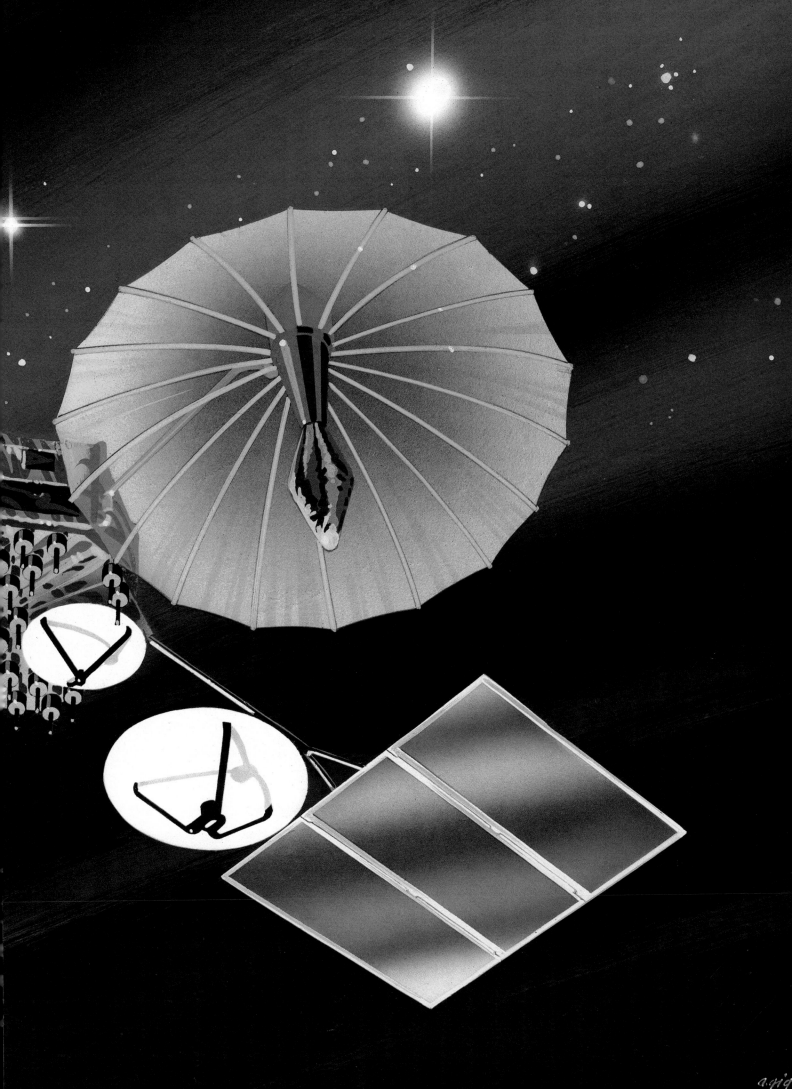

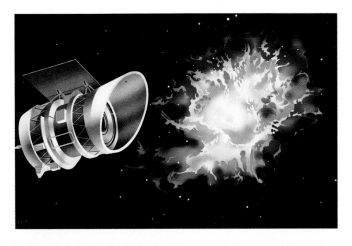

IRAS (Infrared Astronomical Satellite)

This was coproduced by the USA, Holland and Great Britain and sent into a polar orbit in January 1983. It is the first scanner of the Universe to operate in the infrared band of the electromagnetic spectrum. On its first day of operation, IRAS discovered over 4,000 sources of infrared. In this artist's impression, it is set against a backdrop of the Nebula of Cancer.

Exosat

An X-ray astronomical observatory launched on May 26, 1983 from the Vandenberg base using a Delta 3914 carrier; its instruments are capable of locating sources of X-rays throughout the Universe with great precision. In this artist's impression, it is set against the Nebula of Orion.

TDRS (Tracking & Data Relay Satellite)

The first of three telecommunications satellites designed to ensure 100% links between future orbital platforms and Earth stations. It was launched on April 4, 1983 and underwent an orbital correction lasting nearly two months. Here it is seen shortly after release of the second stage of the IUS and after deployment of the antennae and solar panels. It is 17.41m (57.11ft) long from antenna to antenna and weighs 2,120kg (4,674lb).

4

Telecommunications satellites

Space technology discovered its first practical application in the field of telecommunications, also providing unlimited opportunities for business of worldwide proportions. At the beginning of the operational service, only international communications systems have used satellites for some time, and now satellites are being employed increasingly for national requirements. Thanks to them it is simple to overcome difficult situations, such as those posed by mountains, which would have developed into serious problems were it a matter of establishing land links. Furthermore, satellites offer a wide range of services, including telephonic communication, television broadcasting and the transmission of up-to-date information by other means, such as telex, facsimile, etc. It is possible, too, to launch satellites specialized in a particular area, as, for example, those designed to relay news and information between various industries, banks or commercial groups in general; and there are satellites for direct television which use their power to send programs from transmitting stations through domestic aerials into the home. To achieve all this, space communications technology has made notable advances since 1960, the year when the Echo balloon was sent into orbit. These balloons represented the first and simplest attempts at spatial transmission, using a so-called "passive" system which was limited to reflecting toward the Earth electromagnetic waves directed against their aluminum-coated surface.

But this was not the most promising method and indeed it was soon abandoned in favor of "active" systems, namely satellites capable of receiving signals from the Earth with suitable antennae, of amplifying them with onboard instruments, and then of retransmitting them to another part of the planet. This led to the Relay satellites.

There still remained another basic difficulty to overcome, this being related to the satellite's orbit. Rotating in an inclined orbit around the Earth at a height of several hundred kilometers, the satellite, given the Earth's curvature, could be "seen" by ground antennae and thus utilized only for short periods of its orbital journey. This was a significant drawback because it reduced its useful time and so guaranteed only a partial return of the vast amounts of money invested, given the costs of the sophisticated space technology and the expenses incurred in launching.

The solution was found by applying an idea put forward in an essay by the English scientist and author Arthur C. Clarke in 1945. Clarke had suggested placing in equatorial orbit, 42,000km (25,700 miles) from the Earth's center, three satellites, each with an orbital period of 24 hours. Positioned 120° apart, each would be able, from this height, to "observe" one-third of the most populated area of the planet. All three satellites together, which Clarke described as a "chain of space stations", could thus simultaneously "see" the entire Earth, making global communication possible. Each satellite, since it had a 24-hour period of rotation, synchronized with that of the Earth, would thus appear, to an observer on the ground, to be permanently fixed in one spot of the sky. Here, then, was the ideal solution for making full use of a space vehicle so as to allow transmissions between areas that were far apart.

The first satellite to realize Clarke's idea was Syncom-3, which was launched August 19, 1964; it weighed 37.5kg (82.51lb) and, positioned above the Pacific, enabled European viewers to watch the Tokyo Olympic Games live.

In due course intercontinental organizations were formed of groups of nations which launched and managed telecommunications satellites all over the world and which sold their services according to need. The Western nations thus launched the Intelsat, and the socialist countries the Intersputnik programs. These were supplemented by other organizations for regional traffic, such as Eutelsat in Europe, and Arabsat in the Arab countries.

In this way space telecommunications were transformed into a normal work instrument and technology soon had little new to offer. The frequencies assigned for transmission became increasingly crowded because of the growing traffic. Recourse was made to higher and higher frequencies, but this posed new technical problems. For example, frequencies above 10 GHz tend to be disturbed by weather conditions and signals encountering rain are weakened.

So these attenuations have to be measured in order to design systems that can compensate for this loss. One of the first satellites to take account of this phenomenon was the Italian Sirio research satellite which carried on board experiments devised by Professor Francesco Carassa of the Milan Polytechnic. The problem was carefully analyzed and Professor Carassa was given the Marconi Award for his studies, this being an international prize for scientists all over the world who make important contributions to the development of communications. Some years previously the same award had been given to Arthur C. Clarke.

In the meantime there had been changes in the techniques for satellite transmission in order to make maximum use of the invisible channel of electromagnetic waves traveling between Earth and space, carrying both sounds and pictures.

Initially the technique known as "frequency distribution" was adopted, this being the simplest to realize, whereby different carrier waves share the frequency being used. But this system was inadequate for coping with a great volume of traffic and so a new technique called "time division" was put into operation. Here the carrier wave was the only one in the allotted frequency and the different users each shared parts of the transmission time. Every station transmits for a limited period, and in rotation, a parcel of numerical information, making sure that these are perfectly synchronized to avoid overlapping. The receiving station receives the carrier wave coming in from the satellite and extracts from it the parcel of messages destined to it.

This comparatively recent technique permits full advantage to be taken of the satellite's power, also taking advantage of the techniques of compressed information nowadays possible, and taking account of the fact that large parts of our conversations consist of intervals which can also be utilized in this manner.

However, technology sets out to be even more ambitious, aiming at even fuller and more intensive use of available frequencies. Hence the conception of multi-faceted antennae to cover diverse but much smaller surface areas, each becoming active when there is the need to communicate from or to a particular area. Such transmissions, more directive, therefore require the installation on satellites of larger-diameter antennae. Another method being studied is the use of a single frequency in two right-angled positions so as to make twice as much use of the same band without any interference occurring. The objective, broadly speaking, is to make the satellite do most of the technical work of transmission so that ground stations can be smaller and less costly while the satellites themselves become bigger. But the risk is that a steady increase in size may affect the flexibility which is so essential in systems of space telecommunications. Technology thus comes up with clusters of satellites with the same capabilities as the present ones and operating as a system which is sufficiently integrated to handle all the traffic, or huge telecommunications platforms of high capacity in order to deal with different types of traffic. The controlled increase in the number of satellites in geostationary orbit is likewise an objective to be borne in mind because already some orbital positions are regarded as overcrowded.

Letter designations
for bands and frequencies in
transmission via satellite

HF	3-30 MHz
VHF	30-300 MHz
UHF	300-1,000 MHz
L	1-2 GHz
S	2-4 GHz
C	4-8 GHz
X	8-12 GHz
Ku	12-18 GHz
K	18-27 GHz
Ka	27-40 GHz
V	40-75 GHz
W	75-110 GHz
mm	110-300 GHz

ECHO (USA-1960)

The first civil telecommunications satellite sent into orbit. Of the passive type, it merely reflected toward the Earth the electromagnetic signals striking its surface. NASA sent two Echo satellites into orbit. They were shaped like a balloon which was inflated automatically in space by the vaporization of a substance (benzoic acid) contained within them. Echo-1 was 30m (98.42ft) in diameter and weighed 76kg (168lb). The walls were

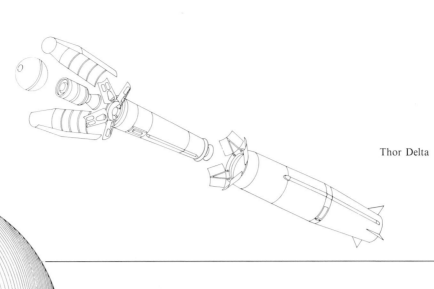

Thor Delta

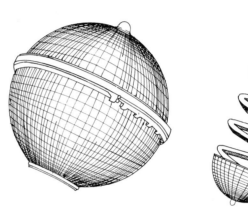

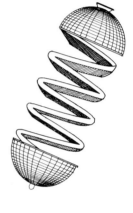

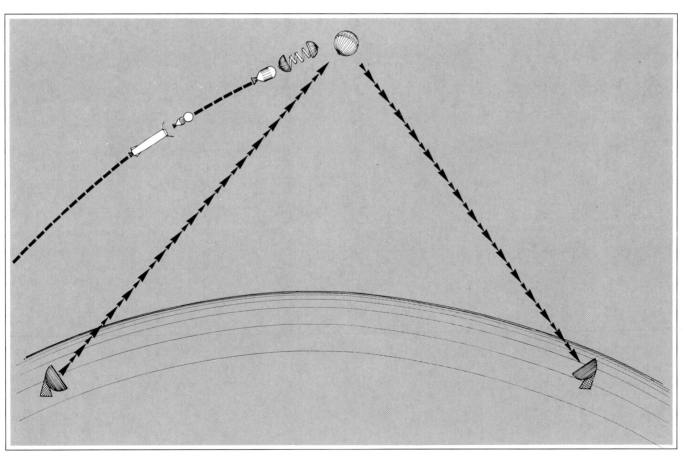

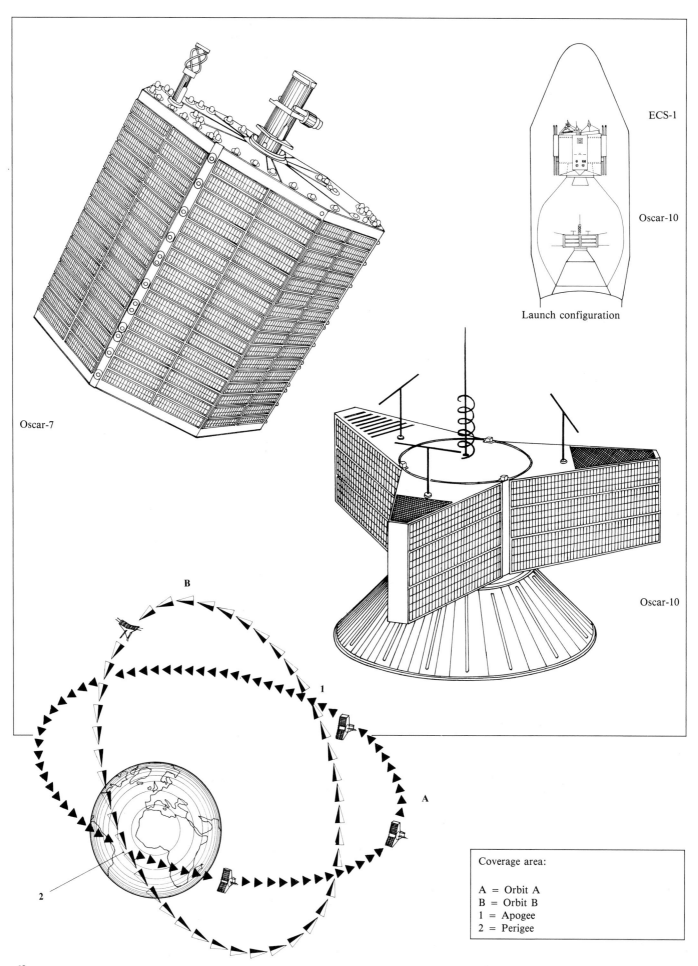

Oscar-7

ECS-1

Oscar-10

Launch configuration

Oscar-10

B

1

A

2

Coverage area:

A = Orbit A
B = Orbit B
1 = Apogee
2 = Perigee

made of mylar polyester film 0.0125cm (0.0049in) thick and coated with aluminum. The surface reflected 98 percent of the radio waves directed against it at a frequency of 20,000 megacycles. Echo-1 was also equipped with 140 solar cells which furnished the necessary power for two transmitters that emitted signals to facilitate survey and tracking operations. The satellite was used for a series of experimental transmissions. The day of the launch (August 12, 1960) a radio message from President Eisenhower was transmitted from one coast of the United States to the other. Subsequently, two Echo AVT's were launched unsuccessfully, the second of which had a diameter of 41m (134.5ft). Echo-2 was derived from this. With a diameter of 41m (134.5ft), it weighed 256kg (564lb) in orbit. The aluminized mylar surface was also treated with alodine which improved its reflective qualities. Interesting research was carried out with Echo-2 on the pressure exercized by solar radiation. The first joint USA-USSR space experiment took place, in the form of a link between the stations of Jodrell Bank in Great Britain and the Zimenski Observatory at Gorki University near Moscow.

Launching and orbital data - Echo-1 was launched August 12, 1960 from Cape Canaveral by a Thor Delta rocket and sent into an orbit initially 1,524km (947mi) high at the perigee and 1,684km (1,046mi) at the apogee. Inclination to the equator was 47.22°, the orbital period being 118 minutes. It reentered the atmosphere May 24, 1968.
Echo-2 left Vandenberg January 25, 1964 by a Thor Agena B rocket. It had a perigee of 1,029km (639mi), an apogee of 1,316km (818mi), a period of 109 minutes and an orbital inclination of 81.5°. It reentered the atmosphere June 7, 1969.
The orbital parameters of the two satellites underwent continual variation due to the pressure of solar radiation.

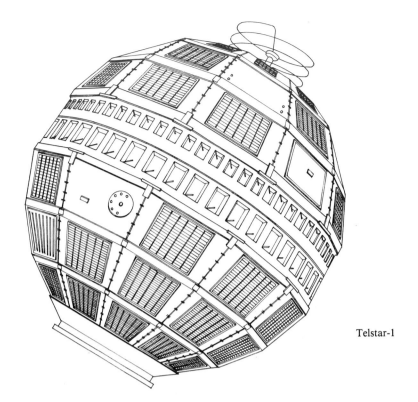

Telstar-1

OSCAR (USA-1961)

The first satellite for radio hams, Oscar-1 from the initials for Orbiting Satellite Carrying Amateur Radio, was launched together with the 36th military vehicle, Discoverer. It was shaped like a box, weighing 5kg (11lb), 0.30m (0.98ft) long, 0.25m (0.82ft) wide and 0.15m (0.49ft) high. With a power output of 100 milliwatts, Oscar-1 transmitted the message "HI," which in Morse code signifies laughter. The satellite operated for 20 days, during which its signals were received by amateur radio enthusiasts from 28 nations. Oscar-2 was similar to the first while Oscar-3 was the first, active telecommunications satellite with free access. It received signals from Earth and retransmitted them with a power output of one watt. It established the first transatlantic link via satellite for radio hams and permitted the first direct links with some East European countries such as Czechoslovakia and Bulgaria. Oscar-4 had two different wavelengths and established the first link with the USSR.

Oscar-5 was designed and built in Australia. Oscar-6, -7 and -8 made up the second group of satellites for radio hams, built in this case under the auspices of the Radio Amateur Satellite Corporation (Amsat) established in 1969. Still shaped like a box, measuring 0.43x0.30x0.15m (1.41x0.98x0.49ft), they weighed 27kg (60lb). In 1981, Oscar-9 was launched. Also known as Uosat, it was built by the students of the University of Surrey in Great Britain and weighed 52kg (115lb). It transmitted data and was equipped with a television camera which sent images of the Earth with a resolution of 2km (1.24mi). It also carried two particles counters for detecting solar and auroral activity in terms of the interference caused to telecommunications. Finally, it also had a magnetometer and a voice synthesizer with a 150 word vocabulary specifying the conditions of the satellite. Oscar-10 was prepared by German radio hams and weighed 44kg (97lb). Oscar-11 (Uosat-2), weighing 60kg (132lb) was developed in Great Britain.

Launching and orbital data - Oscar-1 was launched December 12, 1961 and sent into an orbit with a perigee of 245km (152mi), an apogee of 474km (295mi) and an orbital inclination of 81°. Oscar-2 went up in 1962, Oscar-3 and -4 in 1965, Oscar-5 in 1970, Oscar-6 in 1972, Oscar-7 in 1974, Oscar-8 in 1978 and Oscar-9 in 1981. Oscar-10 was launched by an European Ariane rocket June 16, 1983 from the polygon in French Guiana, together with the ECS European satellite. Its orbit had a perigee of 3,846km (2,390mi), an apogee of 35,609km (22,126mi) and an orbital inclination of 26°. Oscar-11 (Uosat-2) was launched into a polar orbit March 1, 1984, together with the American Landsat-5 satellite.

TELSTAR (USA-1962)

AT&T built the Telstar-1 satellite which was launched and controlled in orbit by NASA. It was in the shape of a polyhedric sphere with 72 sides nearly all covered with solar cells (totaling 3,600). The maximum diameter of the satellite was 0.86m (2.82ft), the weight being 77kg (170lb). With Telstar-1, which had a transmission capacity of 600 telephone channels or one television channel, the first television link between the United States and Europe was established July 10, 1962 and numerous video transmission, telephonic communication and facsimile transmission trials were effected. The satellite, which operated as a repeater (relay station), had a power output of 2.25 watts. Other instruments on board informed the Earth stations of the satellite's conditions and the characteristics of the space environment. Telstar-1 ceased transmission February 21, 1963. A second Telstar was sent into orbit with the same characteristics except for a few improvements, chiefly to the electronic components which were made less vulnerable to radiation. Telstar-2 weighed 80kg (176lb) and permitted the first direct link between Europe and Japan. The choice of a higher apogee than for Telstar-1 gave the satellite a longer operating time in communications between the USA and Europe.

Launching and orbital data - Telstar-1 was launched from Cape Canaveral July 10, 1962 by a Thor Delta rocket and sent into an orbit with a perigee of 952km (592mi), an apogee of 5,632km (3,500mi); the orbital inclination to the equator was 44.79° and the period of 157 minutes.

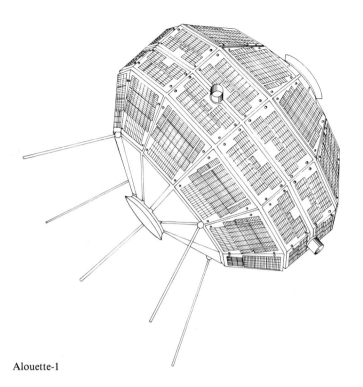

Alouette-1

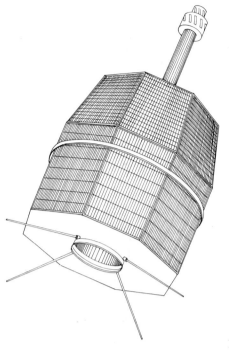

Relay-1

Telstar-2 left Cape Canaveral May 7, 1963 by a Thor Delta rocket and was sent into an orbit with a perigee of 974km (605mi) and an apogee of 10,803km (6,713mi); the orbital inclination was 42.3° and the period of 225 minutes.

ALOUETTE (CANADA-1962)

Two satellites named Alouette were built by Canada according to a Defense Research Board (DRB) program, in collaboration with NASA in the United States, to study the effects of the ionosphere on communications. The Alouettes were shaped like a many-sided

sphere, flattened at the poles, 1.07m (3.51ft) in diameter and 0.86m (2.82ft) high. 6,000 solar cells were fitted to the faceted outer surface. Alouette-1 weighed 145kg (320lb). Once in orbit, two antennae 23m (75.46ft) and 46m (150.91ft) long, projected from the satellite. The two Alouettes were designed and built by the Canadian Research Telecommunications Establishment of the DRB. Alouette-2 remained active for ten years.

Launching and orbital data - Alouette-1 was launched September 29, 1962 from Vandenberg by a Thor Agena B rocket into an orbit with a perigee height of 996km (619mi), an apogee of 1,032km (641mi), an orbital inclination of 80.46° and a period of 105 minutes. Alouette-2 left Vandenberg Novem-

ber 29, 1965, together with Explorer-31 by a Thor Agena B rocket. Its orbit had a perigee of 505km (314mi), an apogee of 2,979km (1,851mi), an inclination of 79.82° and a period of 121 minutes.

RELAY (USA-1962)

Relay-1 was an improvement on Telstar. Built by RCA for NASA, Relay was lighter and placed in a higher orbit to increase the operating time. In the form of a mixed octagonal prism, its outer surface was covered by 8,215 solar cells. The total height was 0.84m (2.75ft), to which was added the

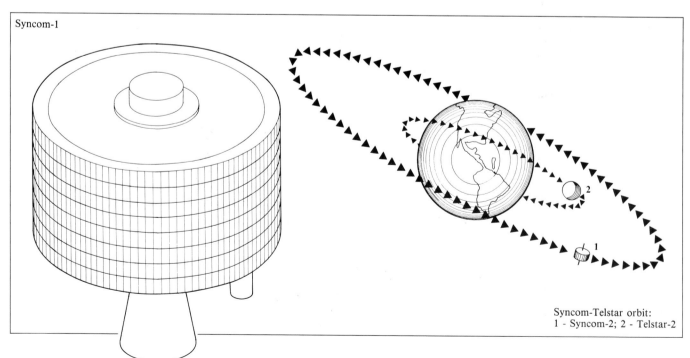

Syncom-1

Syncom-Telstar orbit:
1 - Syncom-2; 2 - Telstar-2

0.45m (1.48ft) long omnidirectional antenna; the maximum diameter was 0.73m (2.39ft), the weight being 78kg (172lb). Equipped with 300 voice channels in one direction only, it retransmitted communications at a frequency of 4,165-4,175 megacycles. Numerous test transmissions in the field of microwaves were conducted with Relay, television and telephone links being established between the United States, Europe and Brazil. A Relay-2 was also launched. This was similar to the first but with improved solar cells. At 83.5kg (184lb), it was slightly heavier than the previous one and established the first link between USA and Japan January 21, 1964.

Launching and orbital data - Relay-1 was launched December 13, 1962 from Cape Canaveral by a Thor Delta rocket. The orbit, inclined 47.49° to the equator, had a perigee of 1,322km (821mi), an apogee of 7,439km (4,622mi) and a period of 185 minutes.
Relay-2 left Cape Canaveral January 21, 1964 by a Thor Delta rocket and was sent into an orbit inclined 46.32°, with a perigee of 2,091km (1,299mi), an apogee of 7,411km (4,605mi) and a period of 194 minutes.

SYNCOM (USA-1963)

A satellite built by Hughes for NASA to test geosynchronous, geostationary orbit in order to create a system of global telecommunications using three satellites, as suggested by Arthur C. Clarke, with an equatorial orbital plane and a maximum altitude of 36,000km (22,369mi). Syncom, meaning "Synchronous (Communications) Satellite," was shaped like a drum 0.64m (2.09ft) high and 0.71m (2.33ft) in diameter. Its weight was 68kg (150lb) including the 41kg (90lb) of the apogee motor. The outer surface was covered with 3,840 solar cells delivering a power of 29 watts. Syncom had a nitrogen peroxide attitude control system. Three Syncom satellites were launched, but communications with the first were lost just after it went into orbit; the second was positioned in an orbit inclined 33.05° to the equator. Apart from a series of experiments, it permitted a telephone conversation between the President of the United States and the Nigerian Prime Minister. Syncom-3, on the other hand, was the first geostationary satellite. Its final position was reached September 23, 1964, five weeks after launching, and permitted transmission of the Tokyo Olympic Games in October 1964. From April 1, 1965, Syncom-3 ceased its civil activity for NASA and became part of the military telecommunications network. The same thing happened with Syncom-2.

Launching and orbital data - Syncom-1 was launched February 14, 1963. Syncom-2 left Cape Canaveral July 26, 1963 by a Thor Delta rocket and was sent into an almost circular orbit with a perigee of 35,584km (22,110mi), an apogee of 36,693km (22,780mi), an orbital inclination of 33.05°

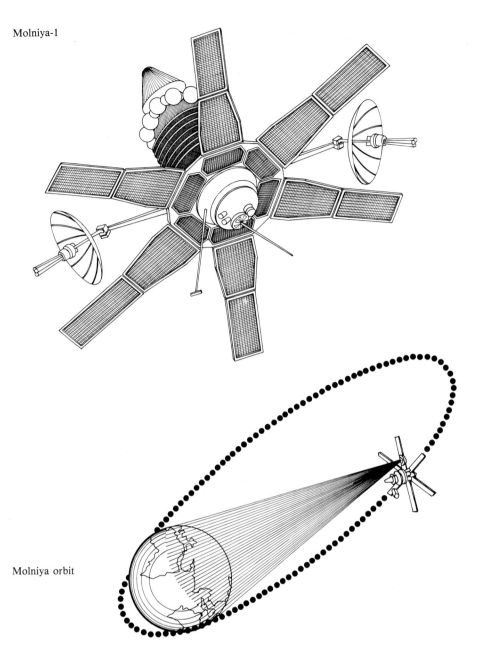

Molniya-1

Molniya orbit

and a period of 1,454 minutes.
Syncom-3 was launched August 19, 1964 by a Thrust Augmented Thor Delta rocket; it entered geostationary orbit over the equator at a height of 35,799km (22,244mi) and an inclination of 0.10°.

MOLNIYA-1 (USSR-1965)

The first Soviet telecommunications satellite. The satellites in this series, being positioned in synchronous orbit, guaranteed communications for eight hours a day, therefore three satellites synchronized in relation to one another could give 24-hour coverage. The Molniya-1 satellites consisted of a central, cylindrical body 1.6m (5.25ft) in diameter and 3.4m (11.1ft) tall, from which six panels of solar cells delivering a power of about 700 watts and two parabolic antennae 0.9m (2.95ft) in diameter projected. The in-

struments on board permitted television transmissions at a frequency of 3.4-4.1 GHz and telephone and telegraph transmissions at frequencies of 0.8-1 GHz both within the Soviet Union through the Orbita network and to a few Communist countries such as Cuba and Mongolia. The power of the onboard transmitter was 40 watts. The Molniya-1 satellites were also equipped with television cameras which sent images of cloud distribution. The satellites were stabilized on three axes.

Launching and orbital data - Molniya-1 was launched April 23, 1965 from Baikonur-Tyuratam polygon by an A-2 rocket. It was positioned in a synchronous, elliptical orbit, 538km (334mi) high at the perigee, 39,300km (24,420mi) at the apogee, inclined 65.5° to the equator.
From 1970, the satellites of the Molniya-1 series were launched from the more northerly polygon of Plesetsk.

Intelsat-1

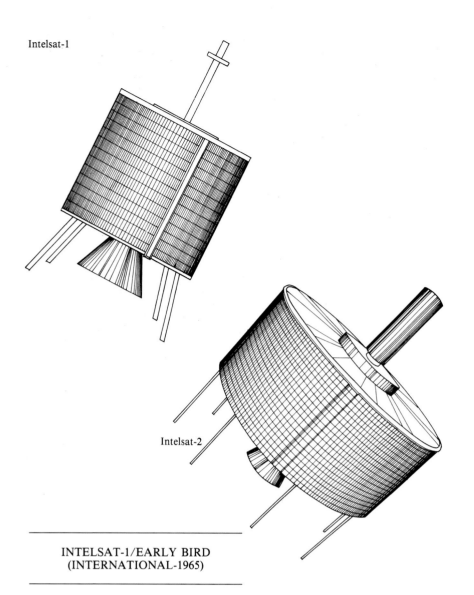

Intelsat-2

0.67m (2.20ft). The solar cells on its outer surface supplied a power of 85 watts. The weight in orbit was 86.4kg (190lb). Intelsat-2 had a capacity of 240 telephone circuits or one television channel. It introduced the possibility of simultaneous links between the Earth stations in the area covered by the antennae, which for the first time could be in the northern or southern hemisphere. Four Intelsat-2 satellites were launched in all, but the first failed to achieve geostationary orbit due to malfunction of the apogee motor. Of the other three, two were positioned over the Pacific and one over the Atlantic. They were built by Hughes.

Launching and orbital data - Intelsat-2 (F-1) was launched October 26, 1966. Intelsat-2 (F-2) went up January 11, 1967 and reached geostationary orbit over the Pacific without incident, becoming operational January 27, 1967. The third (F-3) was positioned over the Atlantic March 22, 1967.
The last Intelsat-2, F-4, was launched over the Pacific September 27, 1967.

ATS-1 to -5 (USA-1966)

The ATS satellites, from the initials for Applications Technology Satellites, were built to test a series of technologies in geostationary orbit regarding telecommunications in particular, but also including navigation, meteorology and system for controlling satellites in orbit. ATS-2 and -4 failed to achieve geostationary orbit. ATS-3 and-4 were

INTELSAT-1/EARLY BIRD (INTERNATIONAL-1965)

This was the first commercial satellite, launched for the international organization Intelsat founded in 1964 to run a space network of global communications. Intelsat-1, initially called "Early Bird," had a capacity of 240 telephone circuits or one television channel. Positioned over the Atlantic to cover the communication requirements between North America and Europe, it only permitted links between two Earth stations at a time. The cylindrical satellite was 0.59m (1.93ft) high and 0.72m (2.36ft) in diameter. Solar cells supplying a power of 46 watts were fitted to the outer surface. The weight in orbit was 38.6kg (85lb). Built by Hughes, it went into service June 28, 1965 and remained operational for three and a half years.

Launching and orbital data - Intelsat-1 was launched April 6, 1965 from Cape Canaveral by a Thrust Augmented Delta (TAD) rocket and sent into geostationary orbit above the Atlantic at longitude 325° E.

INTELSAT-2 (INTERNATIONAL-1966)

Intelsat-2 was also cylindrical in shape with a diameter of 1.42m (4.66ft) and a height of

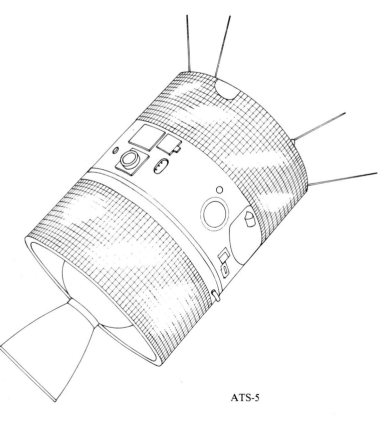

ATS-5

spin-stabilized along their longitudinal axis, while ATS-1, -2 and -5 were gravity stabilized. ATS-1 was in the form of a cylinder weighing 352kg (776lb), 1.45m (4.75ft) high and 1.42m (4.66ft) in diameter. Positioned above the Pacific Ocean, it permitted communications and exchange of information of an educational, medical, scientific and cultural nature between the United States and Australia, New Zealand, Papua New Guinea, Fiji, Tonga, the Solomon Islands, the Gilbert Islands and Samoa. ATS-3 was used to test medical communications in particular between oil platforms and Earth stations or between hospitals and mobile health centers or remote rural areas. ATS-3 was in the shape of a cylinder 1.83m (6ft) tall and 1.42m (4.66ft) in diameter. Its weight was 365kg (805lb). ATS-5 was the same height but slightly larger in diameter (1.52m = 5ft) with a weight of 433kg (955lb). It carried the greatest number of experiments of the series, 13 in all, plus three arms for gravity stabilization: one 38m (125ft) and the other two 14m (45.93ft) long. The solar cells on the outer surface of the satellite generated a power of 254 watts. The experimental apparatus on board included a television system, two transmitters in C-band (6-4 GHz) and L-band (1.5-1.6 GHz), three particle counters and six different types of satellite control system including an ionic propulsor. Hughes was the prime contractor.

Launching and orbital data - The three ATS satellites which achieved geostationary orbit had the following orbital parameters: ATS-1 was launched December 7, 1966 from Cape Canaveral by an Atlas Agena D rocket and sent into geostationary equatorial orbit with a maximum height of 35,817km (22,255mi); ATS-3 left Cape Canaveral November 5, 1967 by an Atlas Agena D rocket, attaining a maximum altitude of 36,130km (22,450mi); ATS-5 was launched August 12, 1969 from Cape Canaveral by an Atlas Centaur rocket and the highest point of the orbit was 35,790km (22,239mi) above the equator. The satellite worked only partially, because it began spinning inadvertently.

INTELSAT-3 (INTERNATIONAL-1968)

The third Intelsat satellite, despite being similar in size to the previous ones, was technologically more advanced and offered greater possibilities. It in fact had 1,500 telephone circuits or four television channels available, or a combination of the two. Also cylindrical in shape, it was 1.04m (3.41ft) high and 1.42m (4.66ft) in diameter with a weight in orbit of 152kg (335lb). It was spin-stabilized and had a contrarotating antenna which greatly improved communications. Intelsat-3 had an increased link capacity between different stations and could transmit telephone conversations, telegraph messages, facsimile, television pictures and high-speed data simultaneously. The satellite was built by TRW Systems. Eight Intelsat-3s were launched but the first, fifth and last failed to achieve geostationary orbit due to failure of the carrier rocket.

Launching and orbital data - The first Intelsat-3 (F-1) launched September 18, 1968 did not reach the established orbit. The second was correctly positioned in geostationary orbit over the Atlantic (maximum altitude, 35,790km = 22,239mi) December 18, 1968 and went into service December 24, 1968; it was active for only a short time due to blockage of an antenna. The last Intelsat-3 (F-8) went up July 23, 1970 but did not achieve geostationary orbit. The carrier rocket used for the launches which took place from Cape Canaveral was the Delta, with stretched fuel tanks.

4

Intelsat-3

Intelsat-3

The Intelsat series

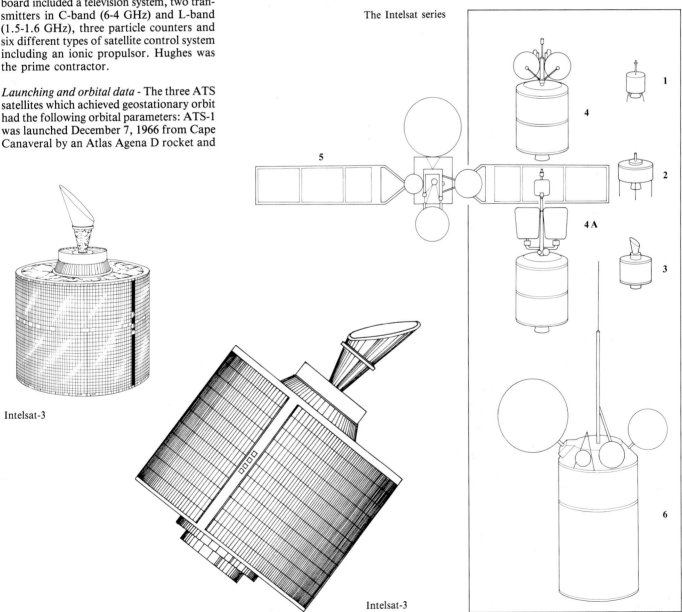

ISIS (CANADA-1969)

Two Canadian satellites of this name were launched, the electronics part of which was built by RCA Limited of Montreal (now Spar Technology Limited) and the structural part by Spar Aerospace Products Limited of Toronto. Isis, from the initials for International Satellites for Ionospheric Studies, continued the research successfully begun by Alouette regarding the influence of solar activity on the ionosphere which directly affected communications. The two Isis satellites were launched as part of an international program. Each satellite weighed 241kg (531lb), was 1.27m (4.17ft) in diameter, 1.07m (3.51ft) high (Isis-2 was 1.22m = 4ft tall) and carried eight Canadian and four American experiments. With them, the density of the electrons in the upper atmosphere, the radio emissions, the cosmic noise and the interaction of charged particles with the atmosphere were continuously measured.

Launching and orbital data - Isis-1 was launched January 30, 1969 from Vandenberg by a Thor Delta rocket into an elliptical orbit inclined 88.42° to the equator, with an apogee of 3,526km (2,191mi) and a perigee of 578km (359mi). The period was 128 minutes. Isis-2 left Vandenberg April 1, 1971 by a Thor Delta rocket and was sent into an almost circular orbit inclined 88.15° to the equator with an apogee of 1,429km (888mi) and a perigee of 1,358km (844mi). The orbital period was 114 minutes.

INTELSAT-4 (INTERNATIONAL-1971)

Intelsat-4 represented the fourth generation of satellites of the international organization for spatial telecommunications. The satel-

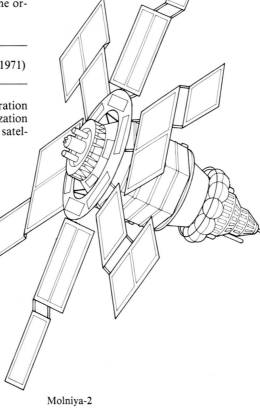

Molniya-2

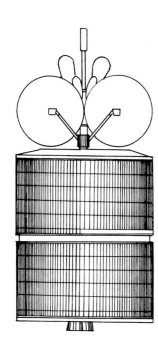

Intelsat-4

Isis-1

lite, which was built by Hughes, was in the form of a cylinder 2.81m (9.22ft) high (but the total height including the antennae was 5.26m = 17.25ft) and weighing 732kg (1,614lb) in orbit. The solar cells covering its outer surface supplied a power of 569 watts. It was spin-stabilized with a hydrazine-fed attitude control propulsion system. Intelsat-4 had 12 transponders supplying 6,000 telephone circuits or 12 video channels (or an average of 4,000 circuits plus 2 video channels). The system containing the antennae was contrarotating relative to the satellite and the two largest antennae had a diameter of 1.2m (3.94ft). The operative life of the satellite was seven years and it offered the possibility of multiple access and simultaneous transmissions. The satellite received at a frequency of 6 GHz and transmitted at a frequency of 4 GHz.

Launching and orbital data - The first Intelsat-4 (F-2) was placed in geostationary orbit (maximum altitude 35,794km = 22,241mi) January 25, 1971. Positioned over the Atlantic at longitude 335.5° E, it went into service March 26, 1971. Seven Intelsat-4s were sent into orbit and the last one, sent up on May 22, 1975, was positioned above the Indian Ocean at longitude 63° E. The carrier rockets used for the launches, which all took place from Cape Canaveral, were the Atlas Centaur.

MOLNIYA-2 (USSR-1971)

The second series of Soviet telecommunications satellites, also stabilized on three axes. Basically similar in structure to the previous ones, they had better attitude control system, onboard power and communications apparatus. All six panels of solar cells had an extra piece to increase their area by one third, bringing the power generated to about 1,000 watts. The frequencies used for transmissions were higher: 4-6 GHz. This enabled radio and television programs, telephonic and telegraphic communications and also entire pages of newspapers and weather charts to be transmitted. The satellites of the Molniya-2 series were also used for the hotline between the White House and the Kremlin which was established for security reasons in 1971.

Launching and orbital data - The first Molniya-2 was launched November 24, 1971 from Plesetsk by an A-2-e rocket and sent into an elliptical orbit inclined 65° to the equator with a perigee of 321km (200mi), an apogee of 24,577km (15,271mi) and a period of 712 minutes.

TELESAT-1 to -3/ANIK-A (CANADA-1972)

Anik-A1 was the first satellite in the world sent into geostationary orbit to be used by a nation for internal commercial telecommunications, that is within national boundaries.

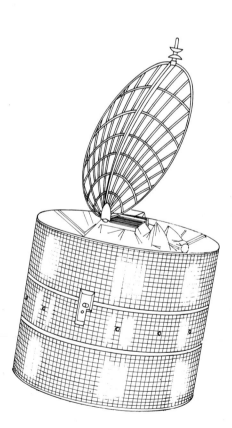

Telesat-1

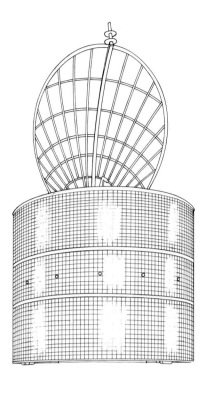

Westar-1

The satellite was built by the American Hughes Aircraft Co., and Spar Aerospace Products Limited of Toronto and the Northern Electric Company Limited of Lucerne (Quebec) were the main Canadian subcontractors. The satellite was cylindrical in form with a diameter of 1.8m (5.90ft) and a total height of 3.4m (11.15ft). The outer surface of the satellite was covered with solar cells which provided a power of 300 watts. It was spin-stabilized. Anik-A1 had 12 channels permitting transmission of as many television channels or the simultaneous transmission of 5,760 two-way telephone conversations. The frequencies used were 6-4 GHz. The weight in geostationary orbit was 295kg (650lb), while the predicted service life was seven years. Anik-A2/Telesat-2 and Anik-A3/Telesat-3 with similar characteristics to the first, were also sent into orbit.

Launching and orbital data - Anik-A1 was launched November 9, 1972 from Cape Canaveral by a Delta rocket and positioned in geostationary equatorial orbit. Anik-A2 and Anik-A3 were launched April 20, 1973 and May 7, 1975, respectively. Their positions in geostationary orbit were 104° (Anik-A1), 109° (Anik-A2) and 114° (Anik-A3) longitude West.

WESTAR-1 to -3 (USA-1974)

Westar-1 was the first internal telecommunications satellite in the United States. Built by Hughes Aircraft Co., it was shaped like a cylinder 1.9m (6.23ft) in diameter and 1.6m (5.25ft) tall, the total height with the 1.5m (4.92ft) diameter antenna fitted to one end of the satellite being 3.42m (11.22ft). Weighing 305kg (672lb) in orbit, it had the outer surface covered with 20,500 solar cells giving a power of 300 watts. Westar-1, which was spin-stabilized, had 12 transponders providing 7,200 telephone circuits or 12 color television channels. The operative life of the satellite was seven years. Westar-2 and -3 were similar in characteristics to the first and used a frequency of 4-6 GHz.

Launching and orbital data - Westar-1 was launched from Cape Canaveral April 13, 1974 by a Delta 2914 rocket. It was positioned in an almost circular geostationary equatorial orbit (maximum height 35,770km = 22,226mi) at longitude 99° W. Westar-2 and Westar-3 also left Cape Canaveral by a Delta 2914, on October 10, 1974 and August 9, 1979, respectively.

ATS-6 (USA-1974)

The sixth satellite in the Applications Technology Satellites (ATS) series which remained active for five years. It permitted one of the most productive series of experiments in the field of communications technology via satellite. With it, educational broadcasts, transmissions from one satellite to another, experiments in air traffic control and teleconferences were conducted. Medical information was also broadcast to remote localities and the satellite was also used during the joint USA-USSR mission with the Apollo-Soyuz spacecraft in July 1975, providing video links for both the United States and Soviet Union. From 1975 to 1976, ATS-6 was also used by India for educational broadcasts directly picked up by the satellite with small stations distributed in 2,500 Indian villages. Other research projects were concerned with climatology and the study of radio interference. ATS-6 was built by Fairchild Industries as prime contractor and Philco-Ford (communication module), IBM (telemetry and control systems), Honeywell Aerospace Div. (attitude control system) and Lockheed Missile Space Company (parabolic antenna reflector). The satellite, which was stabilized on three axes, was made up of a central body called the EVM (Earth Viewing Module) containing the control systems and more than twenty items of research apparatus (from the high resolution radiometer for meteorology to the instruments for direct transmission and sensors for analysis of the space environment). The EVM was box-shaped, 1.4 × 1.4m (4.60 × 4.60ft) at the base and 1.6m (5.25ft) tall, with a weight of 906kg (1,997lb). A 3.96m (13ft) high trellis was fitted to the top which supported the big parabolic antenna which was 9m (29.53ft) in diameter formed of a structure of 48 aluminum ribs covered by copper netting treated with dacron and silicon. An apparatus (EME) for Environmental Measuring Experiments was fitted to the antenna on the outside. Two latticework arms also extended

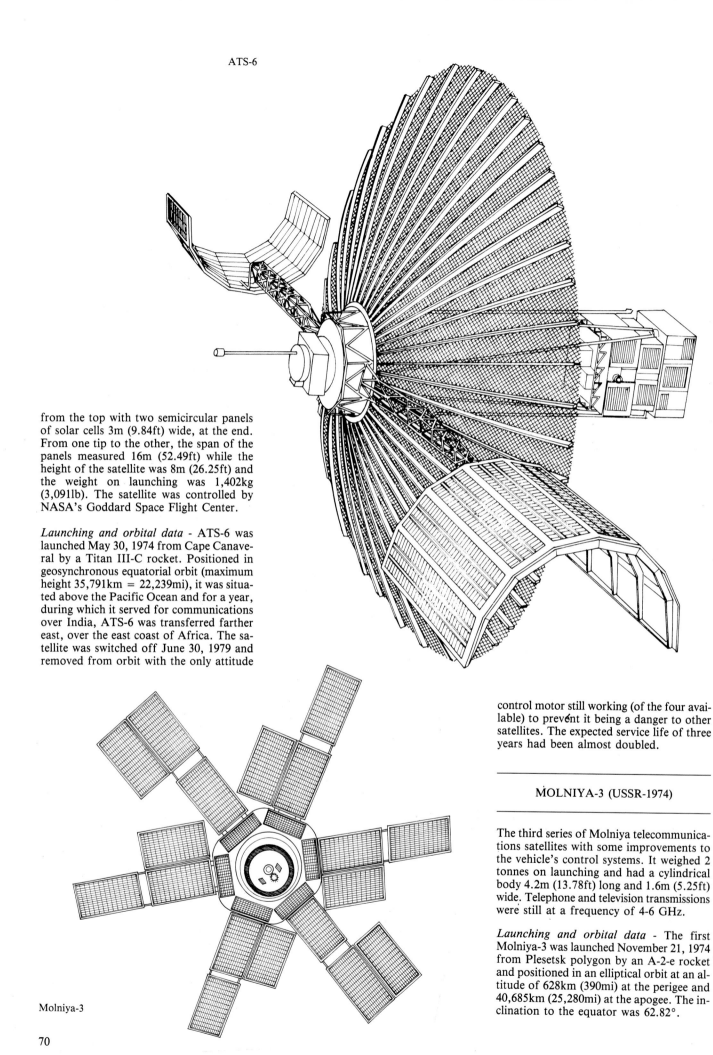

from the top with two semicircular panels of solar cells 3m (9.84ft) wide, at the end. From one tip to the other, the span of the panels measured 16m (52.49ft) while the height of the satellite was 8m (26.25ft) and the weight on launching was 1,402kg (3,091lb). The satellite was controlled by NASA's Goddard Space Flight Center.

Launching and orbital data - ATS-6 was launched May 30, 1974 from Cape Canaveral by a Titan III-C rocket. Positioned in geosynchronous equatorial orbit (maximum height 35,791km = 22,239mi), it was situated above the Pacific Ocean and for a year, during which it served for communications over India, ATS-6 was transferred farther east, over the east coast of Africa. The satellite was switched off June 30, 1979 and removed from orbit with the only attitude control motor still working (of the four available) to prevént it being a danger to other satellites. The expected service life of three years had been almost doubled.

MOLNIYA-3 (USSR-1974)

The third series of Molniya telecommunications satellites with some improvements to the vehicle's control systems. It weighed 2 tonnes on launching and had a cylindrical body 4.2m (13.78ft) long and 1.6m (5.25ft) wide. Telephone and television transmissions were still at a frequency of 4-6 GHz.

Launching and orbital data - The first Molniya-3 was launched November 21, 1974 from Plesetsk polygon by an A-2-e rocket and positioned in an elliptical orbit at an altitude of 628km (390mi) at the perigee and 40,685km (25,280mi) at the apogee. The inclination to the equator was 62.82°.

Molniya-3

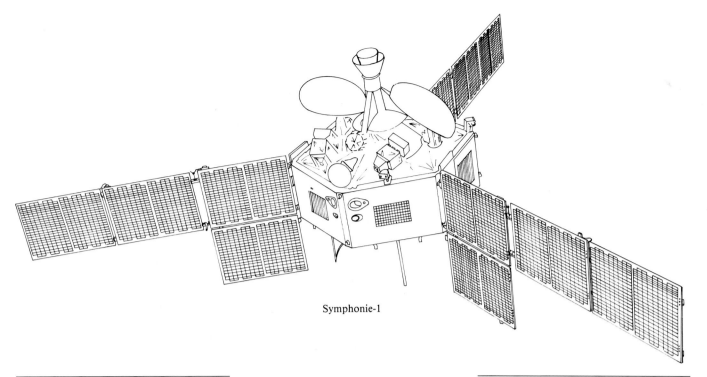

Symphonie-1

SYMPHONIE
(FRANCE/WEST GERMANY-1974)

In June 1967, the Governments of France and West Germany signed an agreement to build an experimental telecommunications satellite. The program was financed in equal parts by both nations and development of the satellite was entrusted to the Franco-German industrial consortium Cifas.

The Symphonie satellite was composed of a central body in the shape of a hexagonal prism with a maximum diameter of 1.7m (5.6ft) and a height of 0.5m (1.64ft). Three panels of solar cells positioned 120° apart projected from the satellite and were extended, in the open position, inside a circle 6.8m (22.31ft) in diameter. The power generated by the 21,888 solar cells was initially 303 watts, falling to 187 watts at the end of the satellite's projected service life of five years. Symphonie, which weighed 230kg (507lb) in orbit, was equipped with a liquid propellant (aerozine 50 and nitrogen peroxide) apogee motor and was stabilized on three axes. The satellite had two transponders at 6-4 GHz and permitted telephone, television, radio, telegraph and data transmission. Two color television programs or 800 telephone conversations could be transmitted by a single transponder through the two main Earth stations used for the experiments (Pleumeur-Bodou in France and Raisting in Germany).

Launching and orbital data - Symphonie-1 and -2 launched from Cape Canaveral by Thor Delta rockets December 19, 1974 and August 27, 1975, respectively. They were both positioned in geostationary, equatorial orbit at longitude 11.5° W above the Atlantic Ocean. At the beginning of 1977, Symphonie-1 was transferred to longitude 49° E above the Indian Ocean, where it remained for two years.

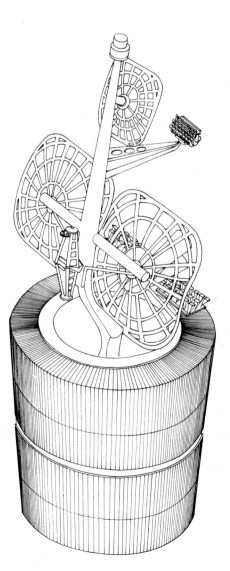

Intelsat-4A

RADUGA/STATSIONAR (USSR-1975)

Statsionar is an international denomination for geostationary. The Radugas were the first Soviet satellites in geostationary equatorial orbit. The Raduga satellites were preceded in 1974 by two experimental satellites: Cosmos-637 and Molniya-1S, which were positioned in geostationary orbit to test the new system. The Radugas, equipped with a system for stabilization on three axes, transmitted in the centimeter waveband and permitted telephone, telegraph and television transmissions inside Soviet territory. Weighing 5 tonnes on launching according to some estimates, they also transmitted newspaper contents to remote cities such as Novosibirsk or Khabarovsk. The vehicle's characteristics were apparently similar to those of the Gorizont satellites.

Launching and orbital data - Raduga-1/Statsionar was launched December 22, 1975 from Baikonur-Tyuratam polygon by a D-1-e Proton rocket, into geostationary equatorial orbit.

INTELSAT-4A (INTERNATIONAL-1975)

Intelsat-4A was in the shape of a cylinder surmounted by a group of antennae of more advanced technology than the earlier Intelsat-4 and offering far greater capacity. The cylinder was 2.38m (7.80ft) in diameter and 2.81m (9.22ft) tall, while the total height was 6.78m (22.24ft). The outer surface of the cylinder was covered by 17,000 solar cells supplying a power of 600 watts. The satellite, which was spin-stabilized, had a service life of seven years and was equipped with 20 transponders providing 6,250 telephone circuits and two television channels. Built by Hughes Aircraft Co., who was the

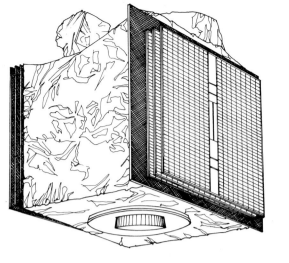

Satcom-2

Satcom in transfer configuration

prime contractor for a group of companies, it weighed 862kg (1,900lb) in orbit. The two larger parabolic antennae were 1.3m (4.26ft) in diameter. Intelsat-4A provided the possibility of multiple access to the satellite and simultaneous transmission. Transmissions to the satellite took place at 6 GHz and it retransmitted to Earth at a frequency of 4 GHz.

Launching and orbital data - The first Intelsat-4A was launched September 25, 1975 from Cape Canaveral by an Atlas Centaur rocket. It went into service in geostationary equatorial orbit (maximum height 35,819km = 22,257mi) February 1, 1976, positioned over the Atlantic Ocean at longitude 335.5° E. The last Intelsat-4A (the sixth in the series) was launched March 31, 1978 and went into service above the Indian Ocean.

SATCOM (USA-1975)

These were internal telecommunications satellites for use within United States boundaries built by the RCA Astro-Electronics Division for RCA American Communications Inc. They handled television broadcasts, telephonic communications and high-speed data transmission. These satellites were used in particular for broadcasting cable television programs. Weighing about 585kg (1,290lb) in orbit, the central body was shaped like a box 1.2m (3.94ft) by 1.6m (5.25ft) at the base and 1.17m (3.84ft) tall. It was stabilized on three axes and the two panels of solar cells measuring 1.55m (5.08ft) by 2.26m (7.41ft) each, supplied a power of 770 watts. The RCA Satcom satellites were built in two initial series (Satcom and Advanced Satcom) with a communications apparatus consisting of 24 transponders with C-band frequencies (6-4 GHz). The third series called Satcom K had a different communications apparatus and used Ku-band frequen-

cies (14-12 GHz). Satcom K permitted direct transmission to homes and used 22 transponders, six of which were in reserve.

Launching and orbital data - Satcom-1 was launched December 13, 1975 from Cape Canaveral by a Delta rocket and positioned in geostationary equatorial orbit at longitude 135° W. The other launch dates, also into geostationary orbit, were: Satcom-2, March 26, 1976; Satcom-3 (lost during transfer to geostationary orbit), December 6, 1979; Satcom-3R, November 19, 1981; Satcom-4, January 15, 1982; Satcom-5, October 27, 1982; Satcom-6, April 11, 1983; Satcom-7, September 8, 1983. The first Satcom K was launched November 28, 1985 by the Shuttle *Atlantis* during mission 61-B.

CTS-HERMES (CANADA-1976)

This satellite was the product of a joint USA-Canada program in which ESA, the European Space Agency, was also involved. The central body measured 1.88m (6.17ft) by 1.83m (6ft) and the span of the two panels of solar cells supplied by the ESA was 16.9m

CTS-Hermes

(55.44ft). The two panels held 27,000 solar cells supplying a power of 1.2 kilowatts. The weight was 675kg (1,488lb). The expected service life was two years but it remained operational until December 21, 1979. CTS (Communications Technology Satellite), later renamed Hermes, was designed according to an agreement between NASA and the Canadian Department of Communications (DOC) to test some special uses of telecommunications, such as long-distance medical work. Hermes concentrated on the testing of three technologies: first transmission at 14-12 GHz with a transmitter supplied by NASA and built by TRW; the use of light panels of solar cells which were built in Europe and deployed in orbit, and stabilization on three axes. Apart from medical work, Hermes provided the possibility of testing communications in the field of education and business transmissions. The Department of Communications was encharged of operating the project, while the Communications Research Center (CRC) was responsible for its design and construction.

Launching and orbital data - Hermes was launched January 17, 1976 from Cape Canaveral by a Delta 2914 rocket and positioned in geostationary equatorial orbit at longitude 116° W.

COMSTAR (USA - 1976)

A group of four satellites built by Hughes Aircraft Co. for Comsat General Corporation which leased them to the two big American telephone companies, AT&T and GTE, for use on the United States territory. The Comstars were in the form of a cylinder 2.44m (8ft) in diameter, with a total height including the antennae of 6.10m (20ft). The weight in orbit was 791kg (1,744lb) and the expected service life was seven years. Each satellite, equipped with 24 transponders, had a capacity of 18,000 circuits equivalent to 18 simultaneous telephone conversations. The C-band was used for transmissions at a frequency of 6-4 GHz and the satellites were spin-stabilized.

Launching and orbital data - Comstar-D1 was launched May 13, 1976 from Cape Canaveral by an Atlas Centaur rocket and positioned in geostationary equatorial orbit at longitude 128° W. It became operative on June 19, 1976. The other three satellites were also sent into geostationary orbit with the same type of carrier and on the following dates: Comstar-D2 July 22, 1976; Comstar-D3 June 29, 1978 and Comstar-D4 February 21, 1981.

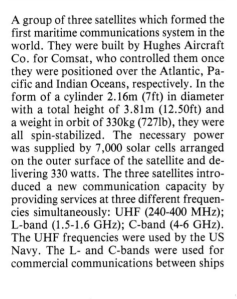

Comstar deployed

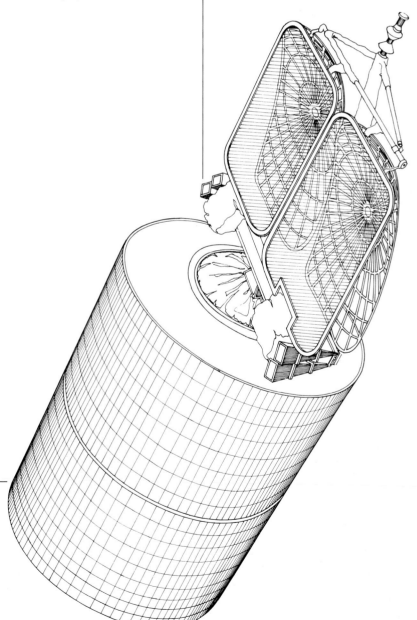

Comstar

MARISAT (USA-1976)

A group of three satellites which formed the first maritime communications system in the world. They were built by Hughes Aircraft Co. for Comsat, who controlled them once they were positioned over the Atlantic, Pacific and Indian Oceans, respectively. In the form of a cylinder 2.16m (7ft) in diameter with a total height of 3.81m (12.50ft) and a weight in orbit of 330kg (727lb), they were all spin-stabilized. The necessary power was supplied by 7,000 solar cells arranged on the outer surface of the satellite and delivering 330 watts. The three satellites introduced a new communication capacity by providing services at three different frequencies simultaneously: UHF (240-400 MHz); L-band (1.5-1.6 GHz); C-band (4-6 GHz). The UHF frequencies were used by the US Navy. The L- and C-bands were used for commercial communications between ships

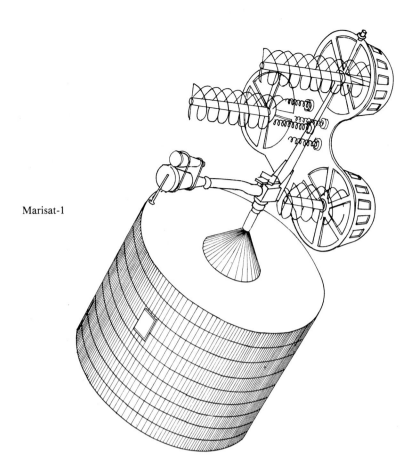

Marisat-1

Satellite for television transmissions within the USSR and bordering countries. The frequency used was 0.7 GHz. The satellite, weighing about 2 tonnes on launching, had a cylindrical body, 5m (16.4ft) long and 2m (6.6ft) wide, at the base of which was a large, rectangular antenna with 96 helicoidal elements. The power output from the antenna was 200 watts. The electric power for operation of Ekran, on the other hand, was supplied by two panels of solar cells at the sides of the vehicle.

Launching and orbital data - Ekran-1 was launched October 26, 1976 from Baikonur-Tyuratam polygon by a D-1-e Proton rocket and positioned in geostationary equatorial orbit at longitude 99° E.

KIKU-2/ETS-2 (JAPAN - 1977)

The first Japanese satellite to be sent into geostationary orbit. Japan thus became the third country capable of positioning satellites in this type of orbit. Cylindrical in sha-

under way and Earth stations, permitting voice, teletype, facsimile and high-speed data transmission services.

Launching and orbital data - Marisat-1 was launched February 19, 1976 from Cape Canaveral by a Delta 2914 rocket, the same as was used for the two subsequent launchings. Positioned in geostationary equatorial orbit at longitude 15° W above the Atlantic Ocean, it began service July 8, 1976. Marisat-3 was launched June 9, 1976 and positioned at longitude 176.5° E above the Pacific Ocean. Marisat-2 was launched October 14, 1976 and positioned at longitude 73° E above the Indian Ocean.

PALAPA-A (INDONESIA - 1976)

A satellite built for the Indonesian Government by the Hughes Aircraft Co., in the shape of a cylinder covered in 20,500 solar cells supplying a power of 300 watts. Palapa was 1.9m (6.23ft) in diameter with a total height including the 1.5m (4.92ft) diameter antenna, of 3.4m (11.15ft), and a weight in orbit of 305kg (672lb). It was spin-stabilized and had 12 transponders providing 5,760 two-way telephone circuit or 12 television channels. Two satellites were launched in the Palapa-A series.

Launching and orbital data - Palapa-A1 was launched July 8, 1976 from Cape Canaveral by a Delta rocket and positioned in geostationary equatorial orbit. Palapa-A2 also left Cape Canaveral by a Delta rocket, March 10, 1977.

Transmissions of TV signals from Earth to Ekran and from Ekran satellite to Earth stations.

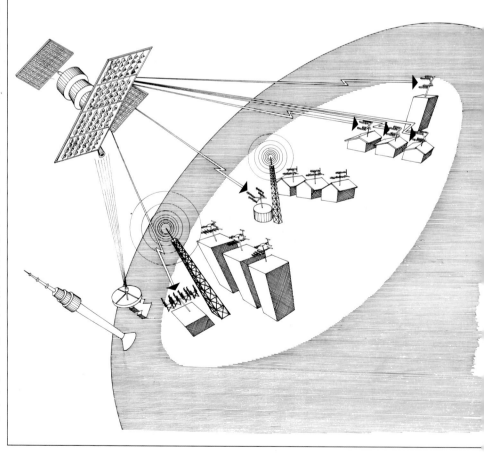

pe with a diameter of 1.4m (4.6ft) and a height of 0.82m (2.7ft), Kiku-2, which was prepared by the National Space Development Agency (NASDA), weighed 130kg (287lb) in orbit. Its outer surface was covered with solar cells. The satellite, also called Engineering Test Satellite (ETS), was launched with the aim of acquiring the technology necessary for insertion into geostationary orbit and subsequent control and tracking during orbital life. Test transmissions were carried out by the Radio Research Laboratory of the Ministry of Post and Telecommunications and the frequencies used were 34.5 GHz, 11.5 GHz and 1.7 GHz. The Mitsubishi Electric Corporation was the prime contractor.

Launching and orbital data - Kiku-2 was launched February 23, 1977 from Tanegashima Space Center by a Japanese N-1 rocket. The satellite was positioned in geostationary equatorial orbit at longitude 130° E.

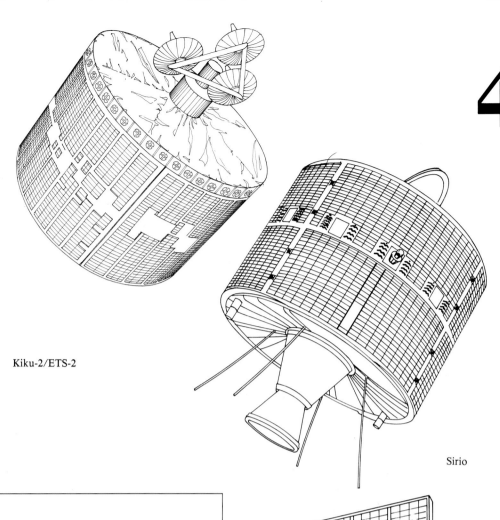

Kiku-2/ETS-2

SIRIO (ITALY - 1977)

Sirio was an experimental telecommunications satellite. Built by Compagnia Industriale Aerospaziale, a consortium of the largest

Sirio

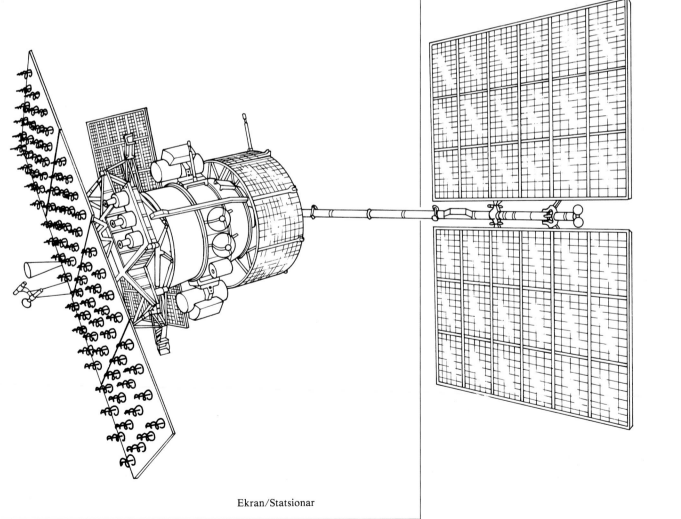

Ekran/Statsionar

Italian aerospace and electronic industries, it carried apparatus to study the attenuations in signals caused by rainfall at frequencies between 12 and 18 GHz. The experiments were carried out with the Earth stations of the Telespazio company at Fucino and Lario, in the center and north of Italy respectively and with many other stations in Europe and in the United States. Sirio was in the shape of a drum 0.95m (3.1ft) tall and 1.43m (4.7ft) in diameter. The outer surface was covered with solar cells supplying a power of 147 watts. The weight in orbit was 220kg (485lb). The life expectancy was two years but the satellite remained perfectly functional beyond that limit and in March 1983, nearly six years after launching, was transferred to longitude 65° E (the original position was 15° E) to permit a series of experiments with China. This continued until February 1985 when Sirio was moved again to 75° E, a more stable position which did not require too many corrections, as by that time the hydrazine propellant of the attitude control system was nearly exhausted.

Launching and orbital data - Sirio was launched August 25, 1977 from Cape Canaveral by a Delta rocket and positioned in geostationary equatorial orbit at longitude 15° East.

SAKURA/CS (JAPAN - 1977)

An experimental telecommunications satellite used for experiments in internal communications employing an almost millimetric waveband and testing a type of technology needed for the production of operational satellites. For the first time Sakura, also known as Communications Satellite (CS), used the 20-30 GHz and 6-4 GHz frequencies for transmission, and contributed to the development of some important technologies such as digital transmission combined with data, voices, and images using the time division multiple access (TDMA) technique. The satellite was cylindrical in shape, 3.5m (11.5ft) tall and 2m (6.56ft) in diameter. It weighed 350kg (772lb) and was spin-stabilized. The experiments were conducted by the Radio Research Laboratories and the Nippon Telegraph and Telephone Corporation. Mitsubishi was the prime contractor. The life expectancy was three years but it was used for longer time. In 1983, two other satellites followed: Sakura-2a/CS-2a and Sakura-2b/CS-2b, with roughly the same characteristics and capabilities. Each had eight transponders, two in C-band (6-4 GHz) and six in Ku-band (14-12 GHz).

Launching and orbital data - Sakura/CS was launched December 15, 1977 from Cape Canaveral by a Delta rocket and sent into geostationary equatorial orbit at longitude 135° E. In September 1983, the satellite was shifted to longitude 150° E.

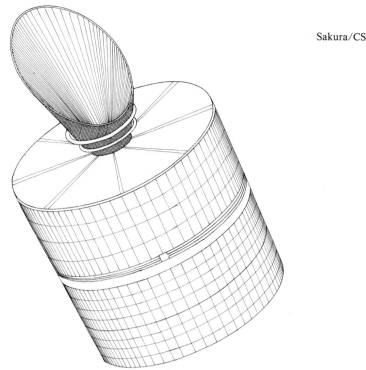

OTS (EUROPE - 1978)

The first European experimental telecommunications satellite from which the ECS (European Communications Satellite) and Marecs (Maritime ECS) were derived. OTS (Orbital Test Satellite) was developed by the ESA (European Space Agency) and built by a consortium of European industries called MESH, with British Aerospace as prime contractor. The central body of the satellite was in the shape of an hexagonal prism 2.39m (7.84ft) wide, 2.13m (7ft) tall and with a total length including the two panels of solar cells when extended of 9.26m (30.38ft). The power supplied by the panels amounted to 594 watts. The satellite was stabilized on three axes and weighed 444kg (978.84lb) in orbit. OTS conducted a series of experiments in the field of television, telephone

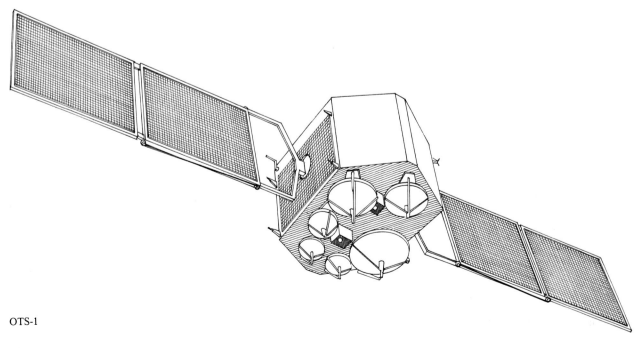

OTS-1

and data transmission using six transponders with frequencies of 14-11 GHz. Its was the third satellite to be used for such studies after the Canadian CTS and Italian Sirio. The postal and telecommunications authorities of the various European countries took part in the research. The time division multiple access technique was also tested. The life expectancy of the satellite was about five years and it remained operational until 1984.

Launching and orbital data - OTS-1 was launched September 14, 1977 from Cape Canaveral by a Delta 3914 rocket which exploded in flight 54 seconds after lift-off. OTS-2, which was identical to OTS-1, was successfully launched May 12, 1978 from Cape Canaveral, also by a Delta 3914 rocket and sent into geostationary, equatorial orbit at longitude 10° E.

GORIZONT/STATSIONAR (USSR - 1978)

A geostationary satellite (excluding Gorizont-1) for telephonic and international television transmission. Weighing about 4 tonnes on launching, it had a central cylindrical main body about 5m (16.4ft) long and 2m (6.56ft) in diameter. Two panels of solar cells fitted at the sides supplied the necessary power. Transmissions took place in the centimetric waveband and the Gorizonts were part of the Intersputnik system which is similar in some respects to the Western Intelsat system.

Launching and orbital data - Gorizont-1 was launched December 19, 1978 from Baikonur-Tyuratam by a D-1-e Proton rocket into an elliptical orbit with an altitude of 22,580km (14,030mi) at the perigee and 48,365km (30,052mi) at the apogee, inclined 11.3° to the equator. Gorizont-2 was launched July 5, 1979 and placed in geostationary equatorial orbit, as were the subsequent models. The positions of the Gorizont-Statsionar satellites were above the Atlantic Ocean at longitude 14° W and above the Indian Ocean at longitude 53° E.

RADIO (USSR - 1978)

Soviet satellites for radio hams built by students, cylindrical in form, 0.42m (1.38ft) in diameter and 0.39m (1.28ft) long, weighing about 40kg (88lb).

Launching and orbital data - Radio-1 and -2 were launched October 26, 1978 from Plesetsk by a F-2 rocket together with the Cosmos-1045 satellites. Both were positioned in an elliptical orbit inclined 82.55° to the equator, with a perigee of 1,688km (1,049mi), an apogee of 1,709km (1,062mi) and a period of 120 minutes.
Six more satellites of this type (from Radio-3 to Radio-8) were launched from Plesetsk December 17, 1981 by a single C-1 rocket. All were positioned in elliptical orbit inclined

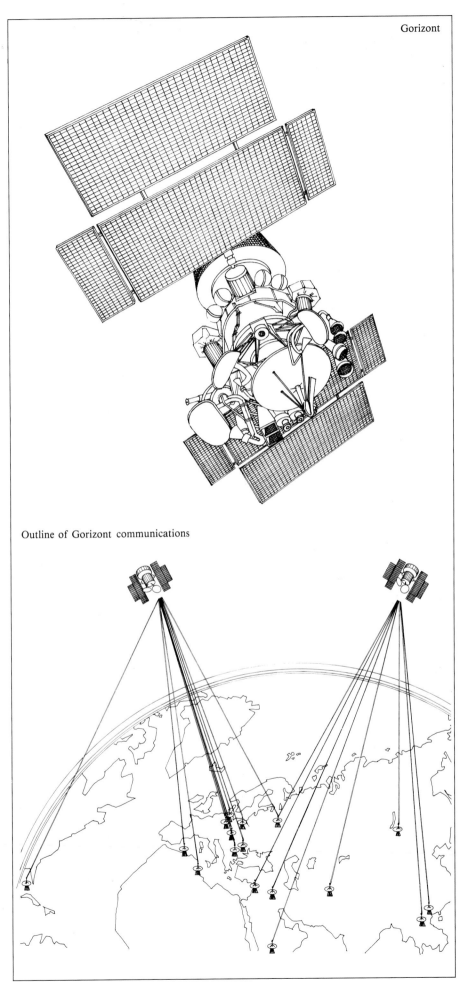

Gorizont

Outline of Gorizont communications

83° to the equator and their parameters were almost the same, with a minimum perigee of 1,561km (970mi) and a maximum apogee of 1,679km (1,043mi). The period was between 118 and 119 minutes.

Yuri/BSE

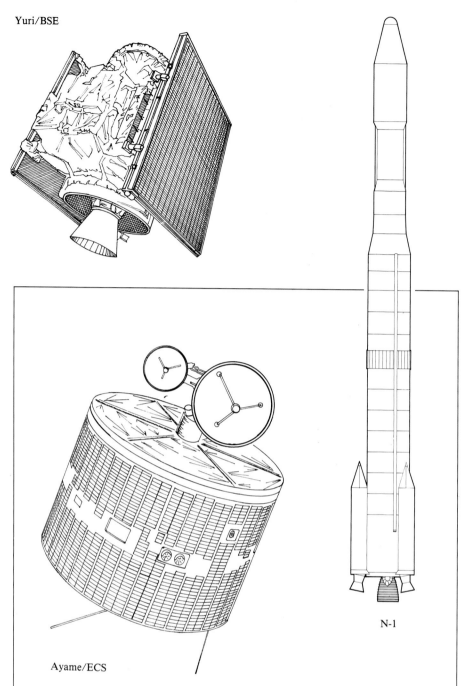

YURI/BSE (JAPAN - 1978)

A satellite used to test direct broadcasting of television programs via satellite. Also known as the Broadcasting Satellite Experiment (BSE), its central body was in the shape of a box measuring 1.3x1.2m (4.3x3.9ft) at the base and 3m (9.84ft) high. Two panels of solar cells attached to the sides supplied the necessary power. Its weight in orbit was 350kg (772lb) and stabilization was on three axes. Toshiba was the prime contractor and the experiments were conducted by the Radio Research Laboratories of the Ministry of Post and Telecommunications in collaboration with the Japan Broadcasting Corporation (NHK). With Yuri, a series of experiments were carried out from 1978 to 1980, transmitting voices and images and using antennae of various types and sizes, including portable ones. These included a meter long antenna for home reception. Yuri used the 14-12 GHz (Ku-band) frequencies for transmission.

Launching and orbital data - Yuri was launched April 8, 1978 from Cape Canaveral by a Delta rocket and sent into geostationary equatorial orbit at longitude 110° E.

Ayame/ECS

N-1

TELESAT-4/ANIK-B (CANADA - 1978)

Anik-B was born after the technology developed for the Hermes satellite program. The central body was shaped like a box 2.17m (7.11ft) wide and 2.14m (7.02ft) tall including the antennae. Two panels of solar cells projected from the sides giving a total length of 11.3m (37ft) from one end to the other. Its weight in orbit was 474kg (1,045lb). Anik-B was stabilized on three axes and equipped with 12 channels, allowing transmission at 6-4 GHz and 14-12 GHz. It permitted various types of internal, commercial transmission (voice, data and video) and also experimented transmission of teleconferences.

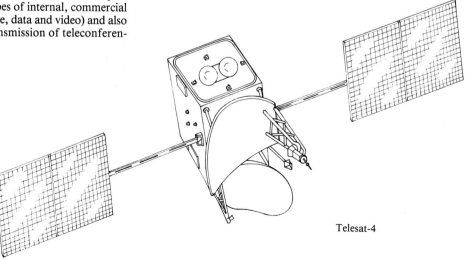

Telesat-4

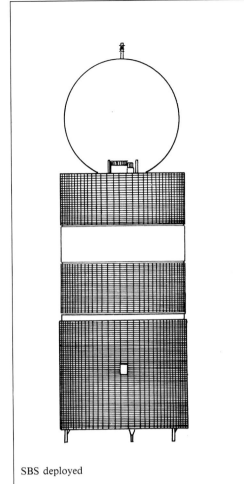

SBS deployed

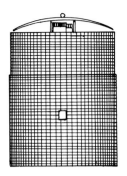

SBS stowed

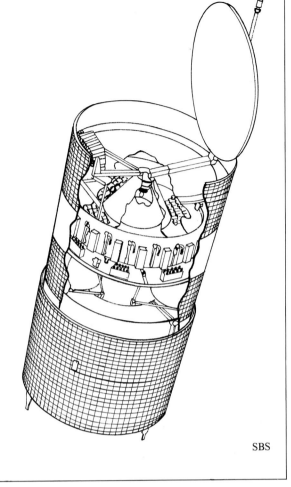

SBS

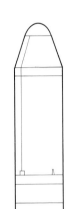

Delta 3910 ▶

Launching and orbital data - Anik-B was launched December 15, 1978 from Cape Canaveral by a Delta rocket and positioned in geostationary equatorial orbit, taking over operations from Anik-A2.

AYAME/ECS (JAPAN - 1979)

Two satellites of this name, also known as Experimental Communications Satellite (ECS) were launched to test certain technologies needed for use in geostationary orbit. But they lost contact with the Earth on ignition of their apogee motors, which should have circularized the orbits to 36,000km (22,369mi) from the Earth. Ayame was cylindrical in shape, 1.4m (5ft) high, 0.95m (3.1ft) in diameter and with a weight of 130kg (287lb). It was spin-stabilized. The frequencies used were 35-32 GHz and 6-4 GHz. Mitsubishi Electric Corporation was the prime contractor.

Launching and orbital data - Ayame-1 and -2 were launched from Tanegashima by a N-1 rocket February 6, 1979 and February 22, 1980, respectively.

SBS (USA - 1980)

A group of satellites built by the Hughes Aircraft Co. on the HS-376 model for Satellite Business Systems, a company formed jointly by the Aetna Life and Casualty Insurance Co., Comsat General Corp. and IBM. The satellites were designed for business services, with fully digitalized transmission permitting telephone conversations, links between computers, sending of electronic post and links for video-teleconferences. The SBSs, which were spin-stabilized (68 rpm) were cylindrical in form with a diameter of 2.16m (7ft) and a total height, including the antenna, of 6.60m (21.65ft). The antenna was 1.82m (5.97ft) in diameter. The weight in orbit was 550kg (1,212lb). The satellite was of telescopic structure, part of it, covered in solar cells, sliding into the open position in space. Other solar cells were located on the remaining outer surfaces of the satellite, giving a total of 14,000 cells supplying a combined power of 1,100 watts. SBS was equipped with ten transponders permitting transmission at the frequencies of 14-12 GHz (Ku-band), also using the TDMA (Time Division Multiple Access) technique. The service life of the satellite was scheduled seven years.

Launching and orbital data - SBS-1 was launched November 16, 1980 from Cape Canaveral by a Delta 3910 rocket and placed in geostationary equatorial orbit at longitude 100° W. SBS-2 left September 24, 1981, also by a Delta 3910 rocket while SBS-3 was carried into orbit November 11, 1982 during the fifth Shuttle mission and SBS-4 was transported by the Shuttle *Discovery* August 30, 1984. Geostationary orbit was achieved in these cases using a PAM-D perigee motor.

INTELSAT-5 (INTERNATIONAL - 1980)

Intelsat-5 was the first satellite of the Intelsat organization to be stabilized on three axes. That is, it was constantly oriented toward the Earth stations by means of Sun and Earth sensors. The previous Intelsats were spin-stabilized and their antennae had to be rotated in the opposite direction to keep them pointing toward the Earth. Intelsat-5 had a total height of 6.6m (21.65ft), while the central body of the satellite was a box measuring 1.66x2.01x1.77m (5.45x6.59x5.80 ft). Two panels of solar cells measuring 15.6m (51.18ft) from one end to the other extended from the sides and supplied a power of 1,560 watts at the beginning of the expected service life of seven years. The weight in orbit was 825kg (1,819lb) including the 227kg (500lb) of hydrazine propellant used for the attitude control motors. Intelsat-5 had 27 transponders operating in the 6-4 GHz and 14-11 GHz frequencies. 12,000 telephone circuits were available (twice as many as for Intelsat-4A) plus two television channels. Intelsat-5, which was built by Ford Aerospace and Communications Corp., who was prime contractor for a group of other companies, was also the first to carry maritime apparatus for maritime communications.

Launching and orbital data - The first Intelsat-5 was launched from Cape Canaveral December 6, 1980 into geostationary equatorial orbit (maximum height 35,707km, 22,187mi) by an Atlas Centaur rocket. It went into service above the Atlantic Ocean.
Nine Intelsat-5s were launched in all. The seventh and eighth by European Ariane rockets from the polygon in French Guiana on October 19, 1983 and March 4, 1984, respectively. The ninth and last Intelsat-5 was launched by Atlas Centaur rocket from Cape Canaveral June 9, 1984.

MARECS (INTERNATIONAL - 1984)

A maritime communications satellite developed by the European Space Agency (ESA) and used by the international organization Inmarsat. British Aerospace was the prime contractor. The satellite used the platform of the ECS European telecommunications satellite which was shaped like a hexagonal prism with a maximum diameter of 2m

(6.56ft) and height of 2.5m (8.2ft). The weight in orbit was 563kg (1,241lb). Stabilized on three axes, its power of 955 watts was derived from two panels of solar cells connected to the sides each of which was 5.2m (17ft) long and 1.3m (4.3ft) wide. The span of the panels when open was 13.8m (45.27ft). The expected service life in orbit was seven years. The onboard telecommunications apparatus used the C-band (6-4 GHz) and L-band (1.6-1.5 GHz). Marecs provided telephone services, telex, facsimile and high speed data transmission (56 kbits per second). It also picked up distress signals from vehicles in difficulty.

Launching and orbital data - Marecs-A was launched December 20, 1981 from the French Guiana polygon by an Ariane rocket. Sent into geostationary equatorial orbit, its operating position was longitude 26° W). Marecs-B2 was launched November 10, 1985 by an Ariane-3 rocket (which also carried the GTE Spacenet-2 satellite) and positioned, also in geostationary orbit, at longitude 177° E. Marecs-B1 was lost due to failure of the Ariane launch.

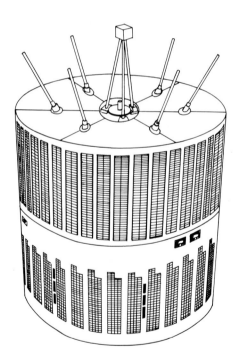

Kiku-3

KIKU-3/ETS-4 (JAPAN - 1981)

An experimental Japanese telecommunications satellite developed by the Japanese space agency, NASDA, in collaboration with NTT (Nippon Telegraph and Telephone Corporation), NAL (National Aerospace

Laboratory) and ETL (Electrotechnical Laboratory) and launched for four reasons: to check the ability of the N-2 carrier rocket to place a satellite in geostationary transfer orbit; to collect data on the launching conditions of the N-2 rocket; to acquire the technological know-how to build and manage telecommunications satellites on a large scale; and to test the telecommunications apparatus carried on the satellite. Mitsubishi Electric Corporation was the prime contractor. Kiku-3 was in the form of a cylinder 2.8m (9.2ft) tall and 2.10m (6.9ft) in diameter. Its weight was 640kg (1,410lb) and it was spin-stabilized. The satellite's mission was concluded May 12, 1981, but it remained in use until December 24, 1984.

Launching and orbital data - Kiku-3 was launched February 11, 1981 from Tanegashima Space Center by a Japanese N-2 rocket and placed in elliptical geostationary transfer orbit inclined 29° to the equator and with a perigee of 220km (137mi) and an apogee of 35,082km (21,799mi).

ISKRA (USSR - 1981)

A small satellite for amateur radio. Weighing 28kg (62lb) it had a telemetric system, a transponder, a memory and a radiodiffusion channel. It was also controlled from Earth by two stations situated in Moscow and Kaluga. It was built by the Ordzhjonikidzé Aviation Institute with the participation of amateur radio enthusiasts. The Iskra satellites were designed for links between radio hams in the Soviet Union, Bulgaria, Hungary, Vietnam, East Germany, Cuba, Laos, Mongolia, Poland, Romania and Czechoslovakia.

Launching and orbital data - Iskra-1 was launched July 10, 1981 from Plesetsk by an A-1 rocket together with the Meteor-Priroda satellite and sent into an orbit 638km (396mi) at the perigee and 663km (412mi) at the apogee, with an orbital inclination of 97.98°. Iskra-2 was launched from the orbiting space laboratory Salyut-7 May 17, 1982 and sent into an orbit 336km (209mi) high at the perigee, 342km (212mi) at the apogee and inclined 51.6°.
Iskra-3 was also released from Salyut-7 November 18, 1982, its orbit being 350km (217mi) at the perigee, 365km (227mi) at the apogee and inclined 51.6°.

APPLE (INDIA - 1981)

The first satellite stabilized on three axes developed by ISRO, the Indian organization for space research. Apple, from the initials for Ariane Passenger Payload Experiment, was an experimental telecommunications satellite equipped with two C-band (6-4 GHz) transponders permitting data transmission experiments, the use of small computer terminals and also long-distance educational

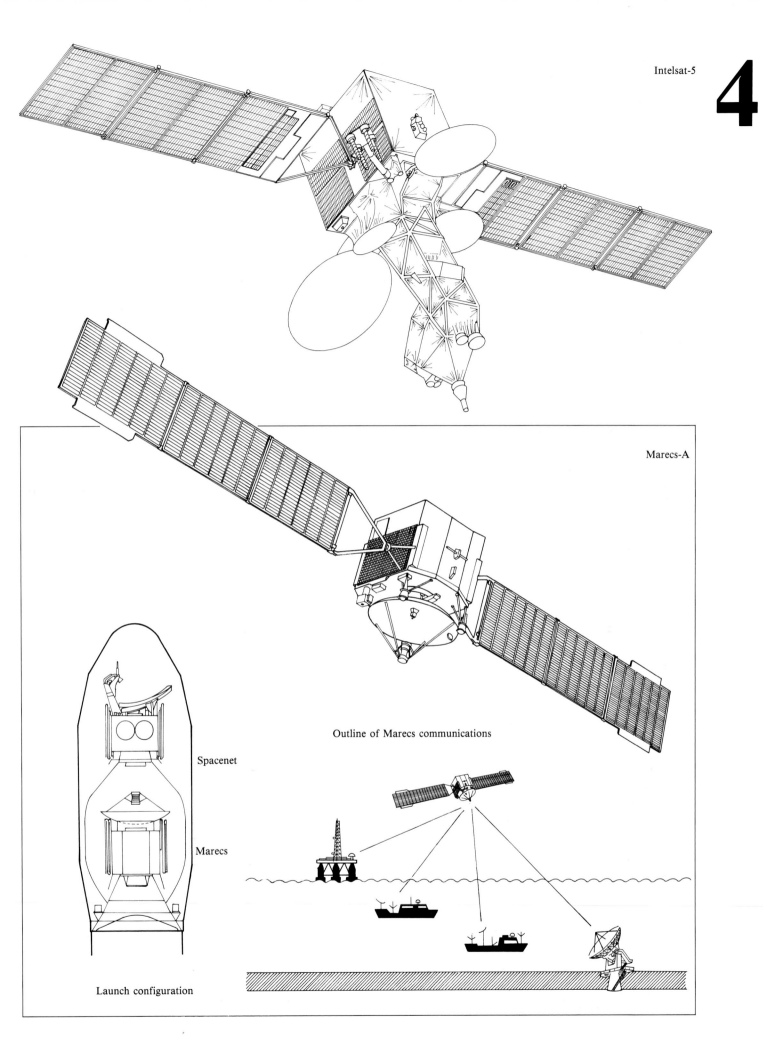

Marecs-A

Spacenet

Marecs

Outline of Marecs communications

Launch configuration

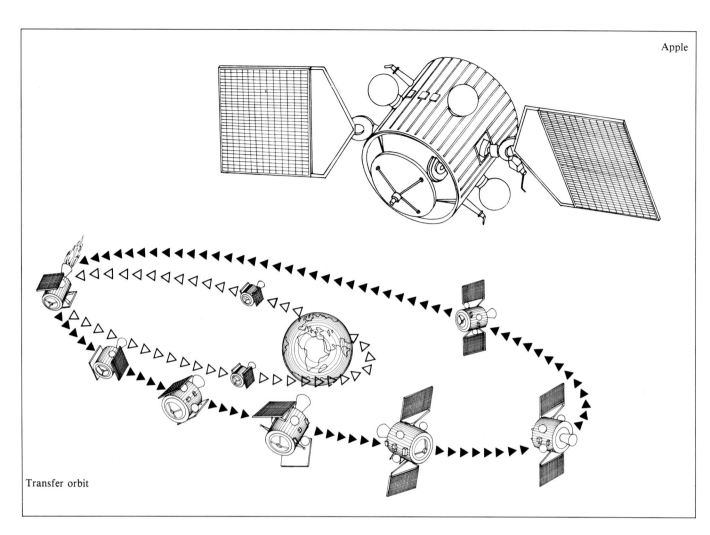

Apple

Transfer orbit

broadcasts. The satellite was cylindrical in structure with a height of 1.2m (3.94ft) and a diameter of 1.2m (3.94ft). A parabolic antenna 0.9m (2.95ft) in diameter was fitted to the top. The exhaust nozzle of the apogee motor, derived from the fourth stage of the Indian SLV3 carrier rocket, projected from the bottom. Two panels of solar cells with a 4.6m (15ft) span extended from the sides of Apple, supplying a power of 280 watts. The weight in orbit was 352kg (776lb). The planned service life was two years.

Launching and orbital data - Apple was launched June 19, 1981 from the Kourou polygon in French Guiana by an Ariane rocket. The Meteosat-2 satellite of the ESA was carried into orbit by the same launch. Apple was positioned in geostationary equatorial orbit at longitude 102° E.

WESTAR-4/-5/-6 (USA - 1982)

The second generation of the United States internal satellites of the Westar series. The new satellite was the model HS-376 built by Hughes Aircraft Co. for Westar Union, the first American company to obtain permission from the U.S. Federal Communications Commission to operate a spatial telecommunications system within the United States. Westar-4 was in the form of a cylinder 2.16m

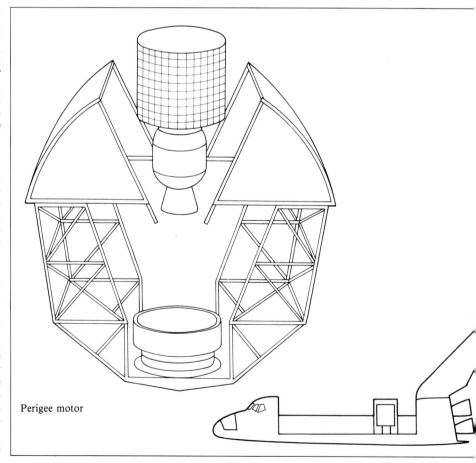

Perigee motor

(7ft) in diameter and 2.84m (9.32ft) high when closed and 6.60m (21.65ft) when open. In the open position, a mobile cylindrical panel containing half the 14,000 solar cells with which the vehicle was equipped and which produced a power of about 1,000 watts was extended, plus the 1.82m (5.97ft) high parabolic antenna. Westar-4 weighed 653kg (1,440lb) in orbit, was spin-stabilized and had 24 transponders capable of controlling 28,000 telephone circuits in the 6-4 GHz frequencies. Apart from sound communications, the Westar system served for color television broadcasts, facsimile and data transmission. The service life envisaged for the satellite was ten years and it could be launched by Delta and Ariane rockets or Space Shuttle. Westar-4, -5 and -6 had the same characteristics.

Launching and orbital data - Westar-4 was launched February 25, 1982 from Cape Canaveral by a Delta/PAM rocket and positioned in almost circular, geostationary equatorial orbit (maximum altitude 35,794km - 22,241mi) at longitude 99° W. Westar-5 went up June 6, 1982, also by a Delta/PAM rocket and was positioned in geostationary orbit at longitude 123° W. Westar-6, on the other hand, went up by Shuttle February 3, 1984 but did not reach geostationary orbit due to failure of the PAM-D perigee motor and was therefore recovered and brought back to Earth in November 1984, by the Space Shuttle *Discovery*, during mission 51-A.

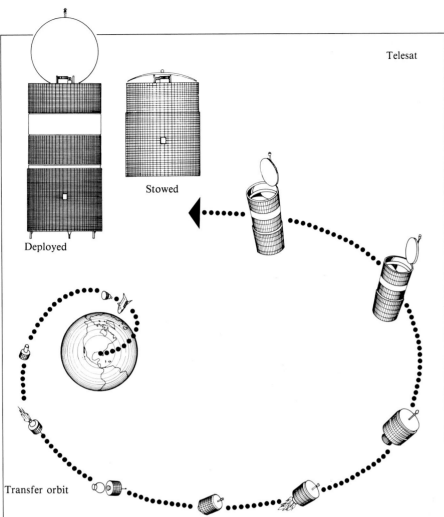

Telesat

4

Stowed

Deployed

Transfer orbit

Westar

Transfer orbit

TELESAT-5,-8/ANIK-D (CANADA - 1982)

This satellite used the Hughes Aircraft Co. HS-376 model. It was cylindrical in form, 2.18m (7.15ft) in diameter and 6.43m (21.09ft) tall. The weight in orbit was 660kg (1,455lb). It was spin-stabilized and had 24 transponders transmitting at a frequency of 6-4 GHz. The outer surface was covered in solar cells supplying a power of 900 watts. A second satellite in the Anik-D series (Telesat-8), also designed for international (telephone or television) communications, was launched in 1984.

Launching and orbital data - Anik-D1 was launched August 26, 1982 from Cape Canaveral by a Delta-PAM rocket and positioned in geostationary equatorial orbit at longitude 104° West. Anik-D2 left the hold of the Space Shuttle *Discovery* November 9, 1984, during mission 51-A, with a PAM-D perigee motor which enabled it to reach geostationary, equatorial orbit.

TELESAT-6/ANIK-C (CANADA - 1982)

A group of three Canadian satellites (Anik-C3, C2 and C1) launched for internal telecommunications in Canada. They used the

HS-376 model built by Hughes Aircraft Co. of cylindrical form, 2.18m (7.15ft) in diameter and 6.43m (21.09ft) tall with the antenna open. The weight in orbit was 632kg (1,393lb), while the expected service life was 8 years. The outer surface was covered in solar cells generating a power of 1,135 watts. These satellites were used for telephone, television and data transmission. Fitted with 16 transponders which used frequencies of 14-12 GHz, they had a capacity of 10,752 simultaneous telephone conversations in two directions or 32 television channels. Telesat-7/Anik-C2 went up in 1983 and Telesat-9/Anik-C1 in 1985.

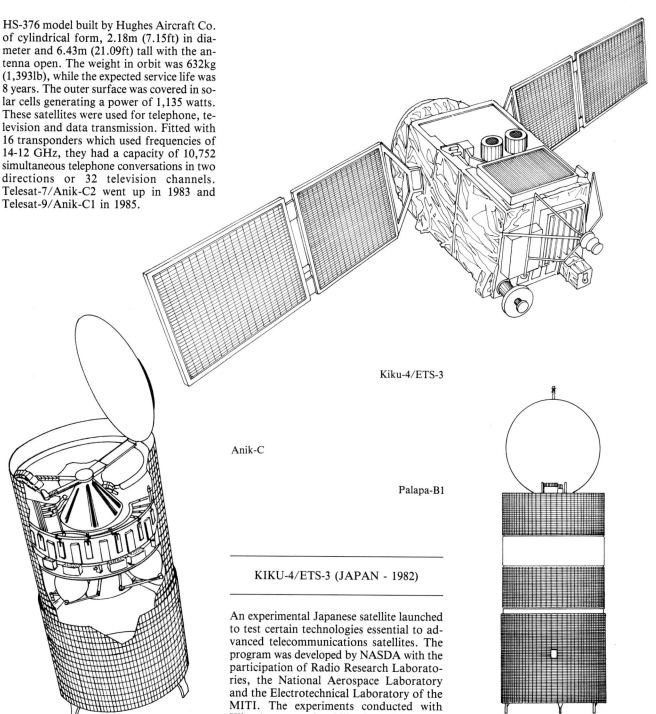

Kiku-4/ETS-3

Anik-C

Palapa-B1

Launching and orbital data - Anik-C3 was launched by the Space Shuttle *Columbia* November 11, 1982 from Cape Canaveral during the first commercial flight of the Shuttle. The satellite was transferred toward geostationary orbit November 12, with a PAM-D perigee motor and finally positioned in geostationary equatorial orbit at longitude 117.5° W. Anik-C2 went up with the Space Shuttle *Challenger* June 18, 1983 and transferred toward geostationary orbit the same day, also using a PAM-D perigee motor. The final position in geostationary orbit was longitude 112.5° W. Lastly, Anik-C1 left in the Space Shuttle *Discovery* on mission 51-D, April 12, 1985. Its position in geostationary orbit was longitude 107.5° W.

KIKU-4/ETS-3 (JAPAN - 1982)

An experimental Japanese satellite launched to test certain technologies essential to advanced telecommunications satellites. The program was developed by NASDA with the participation of Radio Research Laboratories, the National Aerospace Laboratory and the Electrotechnical Laboratory of the MITI. The experiments conducted with Kiku-4 concerned stabilization of the satellite on three axes, production and development of the panels of solar cells, active thermal control and testing of a range of communications equipments. The body of the satellite was box-shaped with a 0.85x0.85m (2.78x2.78ft) base and a height of 1.95m (0.77ft). Its weight was 385kg (848lb). An ion engine was installed and tested on the satellite, to study future attitude control propulsion systems. Toshiba was the prime contractor. The mission was officially concluded September 2, 1983, but the satellite remained in use until March 8, 1985.

Launching and orbital data - Kiku-4 was launched September 3, 1982 from Tanegashima Space Center by a N-1 rocket and sent into a circular orbit 1,000km (629mi) high and inclined 45° to the equator. The period was 105 minutes.

PALAPA-B (INDONESIA - 1983)

Built for the Indonesian Government by the Hughes Aircraft Co., this began the second series of satellites used by Indonesia for commercial telecommunications. Palapa-B used the HS-376 model of cylindrical shape which extended in space to a height of 6.83m (22.40ft) including the 1.83m (6ft) wide parabolic antenna and had a diameter of 2.16m (7ft). The weight in orbit was 630kg (1,389lb) and it was spin-stabilized. Fitted with 24 transponders (twice as many as the earlier Palapa-A), it permitted telephone, television, telegraph and also high speed data

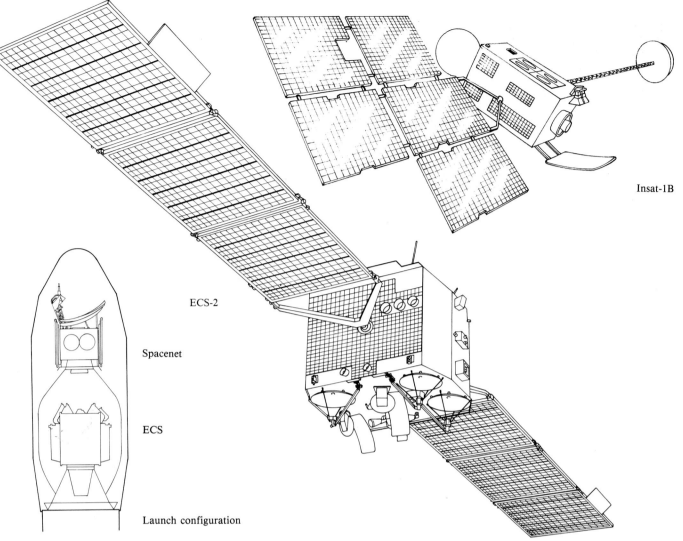

ECS-2

Spacenet

ECS

Launch configuration

Insat-1B

transmissions. The frequency used was 6-4
GHz (C-band). The expected service life is
eight years.

Launching and orbital data - Palapa-B1 was
carried into orbit by the Space Shuttle *Challenger* during the seventh mission which began June 18, 1983.
A PAM-D perigee motor transferred it to
geostationary equatorial orbit where it was
positioned at longitude 108-118° E.
Palapa-B2, also carried by the Space Shuttle *Challenger*, left February 3, 1984 during
mission 41-B.

INSAT (INDIA - 1983)

A satellite built for the Space Department
of the Indian Government by Ford Aerospace Western Development Laboratories Division. Stabilized on three axes, the central
body of the satellite measured 1.42x1.55x
2.18m (4.66x5x7.15ft). A panel of solar cells
was connected to one side and an arm projected from the other side with a solar sail
at the top. The length from one end to the
other was 19.4m (63ft). INSAT-B was a
multipurpose satellite which fulfills various
functions: telecommunications; meteorology; data collection. Twelve C-band (6-4

GHz) transponders permitted telephone, television and data transmission. Two other
S-band (2.5 GHz) transponders permitted direct television transmission from the satellite to small antennae distributed in rural
areas. The second group of instruments carried on board was of the meteorological type.
There was in fact a very high resolution
radiometer (VHRR) with one channel in the
visibile spectrum (0.55-0.75 microns) which
gave images with a resolution of 2.75km
(1.7mi) and a second, infrared channel
(10.5-12.5 microns) which gave images with
a resolution of 11km (6.8mi). There was also an instrument known as a Data Collection Platform (DCP) which collected meteorological information from platforms distributed in various localities. The service life
expectancy of the satellite, which weighed
1,089kg (2,396lb) on launching, was seven
years.

Launching and orbital data - INSAT-A was
launched April 10, 1982 by a Delta rocket
but a fault in the attitude control propulsion
system rendered the satellite unserviceable.
INSAT-B was carried into orbit by the Space Shuttle *Challenger* on the eighth Shuttle
mission and set off toward geostationary orbit August 30, 1983 using a PAM-D perigee
motor. Having reached geostationary, equatorial orbit it was positioned at longitude
74° E.

ECS (EUROPE - 1983)

The first operational European continental
telecommunications satellite. The platform
was derived from that of the OTS, an European experimental satellite and it was built
by an industrial consortium of which British
Aerospace was prime contractor. The ECS
(European Communications Satellite) was
controlled in orbit by the European organization Eutelsat. The central body of the satellite was a hexagonal prism with a maximum diameter of 2.18m (7.15ft) and a height
of 2.4m (7.8ft). Two panels of solar cells
were fitted to the sides, with a span from tip
to tip of 13.8m (45.27ft). Each panel was
5.2m (17ft) long and 1.2m (4ft) wide. The
total power delivered was 1,000 watts. The
weight in orbit of the ECS, which was stabilized on three axes, was 700kg (1,543lb),
while the service life was estimated at seven
years. The satellite was made up of two modules: a service module for the service systems (propulsion, telemetry, trim, etc.) and
another for the telecommunications payload. ECS had 14 Ku-band (14-12 GHz)
transponders and was used for telephone, television, data, facsimile and telex transmissions, computer links and even videoconferences. The area covered apart from Europe included the Middle East and North Afri-

ca. Digital transmissions between small, dedicated Earth stations in Europe are possible within the ECS system.

Launching and orbital data - ECS-1 was launched June 16, 1983 from the French Guiana polygon by an Ariane rocket and positioned in geostationary, equatorial orbit at longitude 10° E. ECS-2, launched August 4, 1984 by Ariane-3 was positioned in geostationary orbit at longitude 7° E.

GALAXY (USA - 1983)

The satellites of the Galaxy series for telecommunications within the USA, which used the Hughes model HS-376, were controlled in orbit by Hughes Communications Services which had its own Operations Control Center (OCC) at Los Angeles in California. Galaxy was cylindrical in form and once the panel of solar cells, which was of the telescopic type and also cylindrical, was extended, it was 6.83m (22.4ft) long and 2.16m (7ft) in diameter. The weight in orbit was 633kg (1,395lb). The solar cells covering the outer surfaces generated a power of 1,000 watts. It was spin-stabilized. The satellite was equipped with 24 transponders, six of which were in reserve and the frequencies for transmission were 6-4 GHz. The expected service life was nine years. The Galaxy satellites were mainly used for broadcasting of cable television programs.

Launching and orbital data - Galaxy-1, -2 and -3 were launched from Cape Canaveral by a Delta-PAM-D rocket June 28, 1983, September 22, 1983 and September 21, 1984, respectively. The three satellites were placed in geostationary equatorial orbit at the following respective longitudes: 134° W; 74° W and 93.5° W.

TELSTAR-3 (USA - 1983)

Internal telecommunications satellites designed by AT&T Bell Laboratories using the HS-376 model built by Hughes Aircraft Corp. The body was a cylinder 2.16m (7ft) in diameter and 6.83m (22.4ft) tall once the cylindrical panel of solar cells and parabolic antenna were deployed. There were 15,558 solar cells. Equipped with 24 transponders, six of which were in reserve, it transmitted in the C-band using frequencies of 6-4 GHz. The satellites are used for transmission of video-teleconferences, 24 color television programs and high speed data in the United States, Hawaii, Puerto Rico and Alaska. The service life is ten years.

Launching and orbital data - Telstar-301 was launched July 28, 1983 from Cape Canaveral by a Delta rocket. Telstar-302 September 2, 1984 during mission 41-D of the Shuttle *Discovery*. Telstar-303 also left in the Space Shuttle *Discovery* June 17, 1985 during mission 51-G. The Telstars launched by

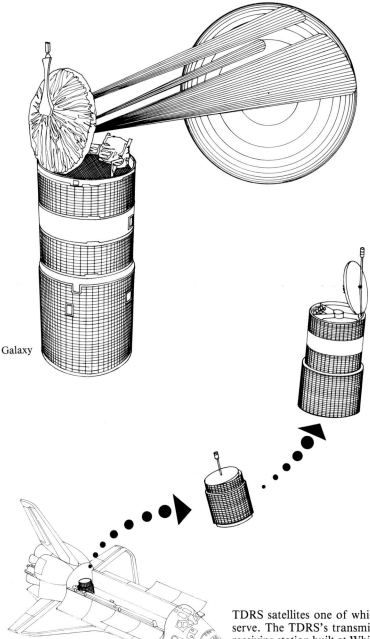

Galaxy

Shuttle used a PAM-D motor for transfer to geostationary orbit. They were all positioned in geostationary equatorial orbit, Telstar 302 at longitude 74° W and Telstar-303 at longitude 125° W.

TDRS (USA - 1983)

A big American satellite used for relay between orbiting space vehicles and an Earth station. TDRS, from the initials for Tracking and Data Relay Satellite, was built by the Space and Technology group of TRW, for a company formed by Continental Telecom Inc. and Fairchild Industries Inc. and called Space Communications Company (Spacecom). Spacecom owned and operated the system which consisted of three orbiting

TDRS satellites one of which will be a reserve. The TDRS's transmitted to a single receiving station built at White Sands in New Mexico. The three satellites were leased to NASA who used them for links between satellites in low orbit or the Space Shuttle, replacing the STDN ground reception network used hitherto and comprising 12 antennae, four of which were on American territory. The TDRS system, apart from providing links for NASA, also offered commercial services in the C- and Ku-bands and could operate with 26 satellites simultaneously, insuring coverage of 85 or 100 percent of their orbital period depending on their altitude. Before that, the STDN ground network guaranteed a mean coverage of 15 percent. TDRS was the largest civil telecommunications satellite launched up to 1983 and the first one capable of operating in three frequency bands at once: S (2.5 GHz) with four transponders; C (6-4 GHz) with 12 transponders and Ku (14-12 GHz) with two transponders. The satellite was formed of a central body in the shape of an hexagonal prism to which seven different types of antenna

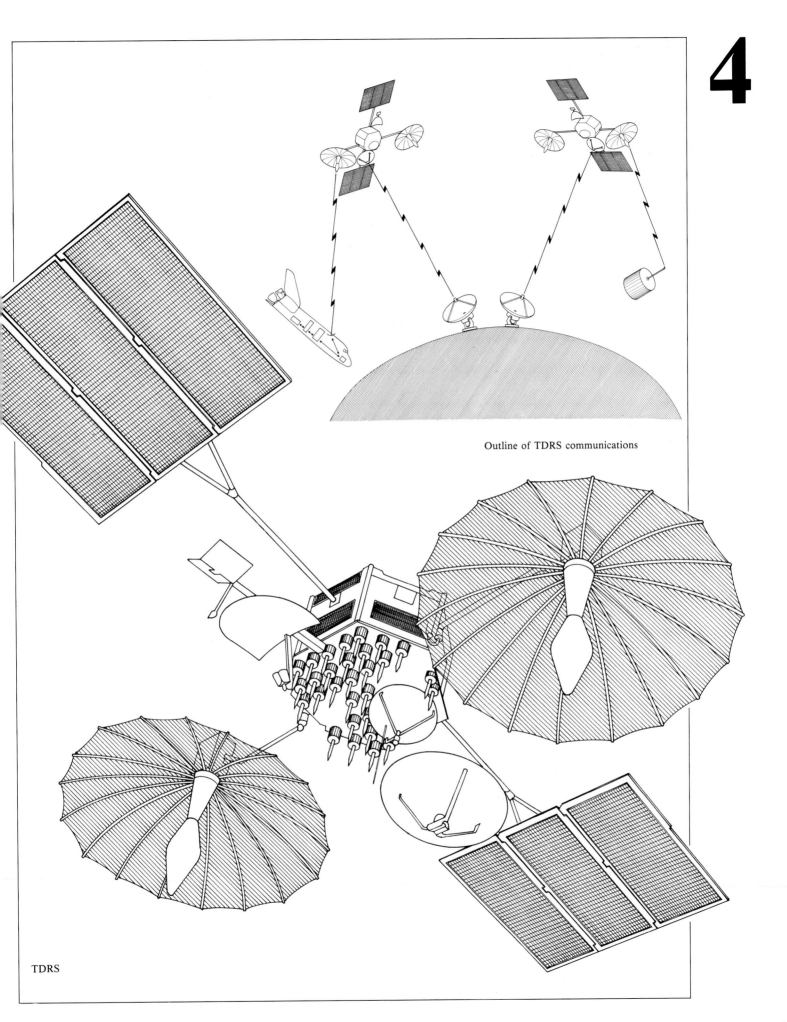

Outline of TDRS communications

TDRS

were connected. When these were opened in orbit together with the two panels of solar cells, the satellite measured 17.41x12.98m (57.11x42.58ft). Two of the seven antennae were parabolic in form with a diameter of 4.9m (16ft) and served for S- and Ku-band links. The transmissive capacity of the satellite (data rates) amounted to 300 Mbps (million bits per second). TDRS weighed 2,120kg (4,674lb) in orbit, had a system of stabilization on three axes and a life expectancy of ten years. The power for its operation was provided by two square panels 3.81m (12.50ft) each side, holding 28,000 solar cells which developed 1,850 watts. Three nickel cadmium batteries came into operation when the satellite was in shadow. Attitude control was by means of 24 thrust motors (0.45kg = 1lb) each of which runned on hydrazine of which 679kg (1,497lb) were carried on board.

Launching and orbital data - TDRS-1 was launched April 4, 1983 by the Space Shuttle *Challenger* during mission STS-6. A two-stage IUS (Inertial Upper Stage) perigee motor was to carry the satellite toward geostationary orbit but due to failure of the second stage, the satellite was sent into an elliptical orbit with a perigee of 21,840km (13,570mi) and an apogee of 35,349km (21,965mi). By a series of ignitions of the attitude control motors over a period of 58 days, the satellite was positioned in the correct geostationary, equatorial orbit at longitude 41° W above the Atlantic Ocean. The second TDRS will be positioned above the Pacific Ocean at longitude 171° W. The reserve TDRS will

be located between the two, over the United States.

YURI-2A/BS-2A (JAPAN - 1984)

A Japanese satellite for direct broadcasting of television programs which was an improved version of the Yuri/BSE experimental satellite of which it kept the box shape measuring 1.3x1.2m (4.3x3.9ft) top and bottom and 3m (9.84ft) high. The weight in orbit was also the same: 350kg (772lb). BS stands for Broadcasting Satellite. Prime contractor for Yuri-2A was Toshiba, with technical assistance from the American General Electric Company. The system of BS satellites which forecasted the use of two orbiting vehicles, one of which was in reserve, was controlled by the Telecommunications Satellite Corporation of Japan (TSCJ), while it was used by the Japan Broadcasting Corporation (NHK). Transmissions from the BS satellites which had three transponders and used the Ku-band (14-12 GHz), can be received on Earth by parabolic antennae with a diameter of approx. 1 meter (3.28ft). The expected service life was five years. Two of the transponders stopped working in March and May, 1984.

Launching and orbital data - Yuri-2A was launched January 23, 1984 from Tanegashima polygon by a N-2 rocket and sent into geostationary equatorial orbit at longitude 110° E.

TELECOM-1 (FRANCE - 1984)

A French satellite built by Matra as prime contractor under the joint responsibility of the Centre National d'Etudes Spatiales (CNES) and the Directorate General of Telecommunications (DGT). Telecom used the body designed for the European ECS. The power supplied by the two panels of 15,816 solar cells was 1,150 watts. Telecom weighed 700kg (1,543lb) in orbit. It was stabilized on three axes and had a life expectancy of seven years. The telecommunications instruments were: six 14-12 GHz transponders; four 6-4 GHz transponders and two 8-7 GHz transponders. The communications permitted include: telephone and television links, data and teletex transmission. Bit rates vary from 2,400bit per second to 2 million for the sending of images. Telecom permitted three types of communication: 1) business transmissions (data and video) between companies at 14-12 GHz; 2) civil transmissions (telephone and television) inside France and with its overseas territories at 6-4 GHz; 3) military transmissions for the Syracuse network (telegraph, data and telephony) at 8-7 GHz.

Launching and orbital data - Telecom-1 was launched August 4, 1984 from the polygon in French Guiana by an Ariane 3 rocket together with the European satellite ECS-2. Telecom-1 was positioned in geostationary equatorial orbit at longitude 5-8° W.

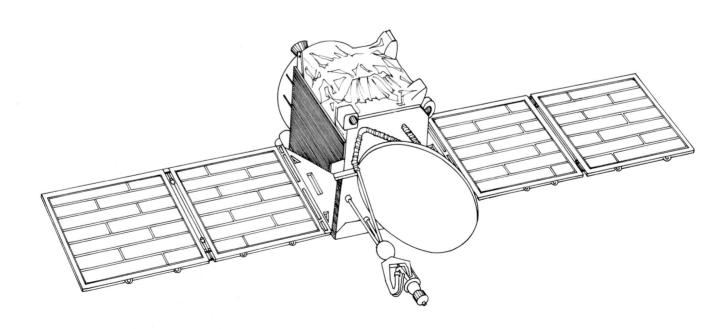

Yuri-2A/BS-2A

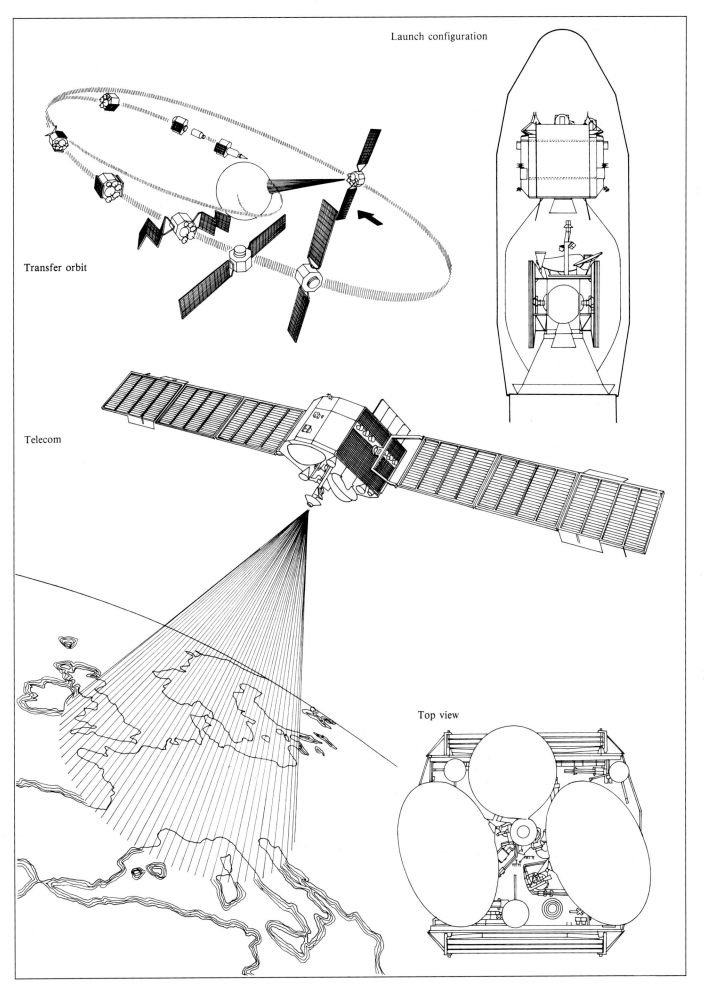

Launch configuration

Transfer orbit

Telecom

Top view

4

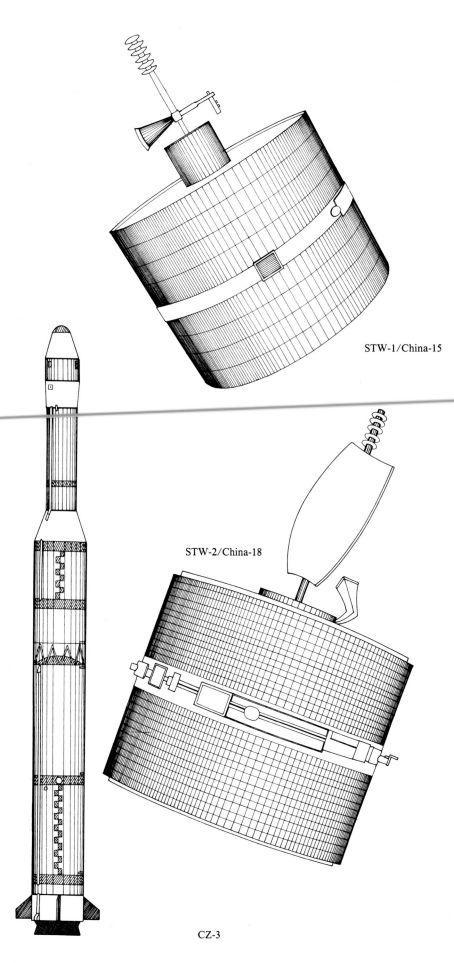

STW/CHINA (CHINA - 1984)

The first Chinese telecommunications satellite in geostationary orbit. Cylindrical in shape with a diameter of about 2.2m (7.22ft), a height of 1.9m (6.23ft), excluding the antenna, and a weight in orbit of 420kg (926lb). The weight on launching was 900kg (1,984lb). STW-1 had a capacity of two television channels or 300 telephone circuits. STW-2, which was the reserve model of STW-1, had almost the same characteristics except for a few elements like the antennae: instead of a small horn-shaped antenna as in the first satellite, there were two parabolic antennae each 1.2m (4ft) in diameter.

Launching and orbital data - STW-1 (China-15) was launched April 8, 1984 from Xichang polygon southwest of Chengdu by a Chinese CZ-3 rocket and sent into geostationary equatorial orbit at longitude 125° E. STW-2 (China-18) left Xichang polygon February 1, 1986, also by a CZ-3 rocket and was sent into geostationary orbit at longitude 103° W.

STW-1/China-15

SPACENET (USA - 1984)

Satellites built by RCA Astro Electronics for the GTE Spacenet Corporation which provided communications services by satellite (high-speed data transmission, telephone and video links) on request within the United States. The satellite was stabilized on three axes and weighed 692kg (1,525lb) in orbit. Its life expectancy was ten years. Spacenet had 18 C-band (6-4 GHz) and 6 Ku-band (14-12 GHz) transponders. The system was designed to have four Spacenet satellites in orbit.

STW-2/China-18

Launching and orbital data - Spacenet-1 was launched May 23, 1984 from the French Guiana polygon by an Ariane 3 rocket and sent into geostationary equatorial orbit at longitude 120° W. Spacenet-2 also went up by an Ariane 3 rocket, November 10, 1984, and was positioned in a similar orbit at longitude 69° W.

INTELSAT-5A
(INTERNATIONAL - 1985)

Intelsat-5A, with almost the same characteristics as its predecessor Intelsat-5, differed mainly in having improved communication reliability and capacity. Its capacity was in fact 25 percent higher than that of Intelsat-5 and 15,000 telephone circuits were available, plus two television channels. Stabilized on three axes and with a weight of 1,098kg (2,420lb) in orbit, it had a maximum height of 6.4m (21ft) and the panels of solar cells had a span of 15.9m (52ft). The Ku-band (14-12 GHz) was used for transmission. Ford Aerospace and Communications Corp. was the prime contractor.

CZ-3

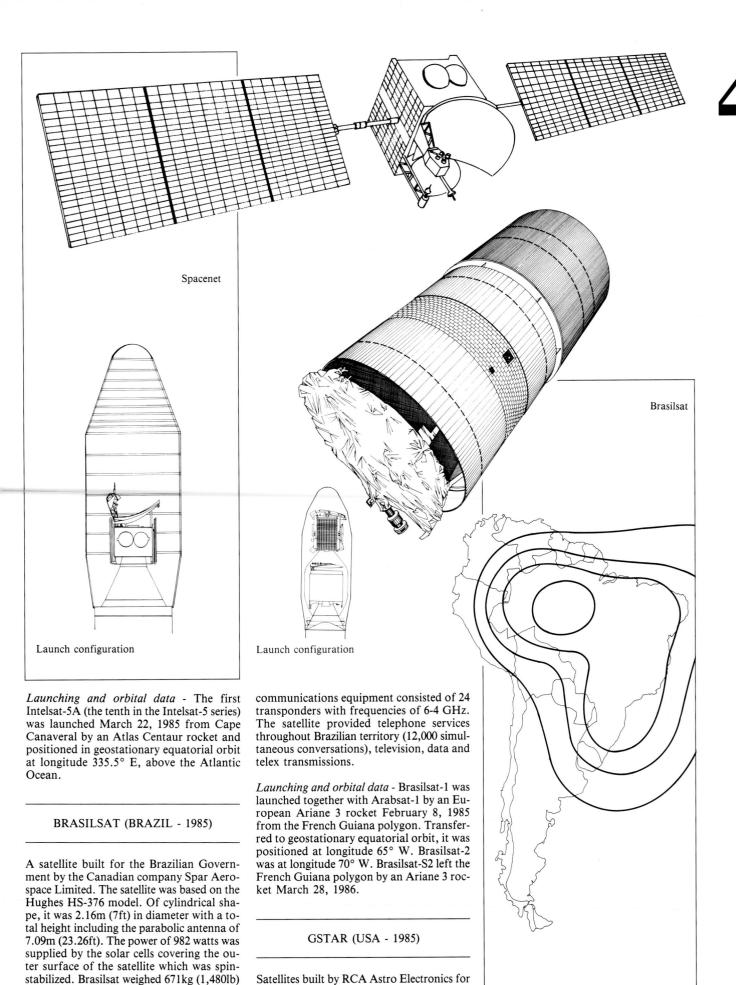

Spacenet

Brasilsat

Launch configuration

Launch configuration

Launching and orbital data - The first Intelsat-5A (the tenth in the Intelsat-5 series) was launched March 22, 1985 from Cape Canaveral by an Atlas Centaur rocket and positioned in geostationary equatorial orbit at longitude 335.5° E, above the Atlantic Ocean.

BRASILSAT (BRAZIL - 1985)

A satellite built for the Brazilian Government by the Canadian company Spar Aerospace Limited. The satellite was based on the Hughes HS-376 model. Of cylindrical shape, it was 2.16m (7ft) in diameter with a total height including the parabolic antenna of 7.09m (23.26ft). The power of 982 watts was supplied by the solar cells covering the outer surface of the satellite which was spin-stabilized. Brasilsat weighed 671kg (1,480lb) in orbit and should have a life expectancy of 8-10 years. The payload in the form of

communications equipment consisted of 24 transponders with frequencies of 6-4 GHz. The satellite provided telephone services throughout Brazilian territory (12,000 simultaneous conversations), television, data and telex transmissions.

Launching and orbital data - Brasilsat-1 was launched together with Arabsat-1 by an European Ariane 3 rocket February 8, 1985 from the French Guiana polygon. Transferred to geostationary equatorial orbit, it was positioned at longitude 65° W. Brasilsat-2 was at longitude 70° W. Brasilsat-S2 left the French Guiana polygon by an Ariane 3 rocket March 28, 1986.

GSTAR (USA - 1985)

Satellites built by RCA Astro Electronics for the American GTE Spacenet Corporation. The company provided communications ser-

Outline of Brasilsat communications

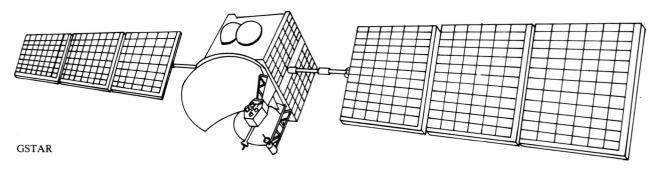

GSTAR

vices within the United States with a system of three GSTAR satellites plus four more of the Spacenet type. The satellites permitted television, telephone (30,000 simultaneous calls) and high-speed data transmission. The body of the satellites measured 1.62x1.32 x0.99m (5.31x4.33x0.28ft) and weighed 699kg (1,541lb) in orbit. They were stabilized on three axes and should have a service life of ten years. Energy was supplied by two panels of solar cells at the sides of the main body of the satellites. 16 Ku-band transponders (14-12 GHz) were available for transmissions.

Launching and orbital data - GSTAR-1 was launched May 1985 from the French Guiana polygon by an Ariane 3 rocket and sent into geostationary orbit at longitude 105° W. GSTAR-2 left French Guiana March 28, 1986, also by an Ariane 3.

MORELOS (MEXICO - 1985)

The first Mexican telecommunications satellite built by the Hughes Space and Communications Group as prime contractor for the Mexican Secretariat of Communications and Transportation. The satellite, built on the Hughes HS-376 model was in the form of a cylinder with a height when fully extended in orbit of 6.58m (21.58ft) and a diameter of 2.2m (7.22ft). Its operating weight was 644kg (1,420lb). Four hydrazine motors, with a 132kg (291lb) fuel supply guaranteed a service life of nine years. It was spinstabilized. Morelos handled telecommunications on Mexican territory, permitting telephone, television, facsimile, data and also business transmissions.

Launching and orbital data - Morelos-1 was carried into orbit by the Space Shuttle *Discovery* during mission 51-G which began June 17, 1985. The satellite was released on the first day of the mission and a PAM-D2 perigee motor transferred it to geostationary equatorial orbit. A second Morelos satellite was launched November 27, 1985 and carried into orbit by the Space Shuttle *Atlantis* during mission 61-B. The first Mexican payload specialist, engineer Rudolpo Neri Vela, took part in the expedition.

ASC (USA - 1985)

A satellite built by RCA Astro Electronics for the American Satellite Co. (ASC) which ran a private telecommunications system using two satellites in orbit and one in reserve on the Earth. The central body of the ASC satellites was a rectangular-based prism, measuring 1.3x1.6x3.2m (4.26x5.25 x10.50ft). Two panels of solar cells with a span of 14.13m (46.36ft) extended from the sides. The weight in orbit was 671kg (1,479lb). The ASC satellites operated both in C-band (6-4 GHz) and Ku-band (14-12 GHz), handling telephone, television (including videoconferences), data and facsimile transmissions for the business sector and government agencies. The ASCs were the first satellites to use encrypted command links for security purposes, to prevent unauthorized access. The vehicles were stabilized on three axes and had a life expectancy of ten years.

Launching and orbital data - The first ASC was launched on the first day of mission 51-I of the American Space Shuttle *Discovery*, which left Cape Canaveral August 27, 1985. The satellite was then transferred toward its final geostationary orbit at longitude 81° W, by a PAM-D perigee motor. The second ASC satellite was assigned the position of longitude 128° W.

ARABSAT (ARAB COUNTRIES - 1985)

A satellite built by the French Aérospatiale for the nations of the Arab League, with the participation of other companies. It provided the possibility of point-to-point communications by telephone, television, radio plus telex and data transmission. The central body of the satellite measured 2.26x1.64x1.49m

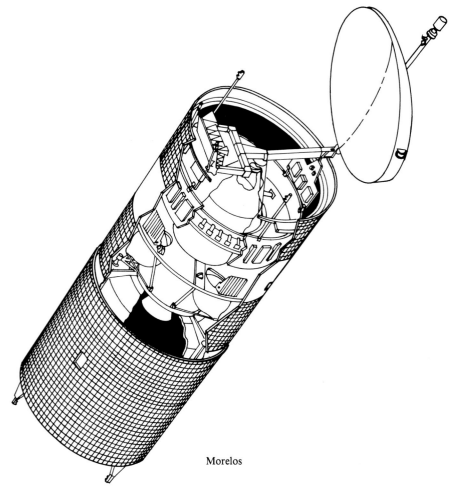

Morelos

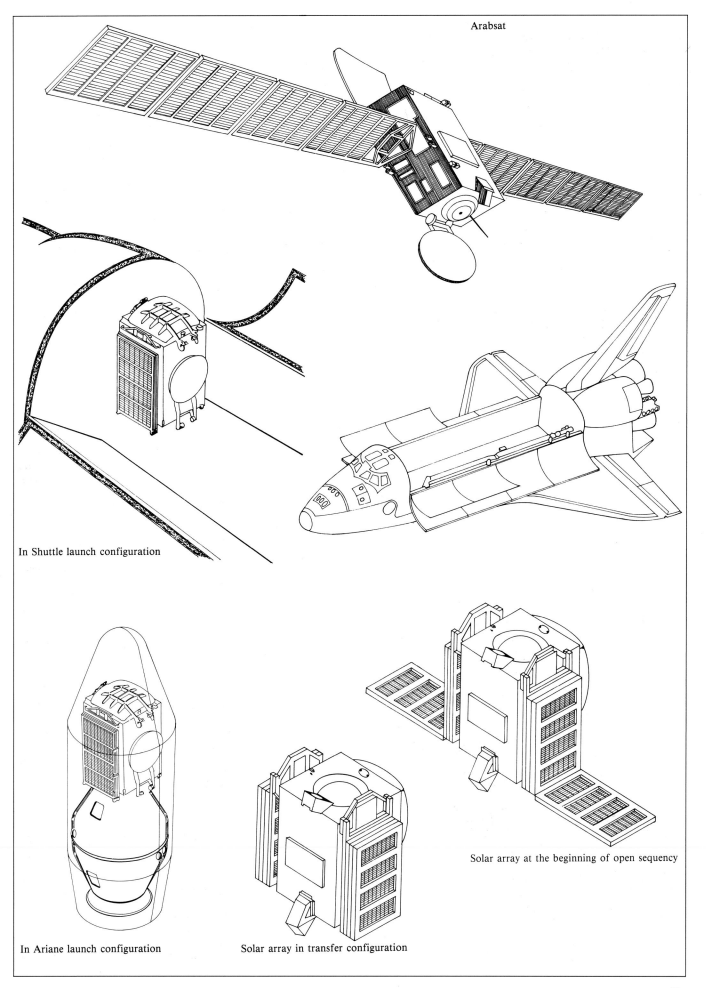

Arabsat

In Shuttle launch configuration

In Ariane launch configuration

Solar array in transfer configuration

Solar array at the beginning of open sequency

4

(7.41x5.38x4.88ft). Two panels of 20,000 solar cells supplying a power of 1.3 kilowatts projected from the sides and had a span of 20.7m (67.91ft). Stabilized on three axes, its weight in orbit was 678kg (1,498lb) and it was designed for a service life of seven years. Arabsat had 25 transponders with frequencies of 4-6 GHz giving 8,000 telephone circuits plus seven television channels and one 4-2.5 GHz transponder with which it was possible to make semi-direct television broadcasts which could be received with parabolic antennae about 3m (9.84ft) in diameter. The satellites could be launched by European Ariane rocket or American Space Shuttle.

Launching and orbital data - Arabsat-1 was launched February 8, 1985 from the French Guiana polygon by an Ariane 3 rocket and was positioned in geostationary equatorial orbit at longitude 19° E. The Brazilian Brasilsat-1 satellite was carried into orbit by the same launching. Arabsat-2 went up by Space Shuttle *Discovery* during mission 51-G which began June 17, 1985.

AUSSAT (AUSTRALIA - 1985)

Aussat was the first Australian satellite of a spatial telecommunications system based on three satellites controlled by the Aussat Proprietary Ltd. company, with a main control station in Sydney and another in Perth. Aussat was built by Hughes Space and Communications Group using the HS-376 model shaped like a cylinder 6.58m (21.58ft) high after deployment in orbit, and 2.2m (7.22ft) in diameter. The weight in orbit was 599kg (1,320lb) and it was spin-stabilized. The necessary power was supplied by two cylindrical panels of solar cells: one was fixed and

the other one movable, of the telescopic type. Aussat, which had 15 transponders operating at a frequency of 14-12 GHz (Ku-band), provided a wide range of communications services throughout Australasia. These included direct television transmission to remote communities, high quality television links between cities and digital transmission of data for normal telecommunications and business services. Plus telephonic links, centralized air traffic control services and assistance to maritime traffic.

Launching and orbital data - Aussat-1 was launched from the American Space Shuttle *Discovery* on the first day of mission 51-I which began August 27, 1985. A PAM-D perigee motor transferred it toward geostationary equatorial orbit where it was positioned at longitude 156° E on the vertical north of Papua (New Guinea). Aussat-2 launched November 27, 1985 by *Atlantis* Shuttle during mission 61-B, was positioned at longitude 164° E. Aussat-3 was assigned the position of longitude 160° E.

COSMOS-1629/-1700 (USSR - 1985)

In 1985, the USSR launched two relay satellites regarded by western observers as similar in characteristics to the American TDRS. Two satellites of this type were probably also launched in 1984.

Launching and orbital data - Cosmos - 1629 was launched February 21, 1985 and placed in geostationary equatorial orbit at longitude 335° E.
Cosmos - 1700 left October 25, 1985 and was placed in geostationary orbit at longitude 95° East.

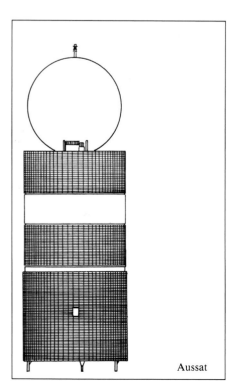

Aussat

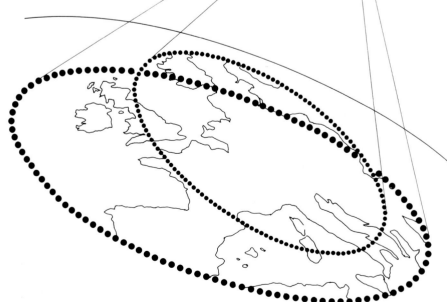

TDF/TV-SAT

TDF

TV-SAT

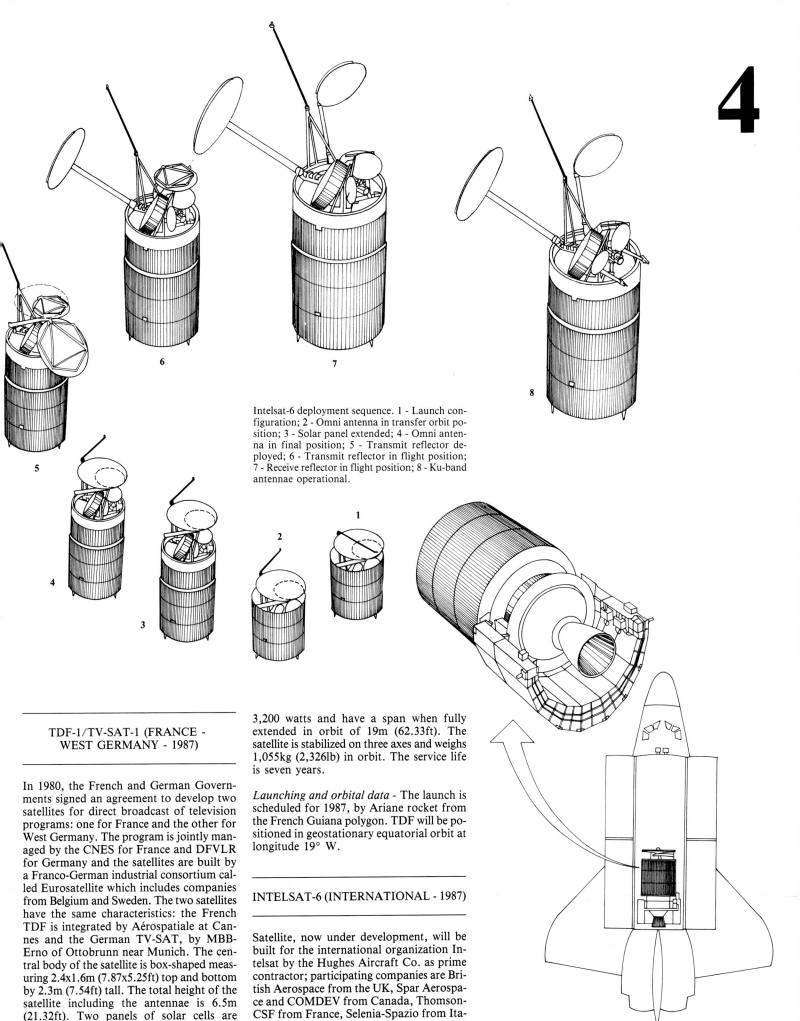

4

6

7

8

5

Intelsat-6 deployment sequence. 1 - Launch configuration; 2 - Omni antenna in transfer orbit position; 3 - Solar panel extended; 4 - Omni antenna in final position; 5 - Transmit reflector deployed; 6 - Transmit reflector in flight position; 7 - Receive reflector in flight position; 8 - Ku-band antennae operational.

1

2

4

3

TDF-1/TV-SAT-1 (FRANCE - WEST GERMANY - 1987)

In 1980, the French and German Governments signed an agreement to develop two satellites for direct broadcast of television programs: one for France and the other for West Germany. The program is jointly managed by the CNES for France and DFVLR for Germany and the satellites are built by a Franco-German industrial consortium called Eurosatellite which includes companies from Belgium and Sweden. The two satellites have the same characteristics: the French TDF is integrated by Aérospatiale at Cannes and the German TV-SAT, by MBB-Erno of Ottobrunn near Munich. The central body of the satellite is box-shaped measuring 2.4x1.6m (7.87x5.25ft) top and bottom by 2.3m (7.54ft) tall. The total height of the satellite including the antennae is 6.5m (21.32ft). Two panels of solar cells are attached to the sides, generate a power of

3,200 watts and have a span when fully extended in orbit of 19m (62.33ft). The satellite is stabilized on three axes and weighs 1,055kg (2,326lb) in orbit. The service life is seven years.

Launching and orbital data - The launch is scheduled for 1987, by Ariane rocket from the French Guiana polygon. TDF will be positioned in geostationary equatorial orbit at longitude 19° W.

INTELSAT-6 (INTERNATIONAL - 1987)

Satellite, now under development, will be built for the international organization Intelsat by the Hughes Aircraft Co. as prime contractor; participating companies are British Aerospace from the UK, Spar Aerospace and COMDEV from Canada, Thomson-CSF from France, Selenia-Spazio from Italy, Nippon Electric from Japan, and MBB

Intelsat-6 launch configuration

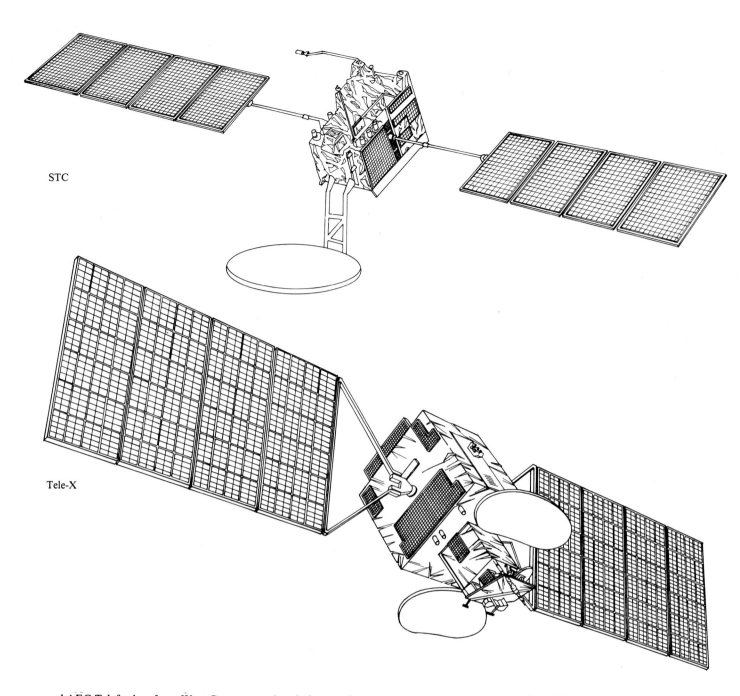

STC

Tele-X

and AEG Telefunken from West Germany. The satellite is a cylinder with a diameter of 3.64m (11.9ft) and a height, when fully extended in orbit, of 11.82m (39ft). A cylindrical panel of solar cells will be lowered into space. All the cells covering the outer surface of the satellite furnish power of 2,200 watts. Weight in orbit will be 2,231kg (1,386lb). A unique system of bipropellant propulsion (with two major and six minor exhaust nozzles) will enable the satellite to reach its definitive geostationary orbit and also maintain attitude control during the projected technical life of ten years. When the satellite, which is spin-stabilized, goes into shadow, two nickel-hydrogen batteries will come into operation. The telecommunications system comprises 50 transponders which will provide a capacity of 40,000 telephone circuits plus two television channels. The satellite uses the TDMA (Time Division Multiple Access) technique and transmits in the 6-4 GHz (C-band) and 14-12 GHz (Ku-band) frequencies.

Launching and orbital data - Intelsat-6 will be launched with the European Ariane 4 rocket or with the American Shuttle. In the latter case a perigee motor will be added to place it in geostationary transfer orbit (GTO). The first launch is planned for 1987.

STC (USA - 1987)

A satellite for broadcasting of television programs within the USA, built by RCA Astro Electronics for the American Satellite Television Corporation (STC). Stabilized on three axes with a weight in orbit of 600kg (1,323lb), the satellite is made up of a central body with two panels of solar cells projecting from it, which have a span of 25m (82ft). The transmission payload has 3 transponders with frequencies of 17.8-12.2 GHz.

Launching and orbital data - STC is due to be launched into geostationary equatorial orbit in 1987 by European Ariane rocket or Space Shuttle.

TELE-X (SCANDINAVIA - 1988)

A satellite for direct television and data transmission financed by Sweden, Norway and Finland. The project, managed by the Swedish Space Corporation, is under development by Aérospatiale in France as prime contractor, assisted by the Swedish company Saab-Scania. Tele-X uses the same bus as the TDF/TV-SAT satellites. The box-shaped central body is 2.4x1.65m (7.87x5.41ft) at top and bottom and 2.4m (7.87ft) tall. With the antenna it is 5m (16.4ft) tall. The two panels of solar cells

96

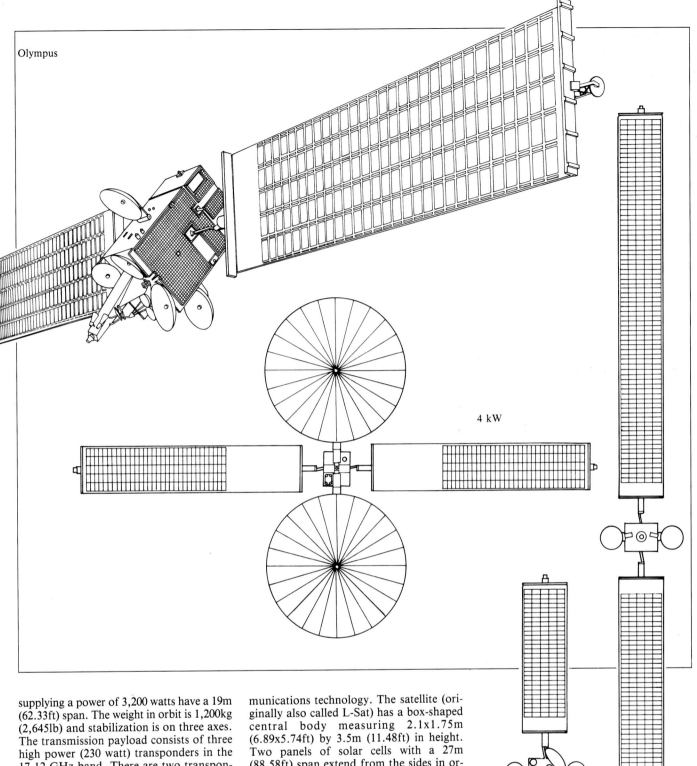

Olympus

4

4 kW

3.5 kW   7.7 kW

supplying a power of 3,200 watts have a 19m (62.33ft) span. The weight in orbit is 1,200kg (2,645lb) and stabilization is on three axes. The transmission payload consists of three high power (230 watt) transponders in the 17-12 GHz band. There are two transponders in the 14-12 GHz frequency band for data transmission. The service life is estimated at 7 years.

Launching and orbital data - Tele-X will be launched in 1988 by an Ariane rocket from the polygon in French Guiana and sent into geostationary equatorial orbit at longitude 5° E.

OLYMPUS (EUROPE - 1988)

A satellite built by the ESA (European Space Agency) to test some advanced telecom-munications technology. The satellite (originally also called L-Sat) has a box-shaped central body measuring 2.1x1.75m (6.89x5.74ft) by 3.5m (11.48ft) in height. Two panels of solar cells with a 27m (88.58ft) span extend from the sides in orbit. The energy delivered by the panels is 3,300 watts. The weight, including the apogee motor, is 2,422kg (5,340lb). Stabilization is on three axes and the expected service life is five years. British Aerospace and Selenia Spazio are the prime contractor. The transmission payload consists of 9 transponders and the satellite has 10 antennae. The mission has four objectives. 1) Direct television: transmissions with frequencies of 11.7-12.5 GHz will take place on two channels. One of the two will be used almost entirely by Italy. The satellite will receive the transmission at 17 GHz. 2) Business transmissions: business service transmissions including video-conference links will take place at frequencies of 14-12 GHz. 3) High frequency com-

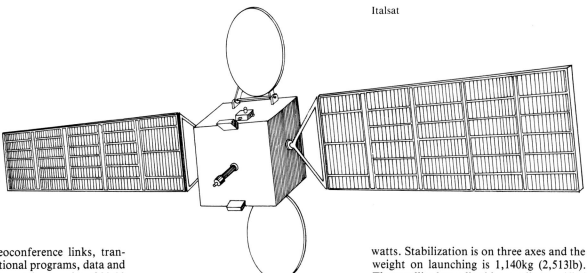

Italsat

munications: videoconference links, transmission of educational programs, data and images will take place at frequencies of 20-30 GHz. 4) Propagation experiments: these will be carried out at frequencies of 20-30 GHz to study the changes caused by the climatic conditions through which the signals pass. Similar experiments will be carried out at a frequency of 12 GHz.

Launching and orbital data - Olympus will be launched into space in 1988 from the French Guiana polygon by an Ariane 3 rocket and sent into geostationary equatorial orbit at longitude 19° W.

ITALSAT (ITALY - 1989)

A preoperational satellite the program for which is managed by the Italian National Space Program (PSN, Piano Spaziale Nazionale). Selenia Spazio is the prime contractor. The satellite has a box-shaped central body 1.8x1.8m (5.90x5.90ft) at the top and bottom and 2m (6.56ft) tall. Two panels of solar cells 2.1x5.5m (6.89x18ft) each extend from the sides with a span in orbit of 13.8m (45.27ft). They provide a power of 1,400

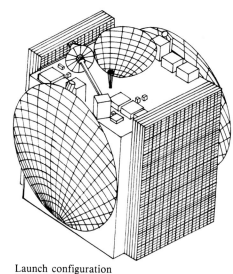

Launch configuration

watts. Stabilization is on three axes and the weight on launching is 1,140kg (2,513lb). The satellite has a liquid propellant unified propulsion system which serves both as an apogee motor and for attitude control. The payload consists of three packs of instruments. The first comprises six 20-30 GHz transponders, which will use the two larger antennae, each 2m (6.56ft) in diameter and will transmit at a speed of 120 Mbps (million bits per second), with a capacity corresponding to 11,000 telephone circuits. Telephone links will be effected with these transponders. The second pack of instruments contains three transponders at 20-30 GHz to cover the whole of Italy, which will permit Time Division Multiple Access (TDMA) communication for special types of data transmission (computer links, electronic post, video and audio conferences and rapid facsimile) with a speed of 25 Mbps. Finally, a third pack of instruments will handle transmission at 40-50 GHz with European coverage for propagation experiments. The service life should be five years.

Launching and orbital data - Italsat will be launched in 1989 from the polygon in French Guiana by an Ariane rocket and positioned in geostationary equatorial orbit at longitude 13° E.

Military satellites

In addition to the network of civil satellites encircling the Earth, there is a second group of space vehicles concerned solely with considerations of defense.

Most of the more advanced space technology was tested and initially used in the military field and subsequently transferred to the civil sector. Thus because of military needs there were rapid developments in electronics, the chemistry of propellants and the science of materials. Even the first telecommunications satellite, Score, was a military craft. The majority of satellites employed for defense are for reconnaissance, familiarly known as "spy satellites." They fulfill the need to survey enemy territory and military movements, and are capable of changing their orbital height according to the task to be performed. In the United States the tendency has been to send into orbit vehicles such as Key Hole capable of carrying out various functions ranging from overall reconnaissance of the area to detailed observation with high-resolution cameras which are able to distinguish objects measuring only a few centimeters. Reconnaissance is possible both by night and day thanks to infrared systems. The technical life of the American Key Hole is around two years.

The system used by the Soviet Union is quite different, resorting more to photography, with the recovery of films through capsules returning to Earth. The orbital life of Soviet spy satellites in the first half of the eighties has been around two months. This is the reason why there have been such frequent launchings of Soviet reconnaissance satellites bearing the generic name of Cosmos. During 1983/1984 there were on average 30-35 satellite launchings each year.

During the eighties much effort has been expended by the United States to develop satellites such as Teal Ruby, for monitoring air and cruise missiles from orbit. This has necessitated the development of special sensors for use in the infrared range, and the use of superfluid helium to cool the system — a technique identical to that employed in the infrared IRAS satellites. In this way it is possible to monitor the fuselage of the spacecraft and not just the heat generated by the engine exhaust. The orbital life of this satellite is about one year.

In addition to reconnaissance, other types of military satellites are concerned with ocean surveillance, electronic listening (eavesdropping on radio communications among armed forces), early warning surveillance against missile attack, observation of nuclear explosions, and antisatellite systems. Then there are navigation satellites also used for civil needs (see chapter on Navigational Satellites.) One sector which seems to have remained a Soviet speciality, and already tested, is that known as FOBS (Fractional Orbit Bombardment System), whereby space vehicles loaded with explosive devices are maneuvered so as to be directed toward any required zone of the Earth.

The West is currently taking a great forward step in military technology with the SDI (Strategic Defense Initiative) program. This entails the installation in orbit of orbiting platforms capable of destroying by laser beams, generated both in space and on the ground, and then reflected against the target by orbital mirrors, missiles that might be launched by the Soviet Union. Research in this field of military lasers is also being conducted in the USSR.

Once feature that is typical of military spacecraft is their use of electronic instruments made to withstand higher than normal radiation levels, such as might be generated by nuclear explosions.

In reading the following table three aspects have to be taken into account. The first is the fact that the Soviet Union often makes use of civil satellites for military purposes as well, for example, in the field of meteorology. The second concerns the launching of a series of unnumbered Cosmos satellites whose destinations remain undefined. The third relates to the launching of many Cosmos satellites broadly described as scientific in purpose but actually employed for military ends.

The term "research satellite" is loosely used for satellites testing new forms of space technology which may be employed for military purposes and which also involves genuine scientific research indirectly associated with defense needs.

Navigational satellites used as well as for military purposes have been listed separately.

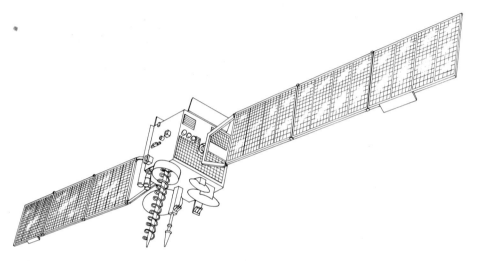

Skynet IV

Telecommunications

Satellite	First launch	Perigee × apogee/inclination degree km (mi)	Nation
Score	2/18/1958	158x1,484 (98x922)/32°	USA
Courier	10/4/1960	938x1,237 (582x769)/28°	USA
LES-1	2/11/1965	2,774x2,811 (1,724x1,747)/32°	USA
IDCSP	6/16/1966	33,656x33,897 (20,914x21,064)/0,09°	USA
Tacsat	2/9/1969	geostationary	USA
Skynet	11/22/1969	geostationary	GB
NATO-A	3/20/1970	geostationary	USA-NATO
Cosmos-336	4/25/1970	1,464x1,490 (910x926)/74°	USSR
DSCS-1	11/3/1971	geostationary	USA
SDS	3/21/1971	390x33,800 (242x21,003)/63°	USA
Fltsatcom	2/9/1978	geostationary	USA
Syncom-4/Leasat	8/31/1984	geostationary	USA
Milstar	1988	geostationary	USA

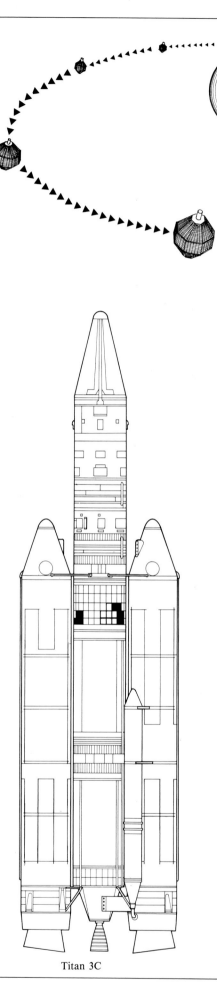

Titan 3C

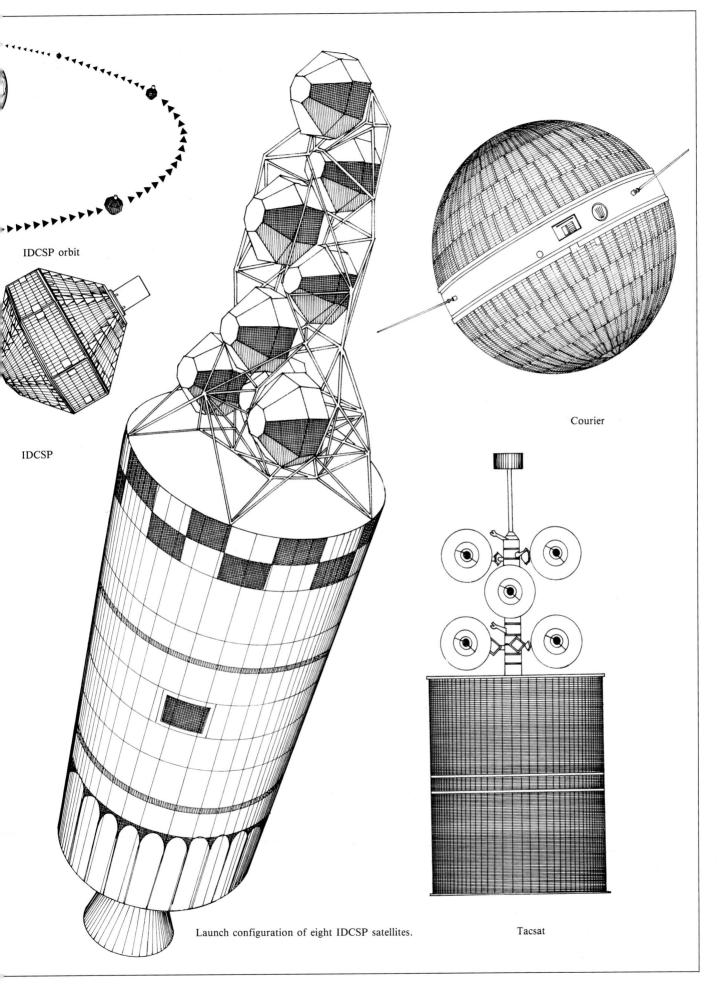

IDCSP orbit

IDCSP

Launch configuration of eight IDCSP satellites.

Courier

Tacsat

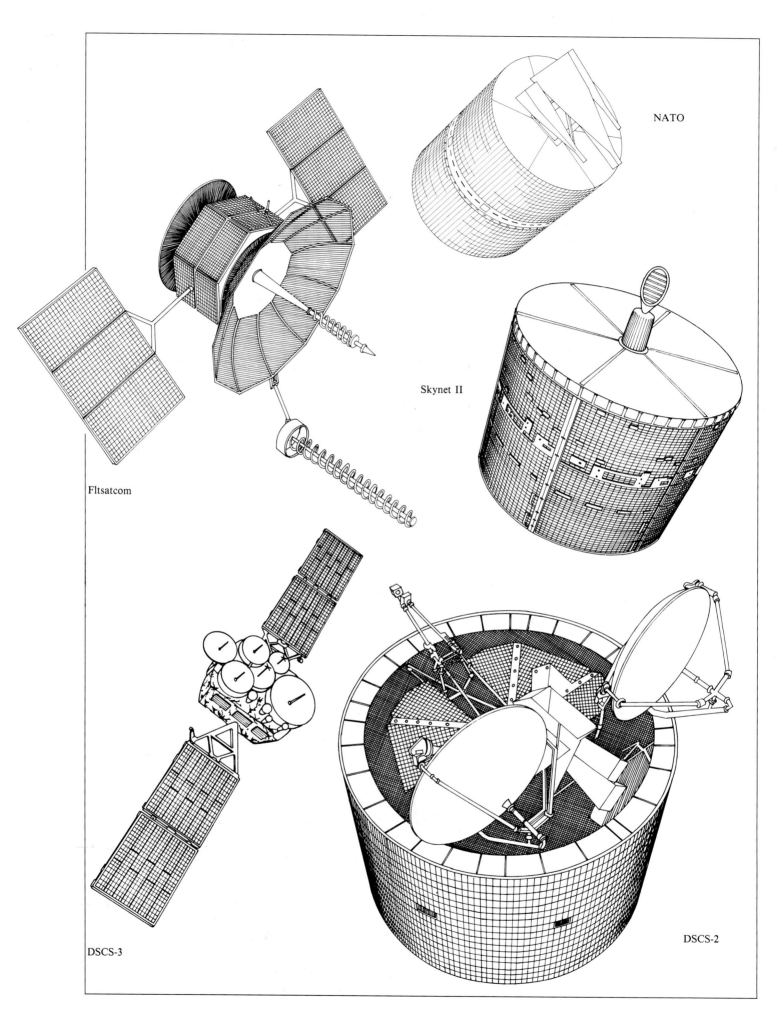

NATO

Skynet II

Fltsatcom

DSCS-3

DSCS-2

IMEWS

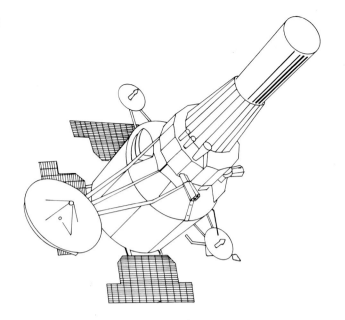

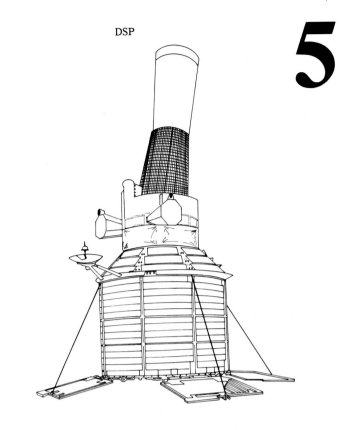

Early-warning

Satellite	First launch	Perigee × apogee/inclination degree km (mi)	Nation
Midas	5/24/1960	484x511 (301x318)/33°	USA
BMEWS	8/6/1968	31,680x39,860 (19,686x24,769)/10°	USA
IMEWS	11/6/1970	26,050x35,886 (16,187x22,300)/8°	USA
DSP	10/14/1971	796x877 (495x545)/98°	USA
Cosmos-520	9/19/1972	227x669 (141x416)/62°	USSR

Nuclear detection

Satellite	First launch	Perigee × apogee/inclination degree km (mi)	Nation
VELA	10/17/1963	102,098x111,137 (63,444x69,061)/38°	USA
Ionds/Gps	2/22/1978	20,095x20,308 (12,487x12,619)/63°	USA

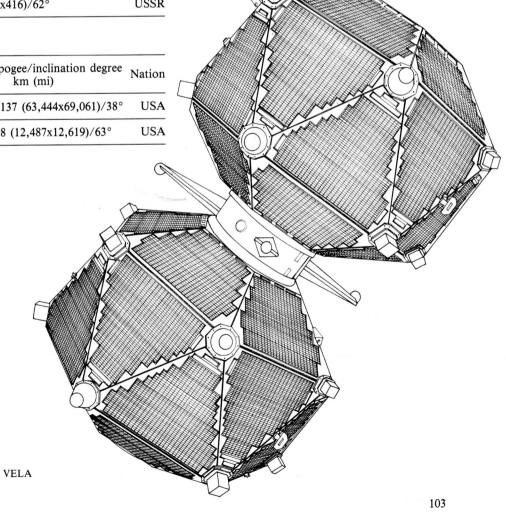

VELA

Ocean-surveillance

Satellite	First launch	Perigee × apogee/inclination degree km (mi)	Nation
RORSAT/ Cosmos-198	12/27/1967	249x270 (155x168)/65°	USSR
SSU	6/8/1975	1,389x1,401 (863x871)/95°	USA
NOSS	4/30/1976	1,092x1,128 (679x701)/63°	USA

Anti-satellite system

Satellite	First launch	Perigee × apogee/inclination degree km (mi)	Nation
Cosmos-249	10/20/1968	254x136 (158x85)/62°	USSR
ASAT	1/21/1984	Over Western Test Range	USA

Bombardment

Satellite	First launch	Perigee × apogee/inclination degree km (mi)	Nation
FOBS/Cosmos-U1*	9/17/1966	163x1,046 (101x650)/49°	USSR

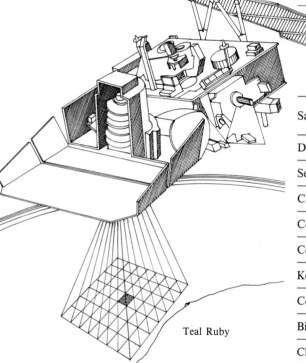

Teal Ruby

Block-5D

Reconnaissance

Satellite	First launch	Perigee × apogee/inclination degree km (mi)	Nation
Discoverer	2/28/1959	163x968 (101x602)/89°	USA
Sentry-Samos	1/31/1961	474x557 (295x346)/97°	USA
Close Look	3/7/1962	251x676 (156x420)/90°	USA
Cosmos-4 (1)	4/26/1962	285x317 (177x197)/65°	USSR
Cosmos-22 (2)	11/16/1963	192x381 (119x237)/65°	USSR
Key Hole/KH-9	7/29/1966	158x250 (98x155)/94°	USA
Cosmos-208 (3)	3/21/1968	208x274 (129x170)/65°	USSR
Big Bird	6/15/1971	184x300 (114x186)/96°	USA
China-3	7/26/1975	184x461 (114x286)/69°	China
Cosmos-758 (4)	9/5/1975	175x326 (108x203)/67°	USSR
KH-11	12/19/1976	247x533 (153x331)/96°	USA
KH-12	1987	250x500 (155x311)	USA
Teal Ruby	1987	740x740 (460x460)	USA

Meteorology

Satellite	First launch	Perigee × apogee/inclination degree km (mi)	Nation
DMSP	9/16/1966	705x891 (438x554)	USA
Block-5D/DMSP	9/11/1976	818x848 (508x527)/98°	USA

* U letter stands for the first Cosmos of the unnumbered series.
(1) first generation; (2) second generation; (3) third generation; (4) fourth generation.

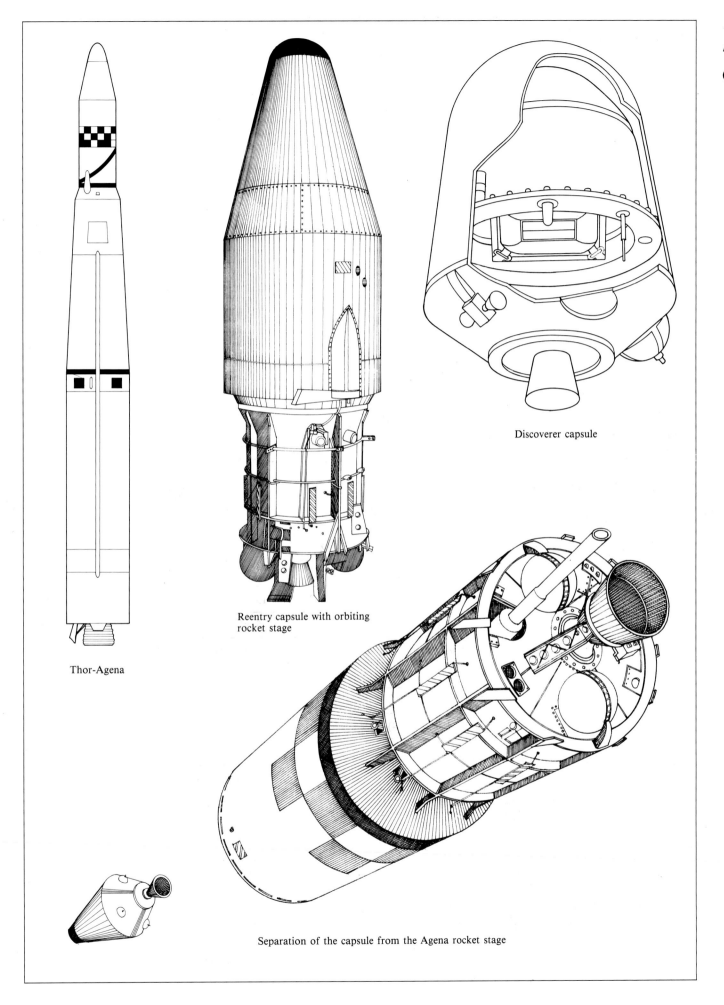

5

Thor-Agena

Reentry capsule with orbiting rocket stage

Discoverer capsule

Separation of the capsule from the Agena rocket stage

105

Electronic intelligence

Satellite	First launch	Perigee × apogee/inclination degree km (mi)	Nation
Elint-Ferrets	5/15/1962	305x634 (190x394)/82°	USA
Cosmos-389	12/18/1970	642x687 (399x427)/81°	USSR

Research

Satellite	First launch	Perigee × apogee/inclination degree km (mi)	Nation
Secor	1/11/1964	904x933 (562x580)/69°	USA
OV-1	10/5/1965	403x3,462 (250x2,151)/144°	USA
OV-2	10/15/1965	706x792 (439x492)/32°	USA
OV-3	4/22/1966	351x5,741 (218x3,567)/82°	USA
OV-4	11/3/1966	294x321 (183x199)/32°	USA
OV-5/ERS	4/28/1967	8,604x111,229 (5,347x69,118)/32°	USA
ASTEX	10/17/1971	773x803 (480x499)/92°	USA
Whitecloud/SSU	4/30/1976	1,093x1,129 (679x702)/63°	USA

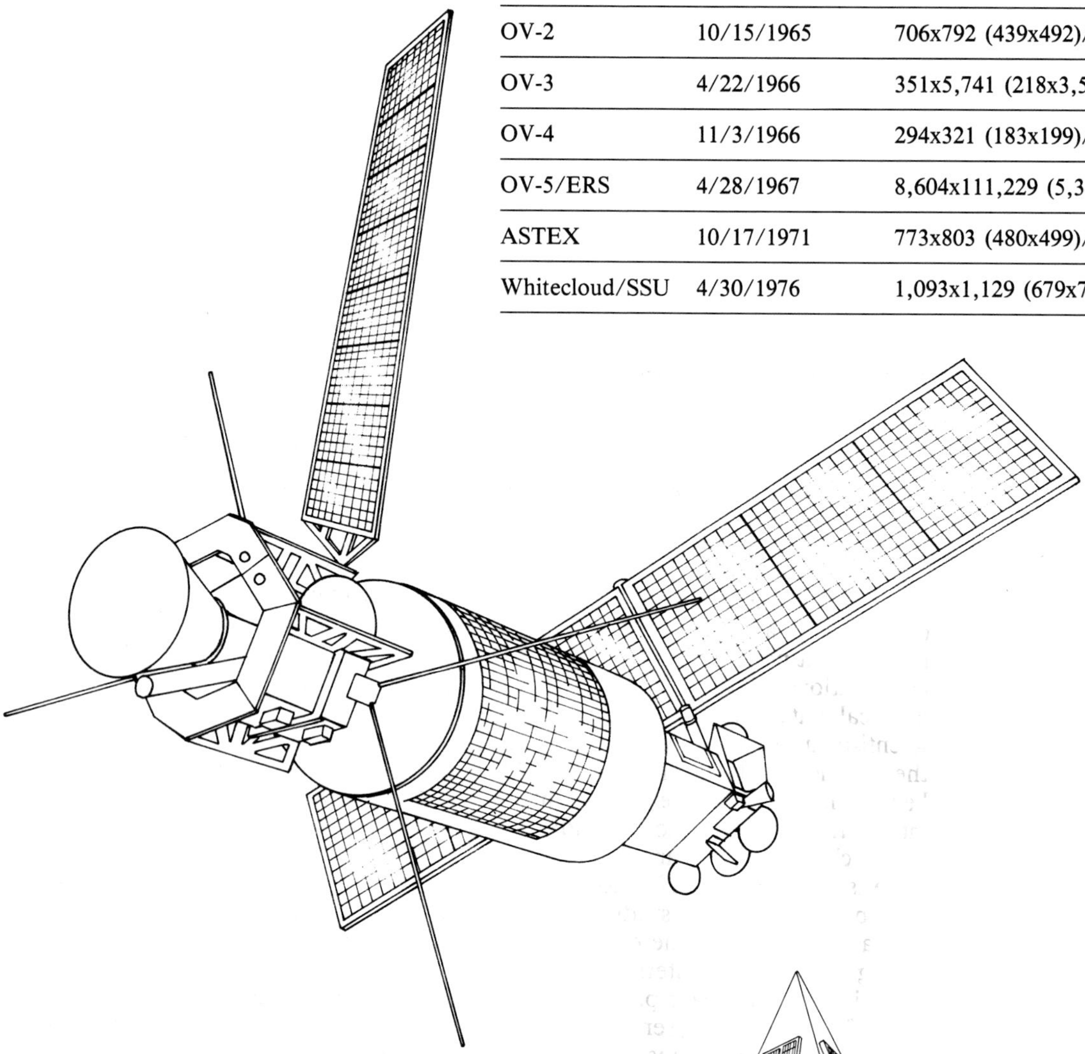

ASTEX

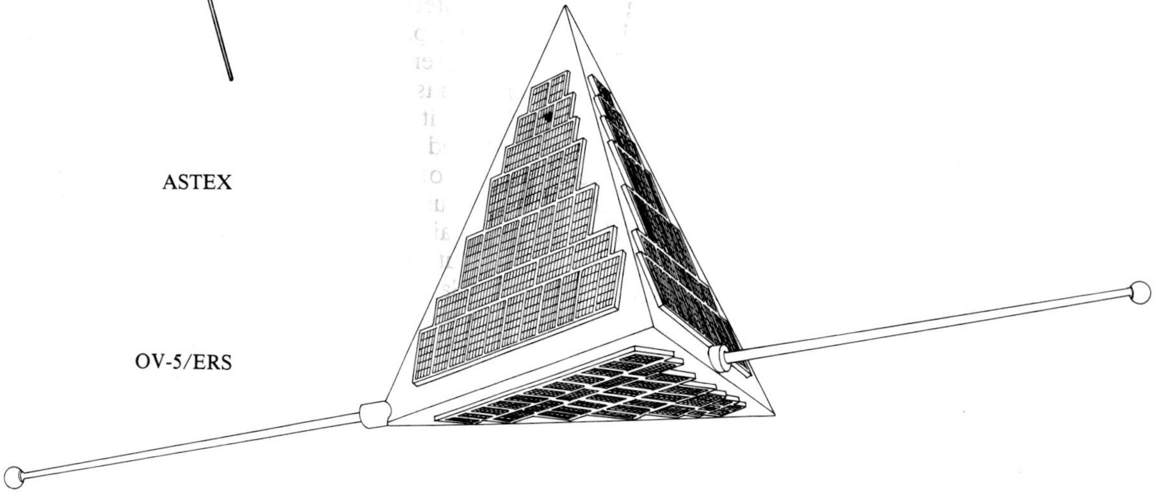

OV-5/ERS

6

Scientific satellites

Scientific satellites play an extremely important role in the field of space activities for two reasons. The first is related to the opportunities they afford to discover facts about the environment in which we live, namely our Earth and those parts of the Universe surrounding it which to some extent condition it. The second reason is that the building of scientific satellites to carry out new research creates technological advances which as a result points the way to further human endeavors and achievements.

There are nowadays many areas of science which rely on satellites to increase knowledge. Earth sciences depend on instruments in space to clarify the characteristics of our planet and the way in which it has evolved. Geodetic satellites, for example, make it possible to survey the movements of the continents and utilize such information for investigating the phenomena of earthquakes and volcanoes. The physical nature of the atmosphere is such that only by using satellites can scientists initiate systematic research on a global basis which can throw light upon the complex workings of our planet. However, the atmosphere is also closely linked to the surrounding environment; and the Sun, which continuously pours out into space a powerful flow of radiations and particles in the course of its eleven-year cycle, provokes changes in the atmosphere which can modify its physical characteristics and even influence the climate. For this reason dozens of satellites have been launched to study the «solar wind» and its influences on the Earth's high atmosphere. But there are also other types of satellites used for investigating with great precision interrelated terrestrial and solar phenomena.

Scientific satellites have probably registered their most spectacular success in the field of astronomy. By sending satellites beyond the protective but limiting screen of the atmosphere, it has been possible to enlarge the boundaries of the known Universe and to reveal it as being incomparably richer in stars and matter than what had been imagined even up to a short time ago. The atmosphere prevented all but a restricted belt of electromagnetic waves to be picked up by groundbased instruments. It was virtually only visible radiation that could tell us anything about the world beyond the air which we actually breathe. X-ray astronomy could not have been born without the use of satellites, and only satellites such as IRAS (Infrared Astronomical Satellite) were capable of picking up infrared rays, functioning at a temperature very close to absolute zero, and thereby providing earliest proof of other solar systems still in course of formation around other stars like Vega. During the 1990s, however, it is envisaged that scientific satellite technology will undergo profound changes. The construction by the United States, in collaboration with Japan, Canada and Europe, of a huge space station will make it possible for scientific activities to be carried out in orbits comparatively close to the Earth from automatic orbital platforms. The necessary research instruments will be assembled on such platforms, inclined either in equatorial or polar orbit, according to need, and exchange of such instruments will also be possible by lowering the platform to the same level as the station or shuttles. In this way scientific activity in space will undoubtedly become more economic, more accessible and wider ranging.

ATMOSPHERIC

SPUTNIK-1 (USSR - 1957)

First artificial satellite in history. It was a sphere with a diameter of 0.58m (1.9ft) and a weight of 83.6kg (184lb). It remained functional for three weeks but stayed in orbit for 92 days until January 4, 1958 when it broke up in the atmosphere. Sputnik-1 carried out the first measurements of atmospheric density and the first investigations into the transmission of electromagnetic waves through the ionosphere.

Launching and orbital data - Sputnik-1 was launched October 4, 1957 from Baikonur-Tyuratam by a Type A rocket. Its orbit had a perigee of 228km (142mi), an apogee of 947km (588mi) and an inclination of 65.1°.

VANGUARD-2 (USA - 1959)

Magnesium sphere with a diameter of 0.508m (1.7ft) and a weight of 10kg (22lb). Spin-stabilized, it carried four photocells and two optical telescopes supplied by the Army Signal Research and Development Laboratory. Mercury batteries provided the power. The satellite carried out experimental observations of the Earth's cloud formations.

Launching and orbital data - Vanguard-2 was launched February 17, 1959 from Cape Canaveral by a Vanguard rocket and was sent into an orbit with a perigee of 559km (347mi), an apogee of 3,320km (2,063mi) and an inclination of 32.88°.

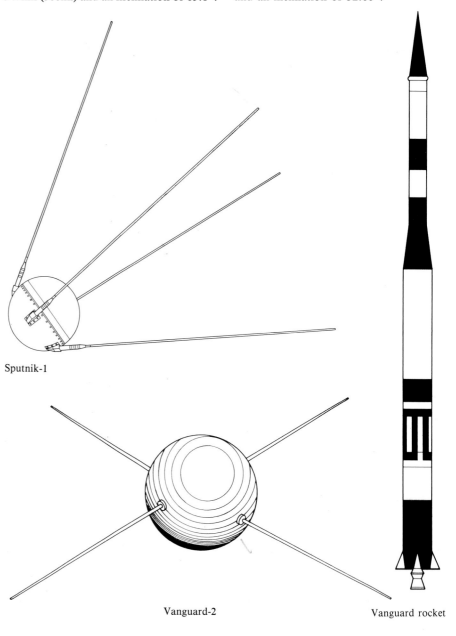

Sputnik-1

Vanguard-2

Vanguard rocket

EXPLORER-9/-19/-24/-39 (USA - 1961)

Mylar spheres covered with aluminum, with a diameter of 3.7m (12.1ft), weighing 7kg (15.4lb), which were inflated automatically in orbit. These satellites measured characteristics and composition of the upper thermosphere and lower exosphere over the entire globe. They studied the density of the air which was found to differ according to latitude, season and local solar time.

Launching and orbital data - Explorer-9 was launched February 16, 1961 and placed in an orbit with a perigee of 634km (394mi), an apogee of 2,583km (1,605mi) and an inclination of 38.86°. Explorer-19 was launched December 19, 1963 and went into a near-circular orbit at an altitude of 905-934km (562-580mi), inclined at 69.91°. Explorer-24 was launched November 21, 1964 and went into an orbit with a perigee of 525km (326mi), an apogee of 2,498km (1,552mi) and an inclination of 81.36°. Explorer-39 was launched August 8, 1968 and was sent into an orbit with a perigee of 670km (416mi), an apogee of 2,538km (1,577mi) and an inclination of 80.66°. All launchings were from Vandenberg by Scout rockets.

EXPLORER-17/-32/-51/-54/-55 (USA - 1963)

Five NASA satellites designed for collecting data on temperature, composition, density and pressure for studies of atmospheric physics on a global basis. Explorer-17 was a sphere of 0.89m (2.9ft) in diameter, weighing 185kg (407lb). Explorer-32 was a sphere of 0.89m (2.9ft) in diameter, weighing 225kg (495lb). Explorer-51 was a 16-faceted cylinder with a diameter of 1.36m (4.5ft) and a height of 1.14m (3.7ft); its weight when empty was 490kg (1,078lb). Explorer-54 was also a 16-faceted cylinder with a diameter of 1.36m (4.5ft), a height of 1.14m (3.7ft), weighing 490kg (1,078lb) when empty, 659kg (1,450lb) when full. Explorer-55 had exactly the same shape, with the same dimensions and empty weight as Explorer-51.

Launching and orbital data - Explorer-17 was launched April 2, 1963 from Cape Canaveral and was sent into an orbit with a perigee of 255km (158mi), an apogee of 917km (570mi) and an inclination of 57.63°.
Explorer-32 was launched May 25, 1966 from Cape Canaveral, its orbit having a perigee of 289km (948mi), an apogee of 2,716km (1,687mi) and an inclination of 64.66°.
Explorer-51 was launched December 16, 1973 from Vandenberg and its orbit had a perigee of 158km (98mi), an apogee of 4,303km (2,673mi) and an inclination of 68.12°.
Explorer-54 was launched October 6, 1975 from Vandenberg and its orbit had a perigee of 155km (96mi), an apogee of 3,816km

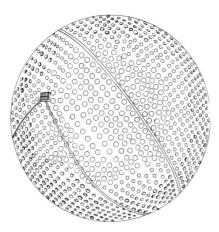

Explorer-9

(2,371mi) and an inclination of 90.1°. Explorer-55 was launched November 19, 1975 from Cape Canaveral into an orbit with a perigee of 156km (97mi), an apogee of 2,983km (1,853mi) and an inclination of 19.7°. Delta rockets were used for all the launchings.

SAN MARCO-1 to -4 (ITALY - 1964)

Group of four Italian satellites in the form of a sphere for studying the atmosphere. They were built by the Aerospace Research Center of the University of Rome as part of a program in collaboration with NASA. San Marco-1 had a diameter of 0.66m (2.2ft) and a weight of 115kg (253lb). On board was a dynamometric balance known as the "Bilancia (Balance) Broglio," because it was designed by Professor Broglio of the University of Rome, which measured variations in the density of the atmosphere and, indirectly, the average temperature and molecular weight of the air. San Marco-2 had a dia-

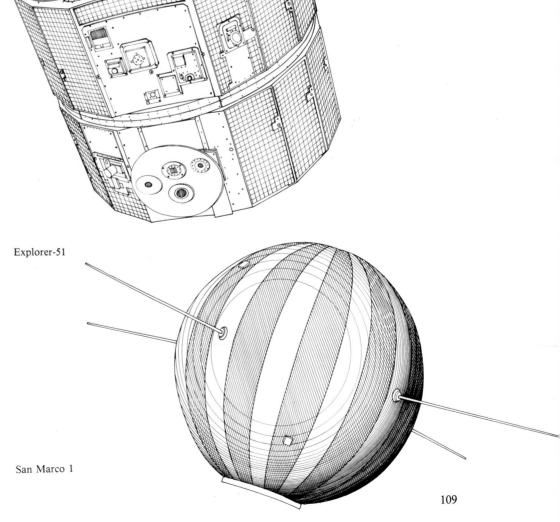

Explorer-51

San Marco-1

meter of 0.66m (2.2ft) and a weight of 129kg (284lb). Mercury batteries furnished the requisite power. On board was the "Bilancia Broglio." San Marco-3 had a diameter of 0.76m (2.5ft) and a weight of 164kg (361lb). On board were three experiments: the "Bilancia Broglio"; an experiment for measuring the composition of the atmosphere, furnished by the Goddard Space Flight Center; and the Omegatron experiment, prepared by the Goddard Center of NASA and the University of Michigan, which measured the temperature and the distribution of molecular nitrogen. San Marco-4 had a diameter of 0.72m (2.4ft) and a weight of 164kg (361lb). On board, in addition to the "Bilancia Broglio," were two instruments supplied by the United States which studied the composition of the upper atmosphere. Around the mid-

dle of the satellite was a series of solar cell panels. All the satellites were spin-stabilized.

Launching and orbital data - San Marco-1 was launched December 15, 1964 into an orbit with a perigee of 198km (123mi), an apogee of 846km (526mi) and an inclination of 33.77°.
San Marco-2 was launched April 26, 1967 into an orbit with a perigee of 217km (135mi), an apogee of 738km (459mi) and an inclination of 2.89°.
San Marco-3 was launched April 24, 1971 and its orbit had a perigee of 222km (138mi), an apogee of 718km (446mi) and an inclination of 3.23°.
San Marco-4 was launched February 18, 1974 into an orbit with a perigee of 231km (144 mi), an apogee of 910km (565mi) and

an inclination of 2.92°. All the satellites were launched with Scout rockets.
San Marco-1 was launched from Wallops Island while San Marco-2/-3/-4 were launched from the Italian base on the San Marco platform anchored in the Indian Ocean off the coast of Kenya.

ARIEL-2 and -3/UK-2 and -3
(GREAT BRITAIN - 1964)

Ariel-2 (UK-2) was a cylindrical satellite with a diameter of 0.58m (1.9ft), a height of 0.9m (2.95ft) and a weight of 68kg (150lb). Four panels of solar cells furnished the necessary power. The satellite was built and tested in

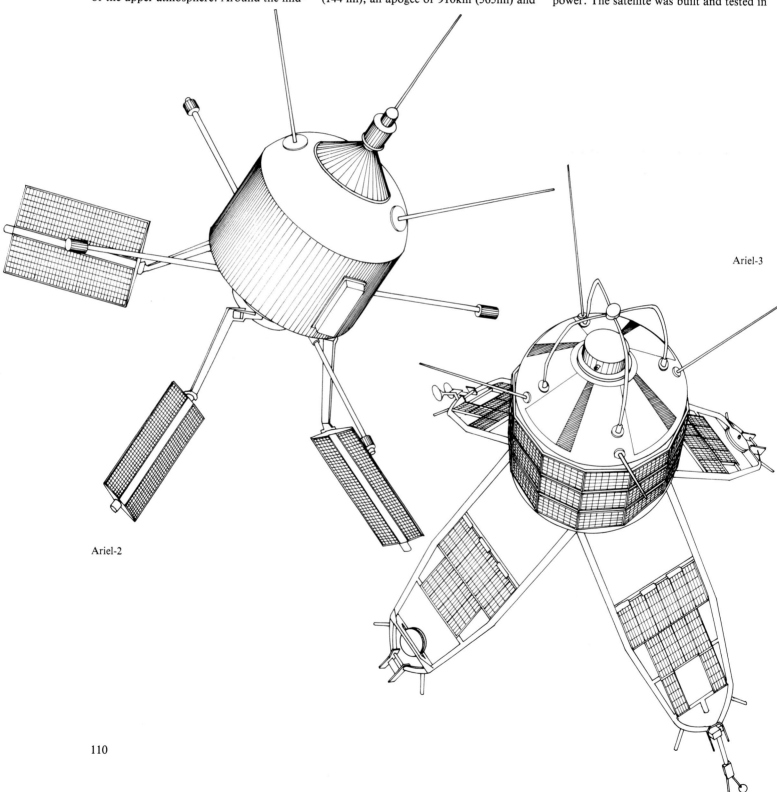

Ariel-3

Ariel-2

the United States. The three experiments conducted related to the measurement of radio noise in the galaxy and exploration of the upper atmosphere, measurement of the vertical distribution of the ozone, and measurement of the flow of micrometeorites. Ariel-3 (UK-3) was a cylinder with a diameter of 0.76m (2.5ft), a height of 0.91m (3ft) and a weight of 89.8kg (198lb). Four panels of solar cells provided the necessary power. Prime contractor was British Aerospace. The satellite measured the vertical distribution of oxygen at the height of 100km (62mi) and above, where the molecular oxygen is destroyed by solar radiation. It measured the emissions of radio noise coming from the galaxy; the intensity of Very Low Frequency (VLF) radiations; the temperature and density of electrons in the ionosphere; and the flow of radiowaves emitted by natural phenomena on the Earth as, for example, violent storms.

Launching and orbital data - Ariel-2 was launched March 27, 1964 from Wallops Island by a Scout rocket into an orbit with a perigee of 285km (177mi), an apogee of 1,362km (846mi) and an inclination of 51.64°. Ariel-3 was launched May 5, 1967 from Vandenberg by a Scout rocket into an orbit with a perigee of 497km (309mi), an apogee of 608km (378mi) and an inclination of 80.17°.

COSMOS-261 (USSR - 1968)

Soviet scientific satellite for studying the atmosphere. Weighing about 400kg (880lb), its diameter was 1.2m (3.9ft) and its height 1.8m (5.9ft). It studied atmospheric density and the polar aurorae.

Launching and orbital data - Cosmos-261 was launched December 20, 1968 from Plesetsk by a B-1 rocket. Its orbit had a perigee of 203km (126mi), an apogee of 642km (399mi) and an inclination of 71.03°.

AEROS (WEST GERMANY - 1972)

Two cylindrical satellites with a diameter of 0.874m (2.9ft), a height of 0.73m (2.4ft) and a weight of 125kg (275lb). The satellites, spin-stabilized, measured the density of electrons, the Sun's ultraviolet radiation and X-rays, the temperature of electrons and ions, the partial density of ions and neutral particles, the temperature of neutral nitrogen and the global density of neutral particles. Prime contractor for the two Aeros satellites, which had identical characteristics, was the German Dornier company.

Launching and orbital data - Aeros-1 was launched December 16, 1972. Its orbit had a perigee of 223km (139mi), an apogee of 867km (539mi) and an inclination of 96.94°. Aeros-2 was launched July 16, 1974 into an orbit with a perigee of 220km (137mi), an apogee of 872km (542mi) and an inclination of 97.44°. Both launchings were from Vandenberg with Scout rockets.

UME/ISS (JAPAN - 1976)

Ionosphere Sounding Satellite (ISS) was the name given to two cylindrical satellites weighing 139kg (306lb) devoted to observing the global distribution of the ionosphere's critical frequencies and to investigating globally the sources of radio interference.

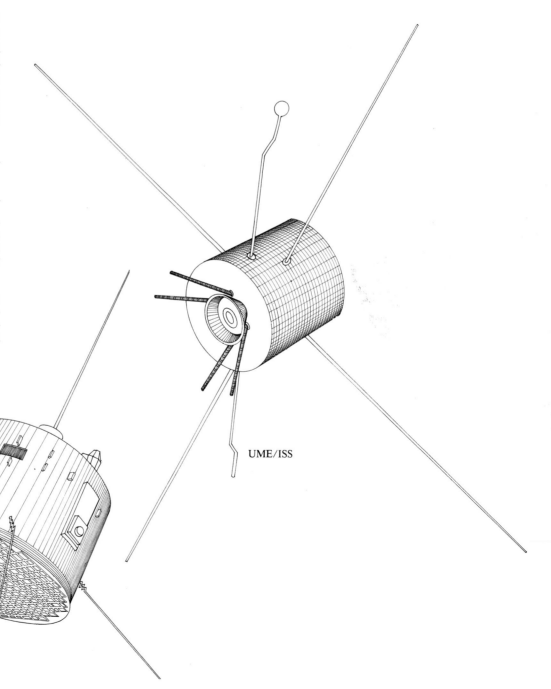

UME/ISS

Aeros

Launching and orbital data - ISS-1 was launched February 29, 1976 from Tanegashima Space Center by a N-1 rocket and sent into a near-circular orbit at a height of 990-1,100km (615-683mi), inclined at 70°. ISS-2 was launched February 16, 1978 from Tanegashima Space Center by a N-1 rocket into a near-circular orbit at a height of 980-1,220km (609-758mi), inclined at 69°.

SAGE/AEM-2 (USA - 1979)

SAGE/AEM (Stratospheric Aerosol and Gas Experiment/Applications Explorer Mission) was a satellite in the shape of an octagonal-based prism weighing 147kg (323lb). Its total height, including antennae, was 1.61m (5.3ft). The satellite was designed by the Goddard Space Flight Center of NASA and built by the Boeing Co. SAGE, the satellite's principal instrument, was a sensor formed of a radiometer with four spectral channels (0.385, 0.45, 0.6 and 1 micron). The object of the mission was to create a vertical map showing the presence in the stratosphere of ozone, aerosols, carbon dioxide and molecular extinction. The spacecraft was spin-stabilized.

Launching and orbital data - SAGE/AEM-2 was launched February 18, 1979 from Wallops Island by a Scout rocket and placed in an orbit with a perigee of 549km (341mi), an apogee of 661km (411mi) and an inclination of 54.93°.

CHINA-9 (CHINA - 1981)

Satellite formed of a balloon linked by thin wire to a metallic sphere. Its purpose was to measure atmospheric density. It reentered the atmosphere six days after being launched.

Launching and orbital data - China-9 was launched September 19, 1981 with the same B-1 rocket which also carried China-10 and -11 into space. It went into an orbit with a perigee of 232km (144mi), an apogee of 1,598km (993mi) and an inclination of 59.47°.

SME (USA - 1981)

SME (Solar Mesosphere Explorer) was a NASA satellite for atmospheric studies, including the reactions between sunlight, ozone and other chemical components of the atmosphere, and the manner in which concentrations of ozone are borne in the atmosphere between altitudes of 30 and 90km (19 and 56mi). Five instruments measured continuously the various elements and their fluctuations. The satellite, spin-stabilized, was cylindrical, with a diameter of 1.25m (4.1ft) and a height of 1.7m (5.6ft), weighing 437kg (961lb). The 2,156 solar cells furnishing the necessary power were placed on a disc 2.2m (7.2ft) in diameter. The program was devised by the Jet Propulsion Laboratory of Pasadena and the satellite was built by the Ball Aerospace System Division.

Launching and orbital data - SME was launched October 6, 1981 from Vandenberg by a Delta rocket and sent into a near-circular orbit at a height of 527-530km (327-329mi), inclined at 97.5°.

SAN MARCO D/L (ITALY - 1986)

Italian satellite with a spherical shape, a diameter of 0.92m (3ft) and a weight of 237kg (521lb), designed by the Aerospace Research Center (Centro Ricerche Aerospaziali - CRA) of the University of Rome in collaboration with NASA and West Germany's DFVLR. Around the middle of the satellite were 28 small panels of silicon solar cells and two panels of gallium arsenide solar cells provided for experiment by the US Air Force Aero Propulsion Laboratory. The cells furnished power of 11 watts in addition to the power provided by the mercury batteries. On board San Marco D/L were six instruments for measuring different characteristics of the atmosphere and the way in which they were modified by the influence of the solar wind. The apparatus comprised a spectrometer prepared by West Germany's DFVLR, the «Bilancia Broglio,» an electrical field surveyor from the Goddard Space Flight Center of NASA, a surveyor of ion velocity from the University of Texas, a star surveyor from the Goddard Center of NASA for controlling position, and a surveyor of solar wind and temperature from the Goddard Center and the University of Michigan. Experimental data were to be transmitted to the Earth at a speed of 72,000 bits per second. The satellite was spin-stabilized and its technical life was intended to be eighteen months.

Launching and orbital data - San Marco D/L is launched at the end of 1986 with an American Scout rocket from the Italian San Marco platform anchored in the Indian Ocean off the coast of Kenya. Its equatorial orbit has a perigee of 240km (149mi) and an apogee of 800km (497mi).

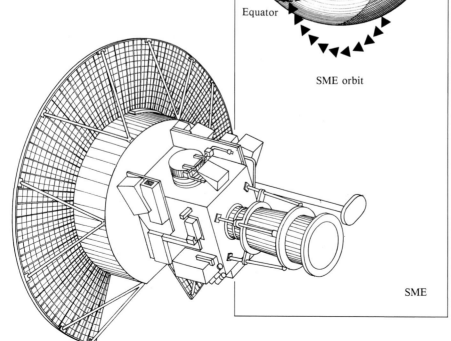
SME

Equator

SME orbit

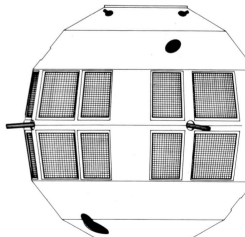
San Marco D/L

GEODETIC SATELLITES

ANNA 1B (USA - 1962)

A satellite almost spherical in shape, 0.91m (3ft) long, with a diameter of 1.22m (4ft) and weight of 161kg (355lb). Built as part of the ANNA project (from the initials for Army, Navy, NASA, Air Force) run by NASA and the Department of Defense (DoD), it carried three types of instruments for geodetic research: an intermittent flash light emitter which lits up at set times for photography from Earth, permitting measurements with a margin of error of 10-30m (32.8-98.4ft); a Secor (Sequential Collocation of Range) radio transmitter for measurements with a margin of error of 10-30m (32.8-98.4ft) and finally, a Doppler system using a transmitter the frequency of which was controlled by a highly stable quartz oscillator. In this case, the accuracy of the findings was within 15-50m (49.21-164ft).

Launching and orbital data - ANNA 1B was launched October 31, 1962 from Cape Canaveral by a Thor Able rocket and sent into an almost circular orbit at 1,077-1,182km (669-734mi) altitude with an inclination of 50.14° and a period of 107.84 minutes. ANNA 1A was launched May 10, 1962 but failed to go into orbit because of malfunction of the carrier.

COSMOS-26/-49 (USSR-1964)

Astronomical satellites equipped with a magnetometer used for magnetic survey of 75 percent of the Earth's surface. These surveys permitted establishment of the coefficient of Gauss and of a set of international values for terrestrial magnetism. The satellites were elliptical in shape, 1.8m (5.90ft) long, 1.2m (3.94ft) across with a weight of approx. 400kg (882lb).

Launching and orbital data - Cosmos-26 was launched March 18, 1964 from Kapustin Yar by a B-1 rocket and sent into an elliptical orbit with a perigee of 271km (168mi), an apogee of 403km (250mi), an inclination of 49° to the equator and a period of 91 minutes. Cosmos-49 left Kapustin Yar on October 24, 1964 in a B-1 rocket and was placed into an elliptical orbit with a perigee of 260km (162mi), an apogee of 490km (304mi), an orbital inclination of 49° and a period of 91.83 minutes.

BEACON EXPLORER-A/-B/-C
(USA - 1964)

Three NASA satellites designed for ionospheric research but also used for geodetic studies. Beacon Explorer-A/S-66 failed to go into orbit because of malfunction of the carrier. Beacon Explorer-B/Explorer-22 with 360 silicon laser reflectors permitted the first measurements from Earth using a laser beam reflected by the satellite. The central body of the vehicle was in the form of an octagonal prism to which four panels of solar cells were attached: it had a diameter of 0.46m (1.5ft), a height of 0.30m (0.98ft), and weighed 52.5kg (116lb). Beacon Explorer-C/Explorer-27 was the same shape as the foregoing, but in addition to the laser reflectors it had an ultrastable oscillator for measurements of the Doppler effect, to detect orbital irregularities, which thus indirectly measured the Earth's gravitational field. The weight of the satellite was 60kg (132lb).

Launching and orbital data - Beacon Explorer-A was launched unsuccessfully March 19, 1964. Beacon Explorer-B left Cape Canaveral October 10, 1964 by a Delta rocket and was placed into an elliptical orbit with a perigee of 889km (552mi), an apogee of 1,081km (672mi), and an inclination of 79.69°. Beacon Explorer-C left Vandenberg April 29, 1965 by a Scout rocket and was sent into an elliptical orbit with a perigee of 941km (585mi), an apogee of 1,317km (818mi) and an orbital inclination of 41.19°.

GEOS-1/EXPLORER-29 (USA - 1965)

Geos-1 (Geodetic Earth Orbiting Satellite) was the first purely geodetic satellite developed by NASA. The central body of the satellite was octagonal in shape with a diame-

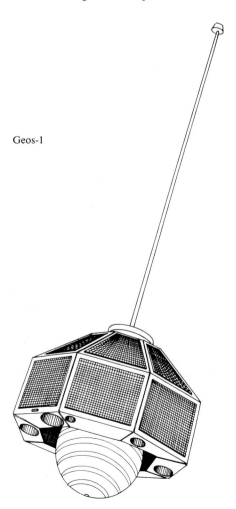

Geos-1

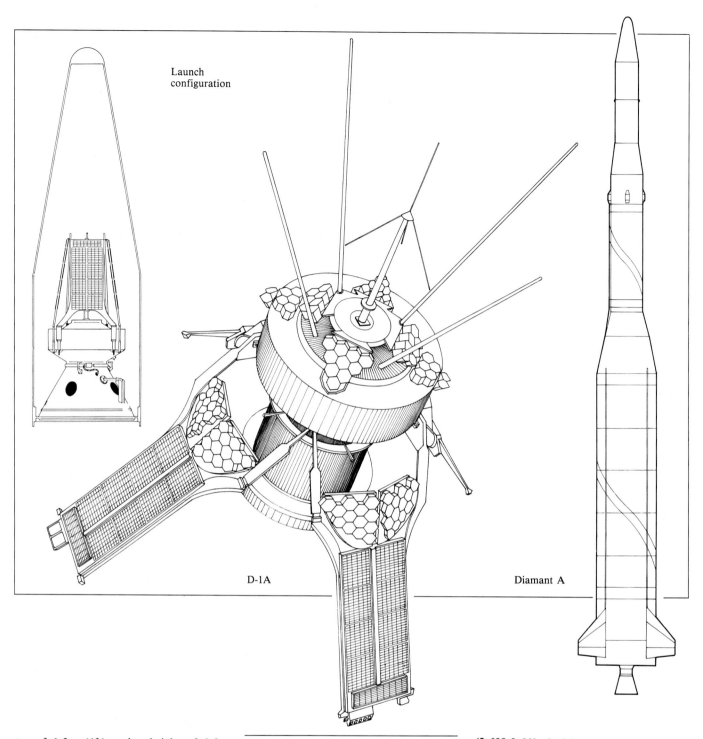

Launch
configuration

D-1A

Diamant A

---

ter of 1.2m (4ft) and a height of 0.8m (2.62ft). The weight in orbit was 175kg (386lb). Gravity gradient stabilization was provided by the addition of an external arm with a mass at the end. In this way, the base of the satellite was constantly turned toward the Earth. Five instruments were installed on board: a light signal emitter which lit up at set times to permit photography from Earth; 440 quartz prism laser reflectors; a transponder; a radio signal transmitter for measurements using the Doppler effect and an antenna for data transmission.

Launching and orbital data - Geos-1 was launched November 6, 1965 from Cape Canaveral by a Delta rocket and sent into an elliptical orbit with a perigee of 1,115km (693mi), an apogee of 2,277km (1,415mi) and an orbital inclination of 59°.

PAGEOS (USA - 1966)

Pageos (Passive Geodetic Earth Orbiting Satellite) was a NASA balloon 30m (98.42ft) in diameter built of mylar and aluminum and inflated automatically in orbit using benzoic acid. The surface of the satellite, which reflected sunlight, was visible from Earth with the brilliance of the Pole star, enabling it to be photographed from Earth from the various points of an observation network. This has made possible repeated measurements of the globe.

Launching and orbital data - Pageos was launched June 23, 1966 from Vandenberg by an Agena D rocket and sent into an almost circular polar orbit at 4,198-4,286km

---

(2,609-2,663mi) altitude and inclined at 87° to the equator.

D-1A DIAPASON (FRANCE - 1966)

A small satellite weighing 19kg (42lb) consisting of a cylinder 0.2m (0.6ft) high and 0.5m (1.6ft) in diameter. Four panels were attached to the central body with 2,304 solar cells in all, each 0.42m (1.37ft) long and 0.21m (0.68ft) wide. The power furnished was 5 watts. It was developed by the Centre Nationale des Etudes Spatiales (CNES) with the participation of various industries. Diapason has permitted geodetic experiments based on systematic study of the Doppler effect on two frequencies (149.70 and 399.920

MHz) coming from the highly stable oscillator installed on board. The satellite was spin-stabilized.

Launching and orbital data - Diapason was launched February 17, 1966 by a French Diamant rocket from the French military base at Hammaguir in Algeria. The satellite was sent into an elliptical orbit with a perigee of 500km (310mi), and an apogee of 2,700km (1,678mi), an orbital inclination of 34.1° and a period of 117 minutes.

D-1C/-1D DIADEME (FRANCE - 1967)

Two satellites similar to Diapason in structure, power source, telemeasurement system and highly stable oscillator emitting the same two frequencies for geodetic research based on study of the Doppler effect. Diademe differed in the installation of laser reflectors where the solar panels started, and on top of the satellite, permitting correlation of the Doppler measurements with the laser measurements. Addition of these reflectors necessitated restabilizing the satellite, whose vertical axis was positioned along the line of force of the Earth's magnetic field. The weight of the satellite was 23kg (50lb). The oscillator stopped transmitting after two months.

Launching and orbital data - D-1C was launched February 8, 1967 and placed into an elliptical orbit 561km (348.58mi) distant at the perigee and 1,231km (765mi) at the apogee. The orbital inclination was 40°.
D-1D was sent into orbit February 15, 1967 with a perigee of 590km (367mi), an apogee of 1,811km (1,125mi) and an orbital inclination of 39.4°. Both satellites were launched by Diamant rockets from the Hammaguir base in Algeria.

GEOS-2/EXPLORER-36 (USA - 1968)

Similar in characteristics to its predecessor Geos-1/Explorer-29. Apart from the traditional instruments on board, it also had a radar transponder to test the use of the C-band in orbital survey of geodetic satellites. The satellite weighed 207kg (456lb).

Launching and orbital data - Geos-2 was launched January 11, 1968 from Cape Canaveral by a Delta rocket and placed into an elliptical orbit with a perigee of 1,084km (674mi), an apogee of 1,577km (980mi) and an orbital inclination of 106°.

PEOLE (FRANCE - 1970)

Peole was the test model for the Eole satellite to be launched subsequently for meteorological experiments using data collected by weather balloons. Peole was thus designed

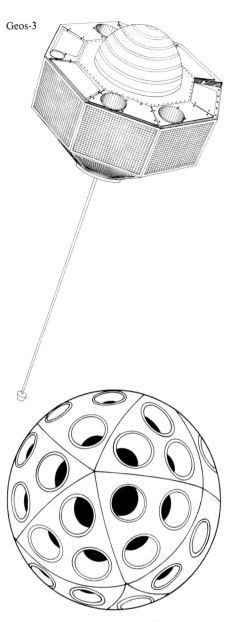

Geos-3

Starlette

to test the transmission systems to be used for this purpose. Laser reflectors were also fitted to Peole for geodetic experiments in space in accordance with the ISAGEC worldwide measurement project involving 16 countries including the Soviet Union. The satellite was in the form of an octagonal prism 1.29m (4.23ft) high including the antenna and with a maximum diameter of 0.62m (2ft). Eight panels with 2,016 solar cells furnishing a power of 20 watts were attached to the base of the satellite and to its outer surface. The 44 laser reflectors were fitted to the edges of the solar panels and the base of the central antenna. The satellite, weighing 60kg (132lb), was gravity gradient stabilized. The French CNES was prime contractor.

Launching and orbital data - Peole was launched December 12, 1970 from the po-

lygon in French Guiana by a French Diamant B rocket and sent into an elliptical orbit with a perigee of 517km (321mi), an apogee of 747km (464mi), an orbital inclination of 15° and a period of 97 minutes.

CHINA-2 (CHINA - 1971)

The second satellite launched by China and intended for scientific research. Its instruments detected cosmic radiation and measured the magnetic field near to the Earth's surface. China-2 was almost spherical in form with a diameter of 1m (3.28ft) and weight of 221kg (487lb). It was spin-stabilized (3 revolutions per minute). Solar cells were attached to its outer surface. The satellite, which transmitted data on a frequency of 20.008 MHz, remained active until June 17, 1979.

Launching and orbital data - China-2 was launched March 3, 1971 by a Long March-1 rocket from Shuang Cheng Tse polygon and sent into an elliptical orbit 268km (167mi) high at the perigee and 1,830km (1,137mi) at the apogee. The orbital inclination was 69.9°.

GEOS-3 (USA - 1975)

Geos-3 (Geodynamics Experimental Ocean Satellite) was a NASA satellite for geodetic and oceanographic research built as part of the EOPAP program (Earth and Ocean Physics Applications Program). Similar in shape to the two earlier Geos (the central body was an octagonal prism), it was 1.32m (4.33ft) in diameter and 0.81m (2.65ft) high with a weight of 340kg (750lb). Gravity stabilized, it had a 6m (19.68ft) long arm with a 45kg (100lb) mass at the end. The outer surface of the satellite was covered with solar cells. There were five instruments on board: a radar altimeter, two C-band transponders, an S-band transponder, laser reflectors and a system for measurement using the Doppler effect. The data obtained by Geos-3, also used in parallel with the Seasat satellite, improved definition of geoid models. Geos-3 was not part of the Explorer satellite series. Prime contractor was Applied Physics Laboratories.

Launching and orbital data - Geos-3 was launched April 10, 1975 from Vandenberg by a Delta rocket and sent into an almost circular orbit at 818-858km (508-533mi) altitude, inclined 115° to the equator.

STARLETTE (FRANCE - 1975)

A spherical satellite 0.26m (0.85ft) in diameter with 60 laser reflectors attached to the surface. A uranium 235 mass was placed at the center of the sphere to increase the

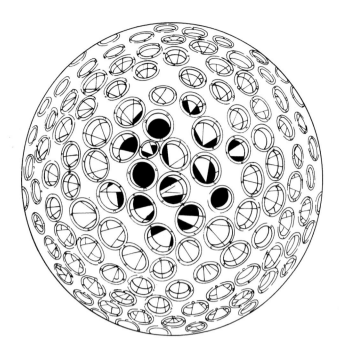

Lageos

weight. The French CNES was prime contractor. Starlette weighed 50kg (110lb) in orbit.

Launching and orbital data - Starlette was launched February 6, 1975 from the Kourou polygon in French Guiana by a French Diamant B-P4 rocket and sent into an elliptical orbit with a perigee of 806km (500mi), an apogee of 1,108km (608mi) and an orbital inclination of 49.82°.

D-5A POLLUX/D-5B CASTOR (FRANCE - 1975)

Two technological satellites launched together to test the SEP hydrazine (D-5A) trim propulsion systems and Onera (D-5B) microaccelerometers. Pollux was in the form of an 18-faceted polyhedron 0.61m (2ft) in diameter, 0.56m (1.84ft) high and weighing 36kg (79lb). 160 solar cells were attached to each facet of the outer surface, furnishing a total power of 10.4 watts. It was spin-stabilized.
Castor was a 26-faceted polyhedron 0.8m (2.62ft) in diameter, 0.71m (2.32ft) high and weighing 76kg (168lb). The satellite was not stabilized. The solar cells attached to the facets furnished a power of 30 watts. 26 laser

reflectors for geodetic research were fitted to Castor's surface. The payload in the form of an accelerometer also permitted aeronomic research. The French CNES was prime contractor for the two satellites.

Launching and orbital data - The two satellites were launched together, one above the other, May 17, 1975 from the Kourou polygon in French Guiana by a French Diamant B-P4 rocket. Pollux was sent into an orbit with a perigee of 269km (167mi), an apogee of 1,283km (797mi) and an inclination of 29.96°. Castor had a similar orbit with a perigee of 272km (169mi), an apogee of 1,268km (788mi) and an inclination of 29,95°.

LAGEOS (USA - 1976)

Lageos (Laser Geodynamics Satellite) was the first NASA satellite designed purely for measurement of movements of the Earth's crust using a laser beam. It was a passive satellite which reflected laser beam sent against its surface to which 426 silicon reflectors were attached. Lageos was an aluminum sphere 0.6m (1.97ft) in diameter with a brass mass at the center. The weight in orbit was 406kg (895lb). The permitted measurements had a

margin of error of 1-2cm (0.4-0.8in). The satellite, placed in a highly stable orbit, permits reliable measurements for about 50 years, but will continue to circle the Earth for about 8 million years before falling. For this reason, two steel plates were fitted inside it with three "Messages to the Future" devised by Professor Carl Sagan of Cornell University and describing the Earth history.

Launching and orbital data - Lageos was launched May 4, 1976 from Cape Canaveral by a Delta rocket and sent into a near circular orbit with a perigee of 5,837km (3,627mi), an apogee of 5,945km (3,694mi) and an orbital inclination of 110°.

COSMOS (USSR - 1978)

The Cosmos series included a few satellites optimized for geodetic research. Among these were Cosmos-1067, weighing about 700kg (1,543lb) and approx. 1.6m (5.25ft) in diameter; Cosmos-1312 and -1410 weighing 2,200kg (4,850lb) and Cosmos-1510. The Soviets had also used other scientific satellites with a laser reflector on board, or some navigational satellites, for geodetic research. In addition, they have employed American Lageos and French Starlette satellites.

Launching and orbital data - Cosmos-1067 was launched December 26, 1978 from Plesetsk by a C-1 rocket and sent into an almost circular orbit 1,154-1,211km (717-752mi) high and inclined 83° to the equator, with a period of 109 minutes.
Cosmos-1312 was launched September 30, 1981, from Plesetsk by a F-2 rocket and sent into an almost circular orbit 1,490-1,499km (926-931mi) high and inclined at 82.6°.
Cosmos-1410 was launched September 24, 1982 from Plesetsk by a F-2 rocket and sent into an almost circular orbit 1,494-1,502km (928-933mi) high and inclined at 82.6°.
Cosmos-1510 was launched November 24, 1983 from Plesetsk by a C-1 rocket and sent into an almost circular orbit 1,479-1,524km (919-947mi) high and inclined at 73.6°.

MAGSAT (USA - 1979)

Magsat (Magnetic Field Satellite) was the first NASA satellite specifically intended for

Magsat

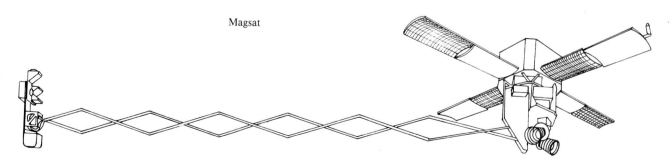

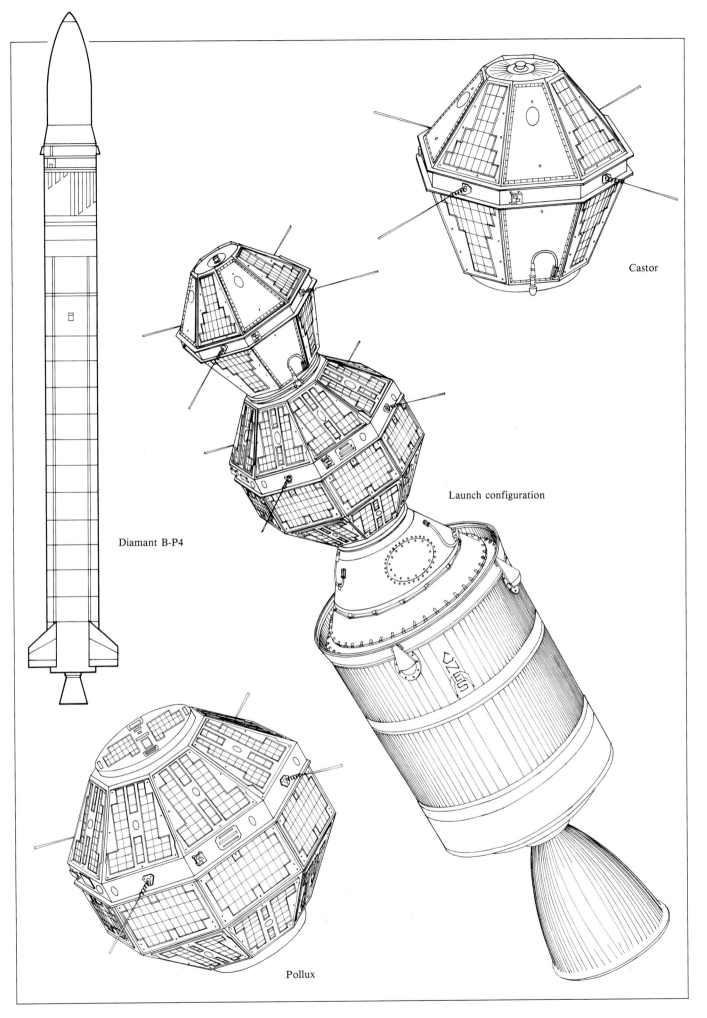

Castor

Diamant B-P4

Launch configuration

Pollux

6

117

both global measurement of the Earth's magnetic field and measurement of magnetic anomalies of the crust with a resolution of 350km (217mi). The central body of the satellite consisted of a basic module and an instrument module. The diameter was 0.77m (2.5ft) and the height 1.64m (5.38ft). Four panels of solar cells furnishing a power of 160 watts were attached to the central body and when open had a span from tip to tip of 3.4m (11ft). The satellite's two main instruments, a vectorial magnetometer and a scalar magnetometer were fitted to the end of a 6.02m (20ft) long arm extending from the satellite. Magsat was stabilized on three axes and weighed 115kg (254lb) in orbit. The minimum mission duration time envisaged was 120 days.

Launching and orbital data - Magsat was launched October 30, 1979 from Vandenberg polygon by a Scout rocket and sent into a polar elliptical orbit with a perigee of 355km (200mi), an apogee of 562km (349mi) and an orbital inclination of 96.8°.

INTERCOSMOS-20/-21 (USSR - 1979-1981)

Soviet satellites produced in conjunction with other Socialist bloc countries. Weighing 550kg (1,212lb), 1.8m (5.90ft) high and 1.5m (4.9ft) in diameter, Intercosmos-20/-21 were designed to study the characteristics of the Earth's land and ocean surfaces.

Launching and orbital data - Intercosmos-20 was launched November 1, 1979 from Plesetsk by a C-1 rocket and sent into an orbit 465km (289mi) at the perigee, 510km (317mi) at the apogee and inclined at 74.05°. Intercosmos-21 left Plesetsk February 6,

1981 by a C-1 rocket. The orbit had a perigee of 473km (294mi), an apogee of 514km (319mi) and an inclination of 74.04°.

INTERCOSMOS-22/BULGARIA-1300 (USSR - 1981)

A scientific satellite for study of the Earth's ionosphere and magnetosphere also equipped with a laser reflector which has permitted a program of geodetic measurements conducted by various Socialist bloc countries. With the studies carried out on the position of the satellite through laser technique with an accuracy of around 5-10m (16.4-32.8ft), it was possible to investigate the atmospheric resistance exercised on the satellite as well. The satellite weighed 1,500kg (3,306lb). Intercosmos-17 also had a laser reflector. (See Space Physics Satellites.)

Launching and orbital data - Intercosmos-22 was launched August 7, 1981 from Plesetsk by an A-1 rocket and sent into an elliptical orbit with a perigee of 800km (497mi), an apogee of 895km (556mi) and an orbital inclination of 81.22°.

GEOSAT (USA - 1985)

A satellite built by Johns Hopkins University under contract from the Naval Research Laboratory and the Naval Electronics Systems Command. The satellite, weighing 636kg (1,402lb), is equipped with a radar altimeter for mapping the exact shape of the Earth's surface, oceans included. Eight pa-

nels of solar cells each 3m (9.8ft) long provided the necessary energy. Geosat was designed with axial symmetry to minimize the orbital variations caused by the effects of atmospheric resistance. It was gravity stabilized by a 50kg (110lb) mass at the end of a 7m (23ft) long arm.

Launching and orbital data - Geosat was launched March 12, 1985 from Vandenberg by an Atlas E rocket and sent into a circular polar orbit 800km (497mi) high.

EGP (JAPAN - 1986)

EGP (Experimental Geodetic Payload) was a passive satellite for geodetic research developed by the Japanese space agency, NASDA. Spherical in shape with a diameter of 2.1m (6.9ft), its surface was covered with two types of reflector: a group of 318 mirrors which reflected sunlight; and a group of 120 CCRs (Corner Cube Reflectors) which reflected a laser beam sent from Earth. The weight in orbit was 685kg (1,510lb) and the expected service life is five years. Kawasaki Heavy Industries Ltd. was prime contractor. The satellite is controlled in orbit by the Geographical Survey Institute of the Ministry of Construction and the Hydrographic Department of the Maritime Safety Agency.

Launching and orbital data - EGP was launched August 8, 1986 from Tanegashima by a Japanese H-1 rocket and sent into circular orbit at an altitude of 1,500km (932mi).

LAGEOS-2 (ITALY - 1988)

Lageos-2 is the result of an agreement between NASA and the Italian Space Plan; it will permit accurate study of geodynamic phenomena, such as the movement of tectonic plates, the movement of the poles and tidal variations. The satellite, of the passive type, is similar to the Lageos launched by NASA in 1976. It is spherical in shape, 0.6m (1.97ft) in diameter, weighs 410kg (904lb) and its surface is covered by 426 silicon mirrors capable of reflecting laser beams coming from Earth stations at various parts of the globe. Aeritalia is the prime contractor.

Launching and orbital data - Lageos-2 will be carried into low orbit by the Space Shuttle. The Italian-built Iris perigee motor will then place it in an elliptical transfer orbit with an apogee of 6,000km (3,728mi). At the apogee, a propulsion module will put Lageos-2 into its final, circular orbit 6,000km (3,728mi) high and inclined at 52° to the equator.

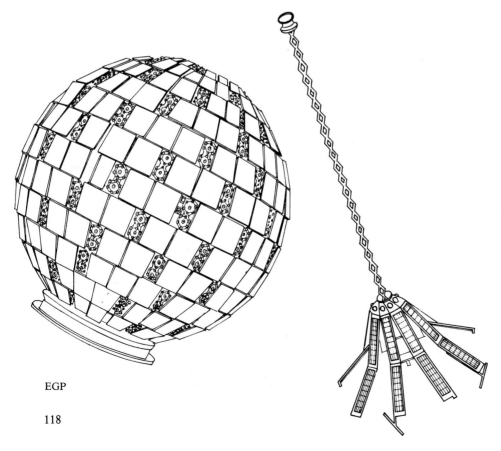

EGP

Geosat

BIOLOGICAL SATELLITES

Group of satellites carrying various animals (monkeys, dogs, guinea pigs and other live organisms) for biological experiments. The object is to conduct tests to find out how living organisms react to conditions in space. Some of these satellites involve international collaboration as, for example, the Soviet Cosmos-110, Cosmos-1514 and Cosmos-1667 satellites, which carried experiments prepared by the United States.

6

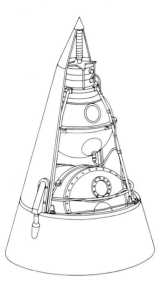

Sputnik-2

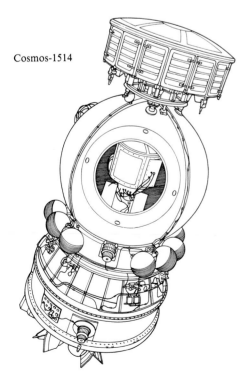

Sputnik-2 re-entry module

Cosmos-1514

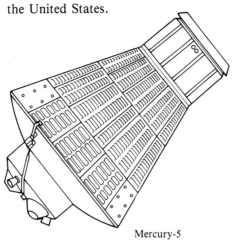

Mercury-5

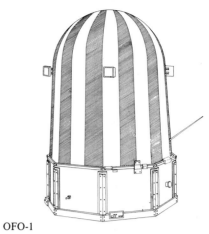

OFO-1

Satellite	First launch	Perigee × apogee/inclination degree km (mi)	Nation
Sputnik-2	11/3/1957	212x1,660 (132x1,032)/65°	USSR
Sputnik-6	12/1/1960	166x232 (103x144)/64°	USSR
Sputnik-9	3/9/1961	173x239 (108x149)/64°	USSR
Sputnik-10	3/25/1961	164x230 (102x143)/64°	USSR
Discoverer-29	8/30/1961	152x542 (94x337)/82°	USA
Mercury-5	11/29/1961	158x237 (98x147)/32°	USA
Cosmos-4	4/26/1962	285x317 (177x197)/65°	USSR
Cosmos-7	6/30/1962	264x344 (164x214)/48°	USSR
Cosmos-92	10/16/1965	201x334 (125x208)/64°	USSR
Cosmos-94	10/28/1965	205x271 (127x168)/64°	USSR
Cosmos-110	2/22/1966	190x882 (118x548)/51°	USSR
Bios-1	12/14/1966	295x309 (183x192)/33°	USA
Bios-2	9/7/1967	286x313 (178x194)/33°	USA
Bios-3	6/29/1969	356x388 (221x241)/33°	USA
OFO-1	11/9/1970	304x518 (189x322)/37°	USA
Salyut-1	4/19/1971	200x210 (124x130)/51°	USSR
Cosmos-605	10/31/1973	213x403 (192x250)/62°	USSR
Cosmos-690	10/22/1974	215x364 (134x226)/62°	USSR
Cosmos-782	10/25/1975	218x384 (135x239)/62°	USSR
Cosmos-936	8/3/1977	219x396 (136x246)/62°	USSR
Cosmos-1129	9/25/1979	218x377 (135x234)/62°	USSR
Cosmos-1514	12/14/1983	214x259 (133x161)/82°	USSR
Cosmos-1667	7/10/1985	222x297 (138x185)/82°	USSR

INTO SPACE

Prognoz-9

An astronomical observatory in highly eccentric, launched by the USSR in July 4, 1983. It can measure irregularities in cosmic radiation by detecting temperature to within approximately one ten thousandth of a degree.

NKC-135

This picture shows the interception and destruction of an intercontinental missile using a laser beam produced by a "laser weapon" fitted to an NKC-135 and concentrated by an orbital paraboloid equipped with positioning and aiming devices. Two other orbital paraboloids are visible in the background; these form part of the antimissile "space shield" under development by American researchers.

SPAS-01A

Challenger (OV.99) during the STS-10 (41-B) mission. In the foreground is the German SPAS-01A satellite which was put into orbit using the RMS (Remote Manipulator System). The two containers for the Westar-6 (USA) and Palapa B-2 (Indonesia) satellites are visible in the Shuttle's cargo bay, together with the maneuvering units (MMU) used, for the first time during this mission, by astronauts McCandless and Stewart.

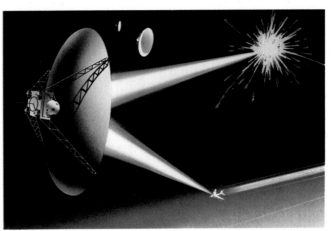

SBS-4 (Satellite Business System)

Ignition of the PAM-D motor of the SBS-4 satellite. The SBS-4 was put into orbit on August 30, 1984, during the 41-D (STS-12) mission of *Discovery*. The picture shows the SBS (Satellite Business System) passing from parking orbit into the transfer orbit which will take it into geostationary orbit.

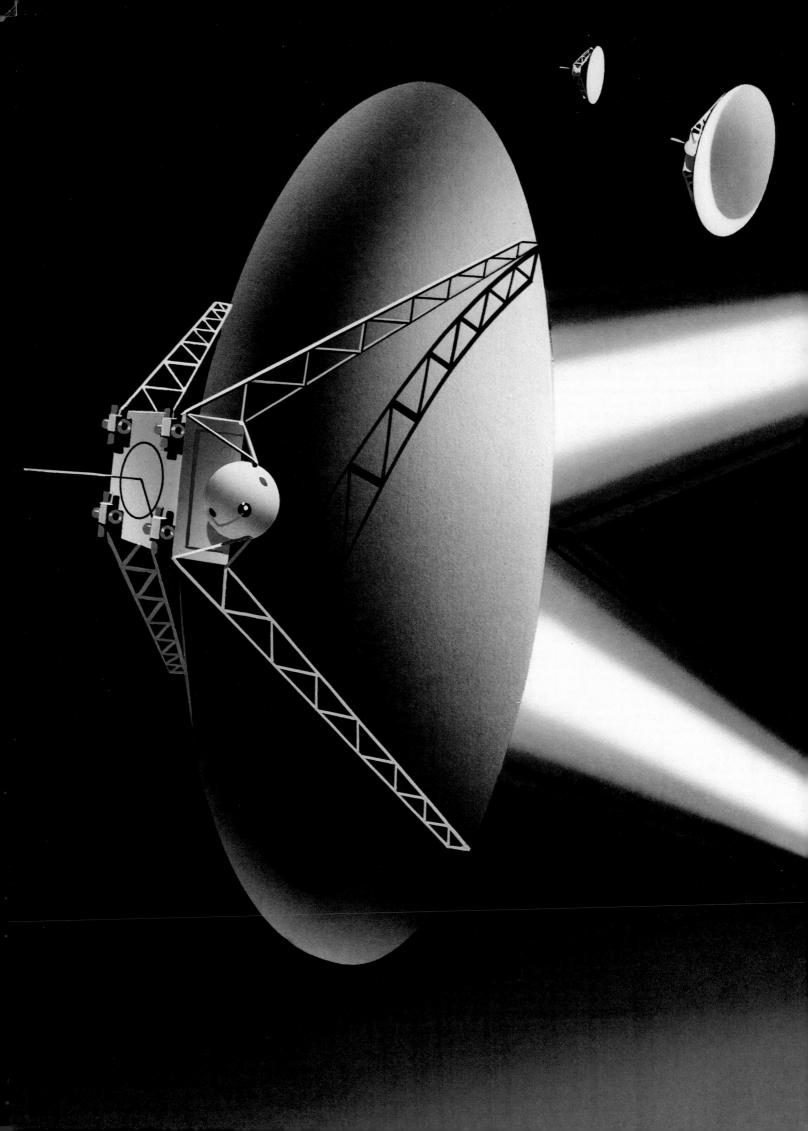

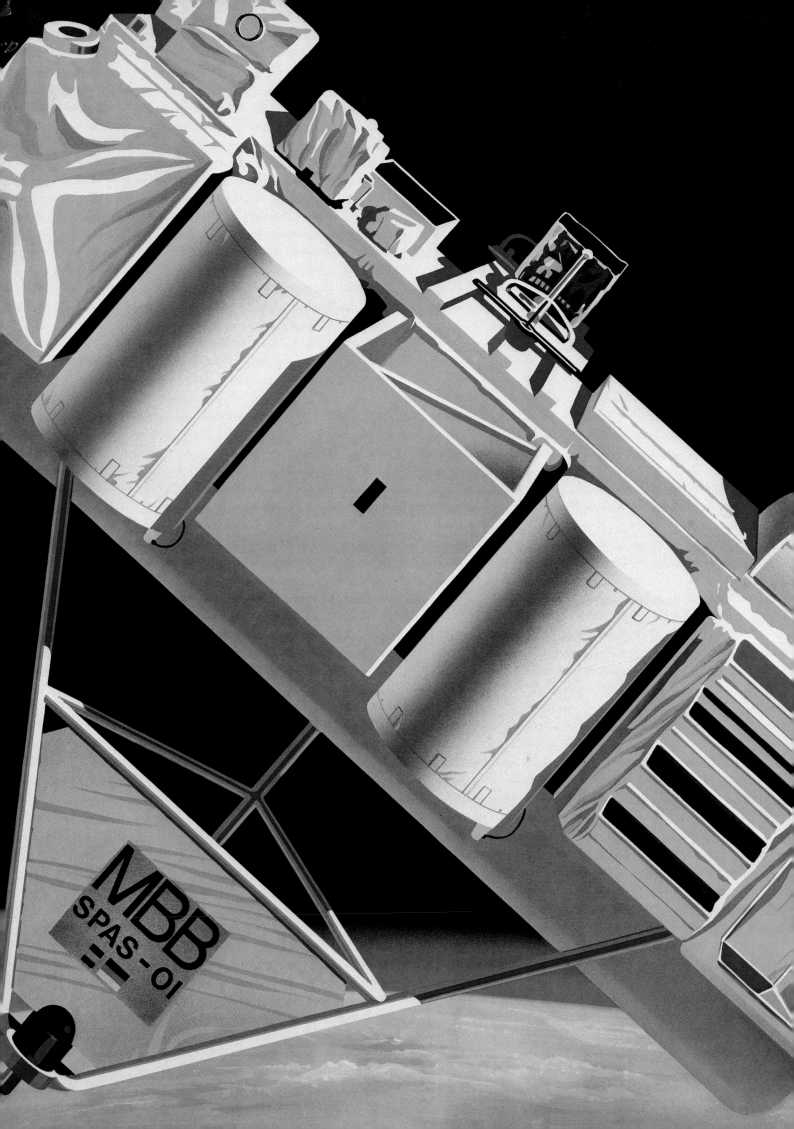

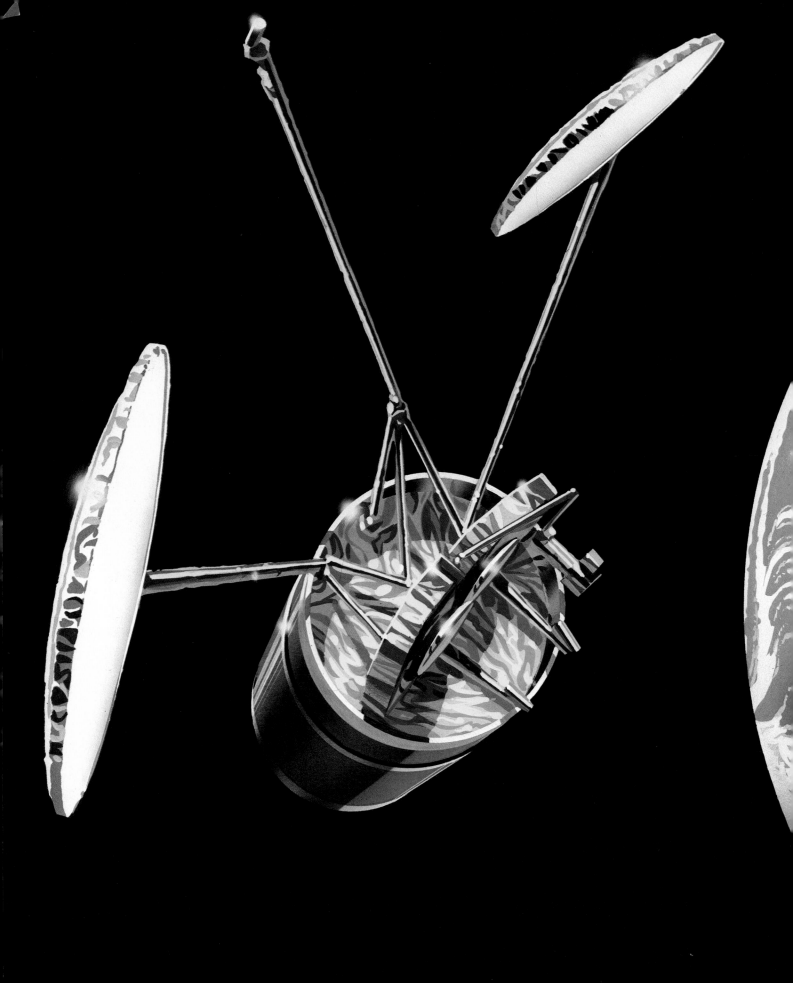

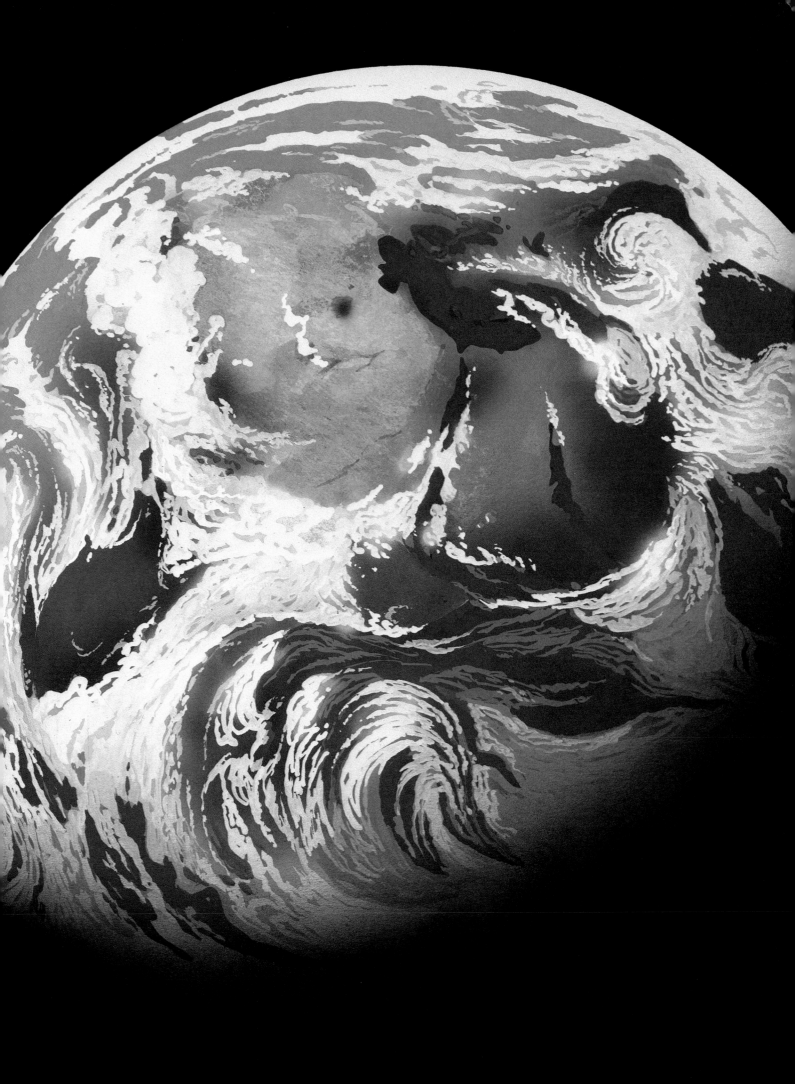

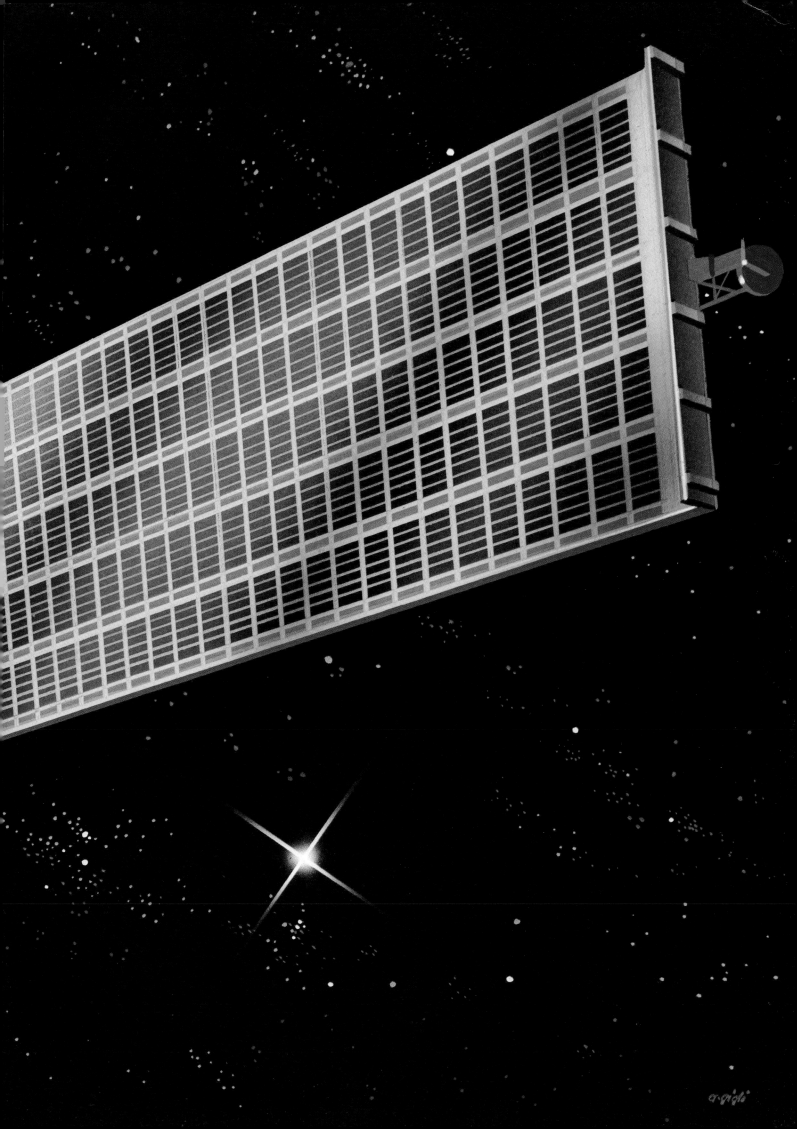

ASAT

The picture shows an anti-satellite attack carried out from a McDonnell Douglas F-15 Eagle armed with a Boeing Thiokol Altair 3 missile. The missile is fired during a "zoom climb" maneuver.
As the missile approaches the target satellite, a capsule called the Miniature Homing Vehicle (MHV) is released from the ogive. This has an infrared ray sensor which steers it to impact. The entire operation is guided and controlled by the NORAD (North American Defense Command) network.

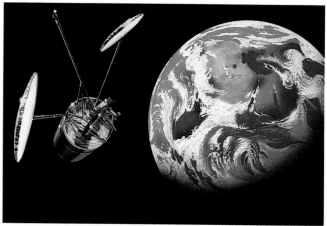

Intelsat-6

This is the largest satellite in the Intelsat series. It is more than 11m (36ft) high and 3.64m (11.9ft) in diameter. Designed for a service life of 10 years, it can be used for various types of intercontinental telecommunications (telephone, telex, telegraph, facsimile, data transmission and television).

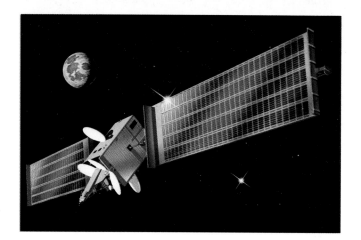

Olympus (L-SAT)

The largest European telecommunications satellite. Still at the preoperational stage, it is a prototype for telecommunications satellites of the nineties. Its maximum span is approx. 27m (88.58ft). British Aerospace and Selenia Spazio are in charge of its development.

SPACE PHYSICS

EXPLORER-1/-3/-4 (USA - 1958)

First satellites placed into orbit by the United States with the rockets developed by Wernher von Braun of the Army Ballistic Missile Agency. Cylindrical in shape (representing the last stage of the Jupiter-C rocket), they were 2.03m (6.7ft) long and had a diameter of 0.152m (0.5ft). Explorer-1 weighed 14kg (31lb), of which 4.8kg (10.5lb) were taken up by instruments. It carried two detectors of micrometeorites and a Geiger counter for studying the charged particles. The experiment with electrically-charged particles, devised by Professor James Van Allen, led to the discovery of the radiation belts around the Earth which were subsequently named after him. The satellite, which was spin-stabilized, transmitted until May 23, 1958. Explorer-3 was like its predecessor but also carried a recorder. Explorer-4, weighing 3kg (6.6lb) more than its predecessors, had improved instruments for studying radiation and detectors of X-rays and cosmic rays.

Launching and orbital data - Explorer-1 was launched January 31, 1958 from Cape Canaveral by a Jupiter C rocket and was placed in an orbit with a perigee of 356km (221mi), an apogee of 2,548 km (1,583mi) and an inclination of 33.24°. Explorer-3 was launched May 26, 1958, and Explorer-4 July 26, 1958.

Sputnik-3

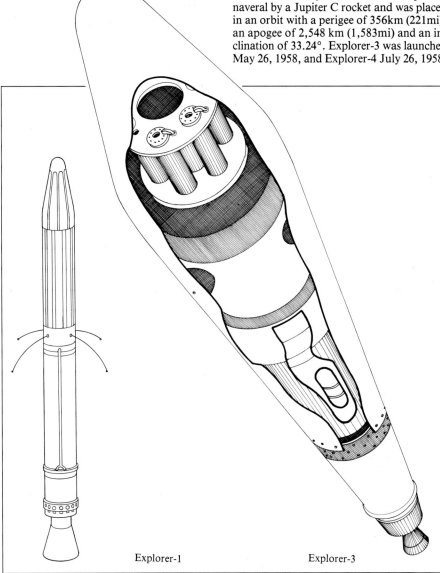

Explorer-1   Explorer-3

SPUTNIK-3 (USSR - 1958)

Satellite 3.57m (11.7ft) long and weighing 1,327kg (2,919lb), of which 968kg (2,129lb) were represented by scientific instruments. It remained in orbit until April 6, 1960, carrying out a research program on the composition of the upper atmosphere, on the concentration of particles charging cosmic rays, on magnetic and electrostatic measurements, and on the flow of micrometeorites.

Launching and orbital data - Sputnik-3 was launched May 15, 1958 from Baikonur-Tyuratam with a Type A rocket and placed in an orbit with a perigee of 226km (140mi), an apogee of 1,881km (1,170mi) and an inclination of 65.1°.

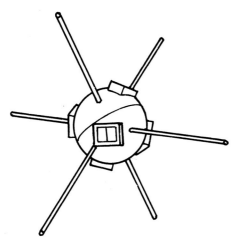

Vanguard-1

VANGUARD-1 (USA - 1958)

Aluminum sphere with a diameter of 16.5cm (6.5in) and weighing 1.5kg (3.3lb), carrying a Geiger counter, a micrometeorite detector and a magnetometer. The information that was assembled revealed the Earth as being slightly pear-shaped. Vanguard-1 was powered by solar cells and mercury batteries. Signals were received up to May 1964.

Launching and orbital data - Vanguard -1 was launched March 17, 1958 from Cape Canaveral by a Vanguard rocket and placed in an orbit with a perigee of 650km (404mi) and an apogee of 3,968km (2,465mi); the inclination was 34.25°.

EXPLORER-6/-10/-45 (USA - 1959)

Group of three NASA satellites for studying the magnetosphere. Explorer-6 was an irregular spheroid, 0.74m (2.4ft) long, diameter 0.66m (2.2ft), weight 64kg (141lb); it studied the electrical fields around the Earth and discovered three radiation levels. Explorer-10, a sphere atop a cylinder with a total length of 2.7m (8.85ft), a diameter of 0.48m (1.6ft) and a weight of 35kg (77lb), studied the interplanetary magnetic field close to the Earth. Explorer-45, in the shape of an octagonal prism 0.76m (2.5ft) long, 0.68m (2.2ft) wide and weighing 52kg (114lb), studied electrical phenomena, magnetic storms, and the relationships between auroral phenomena and magnetic storms with the acceleration of the charged particles within the magnetosphere.

Launching and orbital data - Explorer-6 was launched August 7, 1959 from Cape Canaveral by a Thor Able rocket and sent into an orbit with a perigee of 245km (152mi) and an apogee of 42,400 km (26,343mi). The inclination was 47°. Explorer-10 was launched March 25, 1961, and Explorer-45 November 15, 1971.

EXPLORER-8/-20/-22/-27/-31 (USA - 1960)

Group of five NASA satellites launched in order to study the terrestrial ionosphere. Explorer-8 was in the form of a double cone weighing 41kg (90lb), with a diameter of 0.76m (2.5ft) and a height of 0.76m (2.5ft). Explorer-20 was also in the form of a double cone weighing 44kg (97lb), with a diameter of 0.66m (2.2ft) and a height of 0.83m (2.7ft). Explorer-22/Beacon Explorer-B was in the shape of an octagonal prism 0.3m (0.98ft) high, 0.46m (1.5ft) wide, with a weight of 52.5kg (116lb). Explorer-27/Beacon Explorer-C, also in the shape of an octagonal prism, was 0.3m (1ft) high, 0.46m (1.5ft) wide, with a weight of 60kg (132lb). Explorer-31/ISIS-X (International Satellite for Ionospheric Studies)/ADME was part of a program undertaken with Canada; it studied the density and temperature of ions and electrons, the composition of ions and corpuscular radiation. Explorer-31, an octagonal prism, was 0.63m (2.1ft) high, with a diameter of 0.76m (2.5ft) and a weight of 100kg (220lb).

Launching and orbital data - Explorer-8 was launched November 3, 1960 and went into an orbit with a perigee of 417km (259mi) and an apogee of 2,288km (1,422mi). Explorer-20 was launched August 25, 1964 into an orbit with a perigee of 871km (541mi) and an apogee of 1,018km (632mi). Explorer-22 was launched October 10, 1964 and went into an orbit with a perigee of 889km (552mi) and an apogee of 1,081km (672mi). Explorer-27 was launched April 29, 1965 into an orbit with a perigee of 941km (585mi) and an apogee of 1,317km (818mi). Explorer-31 was launched November 29, 1965 into an orbit with a perigee of 505km (314mi) and an apogee of 2,978km (1,850mi).

EXPLORER-12/-14/-15/-26 (USA - 1961)

Group of four NASA satellites to study the manner in which the radiation belts around the Earth receive, trap and lose their charged particles. Explorer-12 took the shape of an octagonal-based prism 1.29m (4.2ft) high, 0.66m (2.2ft) wide and weighing 38kg (84lb). Explorer-14 was 1.3m (4.2ft) high with a diameter of 0.74m (2.4ft) and weighed 40kg (88lb). Explorer-15 was 1.3m (4.2ft) high with a diameter of 0.74m (2.4ft) and weighed 45.2kg (99lb). Explorer-26 was 0.46m (1.5ft) high, had a diameter of 0.71m (2.3ft) and weighed 46kg (101lb).

Launching and orbital data - Explorer-12 was launched August 16, 1961 into an orbit with a perigee of 314km (195mi) and an apo-

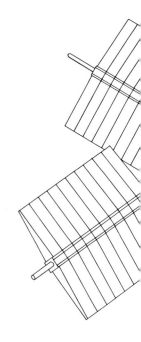

Explorer-6

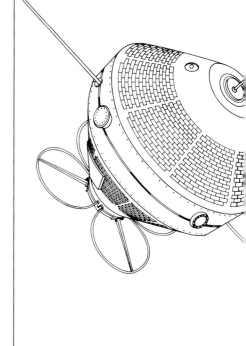

Explorer-8

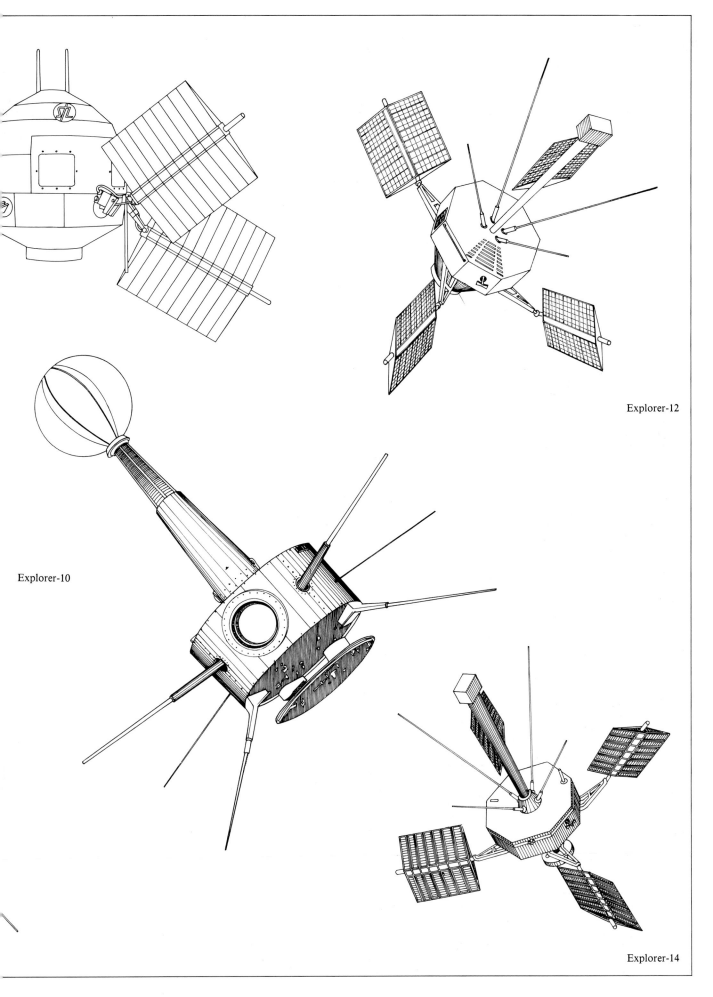

Explorer-12

Explorer-10

Explorer-14

6

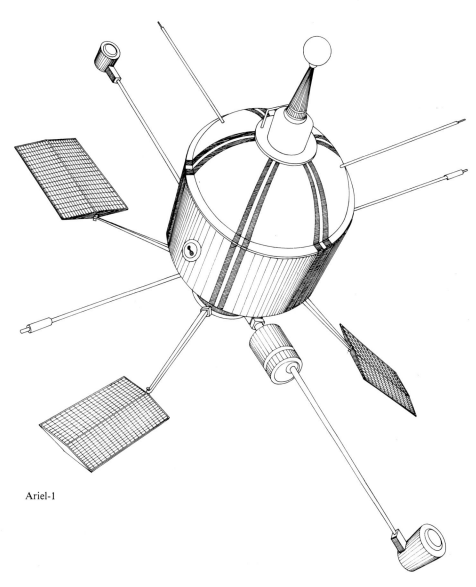

Ariel-1

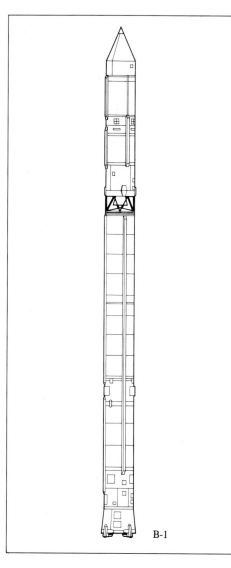

B-1

gee of 77,310km (48,033mi). Explorer-14 was launched October 2, 1962 into an orbit with a perigee of 2,558km (1,589mi) and an apogee of 96,229km (59,787mi). Explorer-15 was launched October 27, 1962 into an orbit with a perigee of 313km (194mi) and an apogee of 17,540km (10,898mi). Explorer-26 was launched December 21, 1964 into an orbit with a perigee of 316km (196mi) and an apogee of 26,191km (16,272mi).

ARIEL-1/UK-1 (GREAT BRITAIN - 1962)

First British satellite. In the shape of a cylinder, diameter of 0.58m (1.9ft) and height of 0.53m (1.7ft), it weighed 60kg (132lb). It carried out four types of experiment: studies of ions and electrons, density of electrons, solar radiations and cosmic rays. It sent back data until November 1964. It was spin-stabilized.

Launching and orbital data - Ariel-1 was launched April 26, 1962 from Cape Canaveral by a Thor Delta rocket and placed in an orbit with a perigee of 389km (242mi), an apogee of 1,214km (754mi) and an inclination of 53.85°.

ALOUETTE-1 (CANADA - 1962)

Studied the physical properties of the ionosphere, carrying out experiments in telecommunications. (See Telecommunications Satellites.)

COSMOS (USSR - 1962)

A number of satellites bearing the name Cosmos were launched into orbit to study the interaction between the Earth and the Sun. Some bore the following series numbers: 1/2/3/26/49/97/321/381/477/481/1463/1508.

Launching and orbital data - Cosmos-1 was launched March 16, 1962 from Kapustin Yar by a B-1 rocket and sent into an orbit with a perigee of 217km (135mi), an apogee of 980km (609mi) and an inclination of 49°.

EXPLORER/IMP-18/-21/-28/-33/-34/-35/-41/-43/-47/-50 (USA - 1963)

Group of ten NASA satellites known as Interplanetary Monitoring Platforms (IMP) launched between 1963 and 1973 in order to study interplanetary radiation and magnetic fields in the vicinity of the Earth and the Moon, and to extend knowledge concerning the relationships between the Sun, Earth and Moon. Explorer-18, weighing 62kg (136lb), confirmed the existence of a shock wave created in the terrestrial magnetosphere by the solar wind. It also revealed the existence of a magnetic tail. Explorer-21, weighing 62kg (136lb), did not reach its projected apogeal height because of a launching error, and was only a partial success. Explorer-28, weighing 59kg (130lb), continued the study of interplanetary radiation between the Earth and Moon, and of the magnetic field. Explorer-33, weighing 57kg (125lb), studied the Earth's magnetic tail and revealed the Moon's magnetic field. Explorer-34, weighing 75kg (165lb), discovered that Saturn, like the Earth and Jupiter, emitted radio waves. Explorer-35 was sent into orbit around the Moon and revealed the existence of the solar wind directly behind the

140

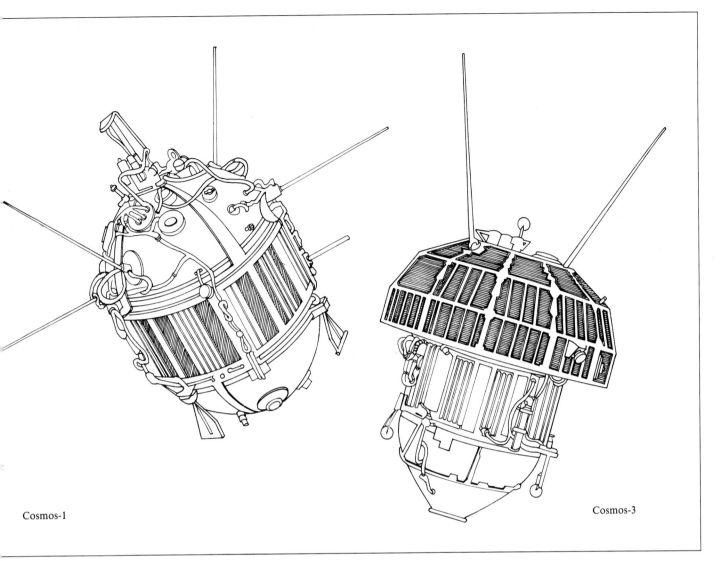

Cosmos-1

Cosmos-3

Explorer-35

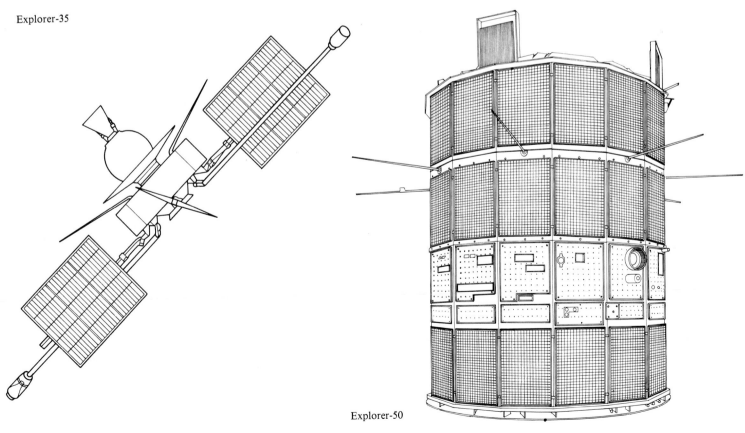

Explorer-50

Moon of which it studied the electrical conductivity and internal temperature. Explorer-41 and -43, weighing respectively 79kg (174lb) and 288kg (634lb), continued to measure interplanetary radiation. Explorer-47, sent into a near circular orbit, and Explorer-50 studied both the middle field of radiation between the Earth and the Moon, and also the Earth's magnetic tail.

Launching and orbital data - Explorer-18 was launched November 27, 1963 into an orbit with a perigee of 192km (119mi) and an apogee of 197,616km (122,779mi).
Explorer-21 was launched April 10, 1964. Perigee 190km (118mi), apogee 95,595km (59,393mi).
Explorer-28, May 29, 1965. Perigee 190km (118mi), apogee 264,000km (164,023mi).
Explorer-33, July 1, 1966. Perigee 30,532km (18,970mi), apogee 494,230km (307,065mi).
Explorer-34, May 24, 1967. Perigee 242km (150mi), apogee 214,383km (133,196mi).
Explorer-35, July 19, 1967. Lunar orbit.
Explorer-41, June 21, 1969. Perigee 378km (235mi), apogee 176,434km (109,618mi).
Explorer-43, March 13, 1971. Perigee 353km (219mi), apogee 204,577km (127,104mi).
Explorer-47, September 22, 1972. Perigee 201,100km (124,943mi), apogee 235,600km (146,378mi).
Explorer-50, October 25, 1973. Perigee 141,185km (87,718mi), apogee 288,857km (179,467mi).
All ten satellites were launched from Cape Canaveral by Delta rockets.

EXPLORER-25/-40/-52 (USA - 1964)

Group of three NASA satellites for studying the magnetosphere. Explorer-25 and -40 measured the flow of corpuscular radiation entering the Earth's atmosphere, and the concentration and distribution of energy of the charged particles. Explorer-25/Injun-4

was spherical in shape with a diameter of 0.61m (2ft) and a height of 0.76m (2.5ft), weighing 40kg (88lb). Explorer-40/Injun-5 had the shape of a hexagonal prism, 0.74m (2.4ft) high, 0.76m (2.5ft) wide, weighing 69.6kg (153lb). Explorer-52/Hawkeye studied the interaction between the solar wind and the magnetic field in the polar regions, determining points and neutral lines during the periods of the Sun's maximum and minimum activity. The satellite was cylindrical-conical in shape, with a maximum diameter of 0.75m (2.46ft) and a height of 0.75m (2.46ft); it weighed 25kg (55lb).

Launching and orbital data - Explorer-25 was launched November 21, 1964 from Vandenberg by a Scout rocket and went into an orbit with a perigee of 522km (324mi) and an apogee of 2,494km (1,550mi), inclined at 81.36°. Explorer-40 was launched August 8, 1968. Its orbit had a perigee of 681km (423mi) and an apogee of 2,533km (1,574mi). Explorer-52 was launched June 3, 1974 and placed in a markedly elliptical polar orbit with a perigee of 513km (319mi), an apogee of 126,896km (78,840mi) and an inclination of 89.9°.

OGO (USA - 1964)

Group of six satellites launched by NASA under the name of Orbiting Geophysical Observatory (OGO) for studying the Earth's atmosphere, magnetosphere and space between the Earth and the Moon. The satellites also tested the tecnique of three-axis stabilization. All were similarly box-shaped, measuring 0.9x0.9m (2.95x2.95ft) at the base, and 1.8m (5.9ft) high. On the outside were two arms of 6.7m (22ft) and another four arms of 1.8m (5.9ft) which accomodated various experiments. OGO-1 weighed 487kg (1,071lb) and carried twenty experiments, twelve for studying particles, two for

the magnetic field and one each for interplanetary dust, electric fields, Lyman-Alpha emissions, the Gegenschein effect, atmospheric mass and radio astronomy. The three-axis stabilization failed to function and one of the arms did not open. It remained operational, even if only partially, until November 1971. OGO-2 weighed 520kg (1,144lb) and carried twenty experiments for studying the atmosphere, the ionosphere, the magnetic field, the radiation belts, cosmic rays, micrometeorites and solar emissions. The mechanisms functioned partially, and the stabilization failed to operate after ten days in orbit so that the satellite had to be spin-stabilized. Activities terminated in November 1971. OGO-3 weighed 515kg (1,133lb) and carried the same instruments as in OGO-1. The three-axis stabilization functioned partially, and operations were concluded in February 1972. OGO-4 weighed 562kg (1,236lb) and carried similar instruments to those of OGO-2. The three-axis stabilization only functioned partially and operations came to an end in September 1971. OGO-5 weighed 611kg (1,344lb) and carried twenty-five experiments, seventeen of them for studying particles, two for the magnetic field, and one each for radioastronomy, the ultraviolet spectrum, Lyman-Alpha emissions, solar X-ray emissions, plasma waves and electric fields. This was regarded as the most successful mission. The three-axis stabilization functioned for some time, and twenty-two of the twenty-five experiments worked properly. Operations came to an end in July 1972. OGO-6 weighed 632kg (1,390lb) and carried twenty-six experiments devoted to geophysical phenomena and Sun-Earth interaction. The stabilization system functioned for almost the whole time. Nine experiments were failures and operations were concluded in July 1972.

Launching and orbital data - OGO-1 was launched September 5, 1964, its orbital perigee being 35,743km (22,207mi), apogee 114,040km (70,853mi), inclination 57.5°.

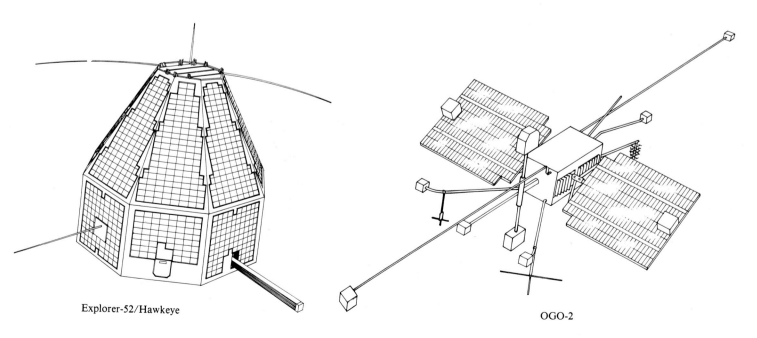

Explorer-52/Hawkeye

OGO-2

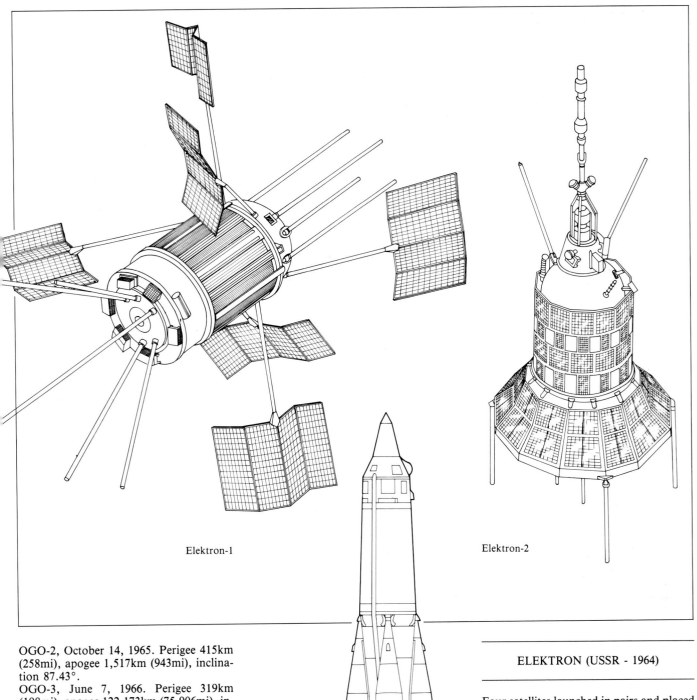

Elektron-1

Elektron-2

A-1

OGO-2, October 14, 1965. Perigee 415km (258mi), apogee 1,517km (943mi), inclination 87.43°.
OGO-3, June 7, 1966. Perigee 319km (198mi), apogee 122,173km (75,906mi), inclination 31.39°.
OGO-4, July 28, 1967. Perigee 411km (255mi), apogee 903km (561mi), inclination 86.03°.
OGO-5, March 4, 1968. Perigee 232km (144mi), apogee 148,228km (92,094mi), inclination 31.13°.
OGO-6, June 5, 1969. Perigee 397km (247mi), apogee 1,089km (677mi), inclination 82°.
OGO-1/-3/-5 were launched from Cape Canaveral by Atlas Agena rockets and OGO-2/-4/-6 from Vandenberg by Thor Agena rockets.

ELEKTRON (USSR - 1964)

Four satellites launched in pairs and placed in different orbits so as to make simultaneous studies of the outer and inner zones of the Van Allen radiation belts surrounding the Earth. Elektron-1 and -3 weighed 350kg (770lb), with a diameter of 0.75m (2.5ft) and a length of 1.3m (4.3ft). They were concerned with studies inside the radiation belts. Elektron-2 and -4 weighed 445kg (979lb), with a diameter of 1.8m (5.9ft) and a height of 2.4m (7.9ft). They examined the outer zone of the Van Allen radiation belts and the areas of cosmic space beyond the belts.

Launching and orbital data - Elektron-1 and -2 were launched January 30, 1964 from Baikonur-Tyuratam by an A-1 rocket. Elektron-3 and -4 were launched July 11, 1964 from Baikonur-Tyuratam, likewise by an A-1 rocket. Elektron-1 and 3 were placed in orbit with a perigee of 400km (248mi), an apogee of 7,000km (4,349mi), inclined at 60.83°. Elektron-2 and -4 were sent into more elliptical orbits with a perigee of 460km (286mi), an apogee of 68.000km (42,248mi) and 66,000km (41,006mi) respectively, inclined at 60.87°.

HEOS (EUROPE - 1968)

Two satellites (HEOS-1, HEOS-A2) developed by the European Space Agency, with almost identical characteristics, each carrying a payload of seven experiments for studying the interactions between solar particles and the magnetosphere. The central body of the satellite was a sixteen-faced cylinder with a diameter of 1.3m (4.3ft), to which was attached a tubular structure supporting various instruments. The overall height of the satellite was 2.4m (7.9ft) and the weights in orbit were, for HEOS-1, 108kg (255lb), 27kg (59lb) of this being represented by the payload, and, for HEOS-A2, 117kg (257lb), with 30.5kg (67lb) of payload. HEOS (Highly Eccentric Orbit Satellite) was spin-stabilized, and the outside was covered with solar cells furnishing power of 55 watts. Technical life was eighteen months.

Launching and orbital data - HEOS-1 was launched December 5, 1968 from Cape Canaveral by a Delta rocket and was placed in a highly eccentric orbit with a perigee of 424km (263mi), an apogee of 223,428km (138,816mi) and an inclination of 28.28°. HEOS-A2 was launched January 31, 1972 by a Delta rocket from Vandenberg and sent into an orbit with a perigee of 359km (223mi), an apogee of 238,199km (147,993mi) and an inclination of 90°.

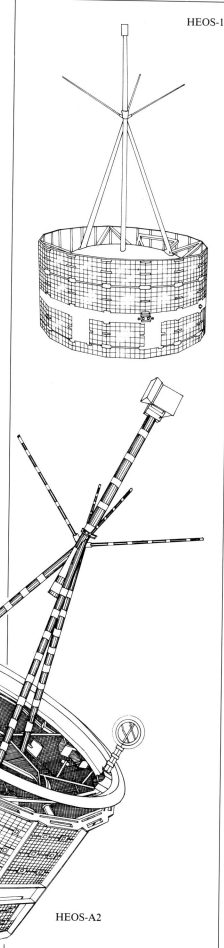

HEOS-1

HEOS-A2

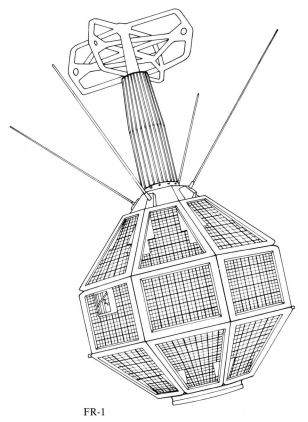

FR-1

FR-1 (FRANCE - 1965)

A French satellite for studying irregularities of ionization in the magnetosphere and ionosphere, developed by CNES (Centre National d'Etudes Spatiales). The satellite experimented in particular with the transmission of very low-frequency waves. In the shape of a polyhedron, its diameter was 0.68m (2.2ft) and its height 1.32m (4.3ft). The weight was 60kg (132lb). It remained functional until February 1969.

Launching and orbital data - FR-1 was launched December 6, 1965 from Vandenberg by a Scout rocket and placed in a near-circular orbit 746-762km (463-473mi) high, with an inclination of 75.87°.

ESRO (EUROPE - 1968)

Group of four satellites launched by the European Space Agency for the study of space physics. Esro-II/Iris was the first satellite launched by what was then called ESRO (European Space Research Organization). Weighing 75kg (165lb), it was a twelve-sided cylinder with a height of 0.85m (2.8ft) and a diameter of 0.76m (2.5ft). The outside was covered with solar cells that furnished power of 40 watts. On board were seven experiments devoted to the study of radiations and of cosmic and galactic particles.

Esro-I/Aurorae, weighing 86kg (189lb), was cylindrical, with a total height of 1.52m (5ft) and a diameter of 0.76m (2.5ft). The solar cells attached to the outside furnished power of 21 watts. The eight experiments on board were devoted to the study of the polar ionosphere and phenomena of the polar aurorae.

Esro-I/Boreas, weighing 108kg (238lb), was 1.52m (5ft) high, and its cylindrical body had a diameter of 0.76m (2.5ft). Its external solar cells provided power of 21 watts. It too carried eight instruments for studying the polar ionosphere and the polar aurorae.

Esro-IV, cylindrical in form, had a diameter of 0.76m (2.5ft), a height of 0.9m (2.95ft) and a weight of 113kg (248lb). There were six experiments on board for studying the ionosphere and solar particles. The solar cells on the outside furnished power of 60 watts. All the Esro satellites were spin-stabilized.

Launching and orbital data - Esro-II/Iris was launched May 17, 1968 into an orbit with a perigee of 332km (206mi), an apogee of 1,094km (680mi) and an inclination of 97.21°.

Esro-I/Aurorae was launched October 3, 1968 into an orbit with a perigee of 253km (157mi), an apogee of 1,534km (953mi) and an inclination of 93.76°.

Esro-I/Boreas was launched October 1, 1969 into an orbit with a perigee of 306km (190mi), an apogee of 393km (244mi) and an inclination of 85.13°.

Esro-IV was launched November 22, 1972 into an orbit with a perigee of 280km (174mi), an apogee of 1,100km (683mi) and an inclination of 90°.

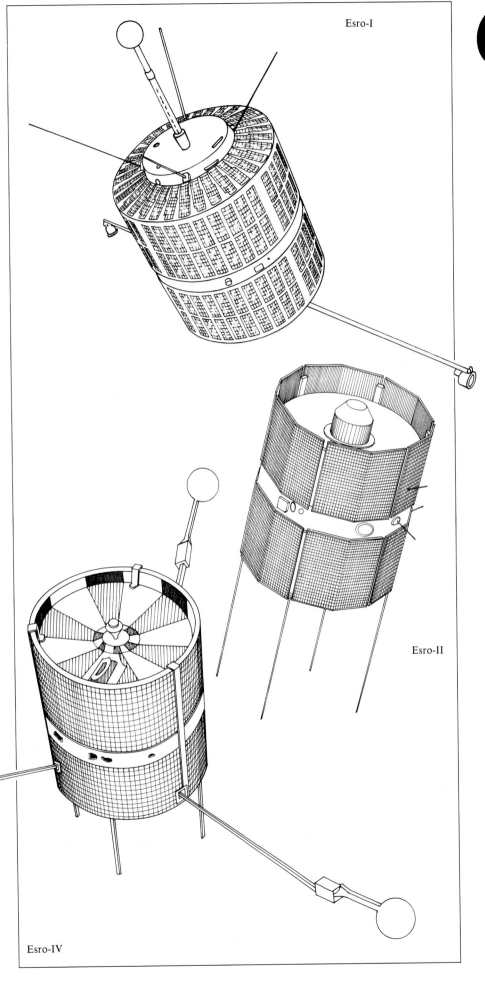

Esro-I

Esro-II

Esro-IV

6

ISIS-1/-2 (CANADA - 1969)

Canadian satellites for studying the ionosphere, Isis-1/-2 carried out experiments in telecommunications. (See Telecommunications Satellites.)

AZUR-1
(WEST GERMANY - 1969)

German satellite for studying the magnetosphere and Earth-Sun relationships, and for taking measurements in the Earth's magnetic field. Experiments carried out related to angular distribution and time variations in the flow of protons and alpha particles in the Van Allen belts, omnidirectional flow of protons and electrons in the belts, variations in the flow of incident and reflex electrons in the polar zones, and light intensity in the auroral zones and correlation with flow of electrons. The satellite was cylindrical-conical in form, diameter 0.76m (2.5ft), height 1.13m (3.7ft), weight 71kg (156lb), and was spin-stabilized.

Launching and orbital data - Azur-1 was launched November 8, 1969 from Vandenberg by a Scout rocket and placed in an orbit with a perigee of 387km (240mi), an apogee of 3,150km (1,957mi) and an inclination of 102.96°.

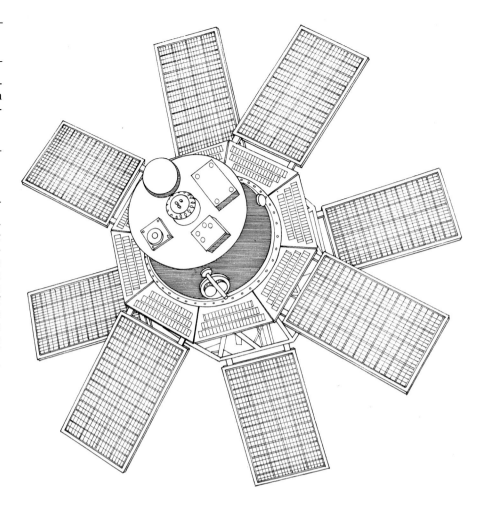

Intercosmos-1

Azur-1

INTERCOSMOS-1/-2/-3/-4/-5
(USSR - 1969)

Group of five satellites built in collaboration with various countries in Eastern Europe. Intercosmos-1 had a diameter of 1.35m (4.4ft), a length of 1.5m (4.9ft) and a weight of 350kg (770lb). Built in collaboration with East Germany and Czechoslovakia, it studied ultraviolet rays and X-rays from the Sun, and their effects upon the structure of the Earth's upper atmosphere.
Intercosmos-2 had a diameter of 1.2m (3.9ft), a length of 1.8m (5.9ft) and a weight of 400kg (880lb). Built in collaboration with East Germany, Bulgaria and Czechoslovakia, it studied the concentration of electrons and positive ions in the ionosphere, the temperature of electrons close to the satellite, the concentration of electrons between the satellite and the Earth. Intercosmos-3 had a diameter of 1.2m (3.9ft), a height of 1.8m (5.9ft) and a weight of 400kg (880lb). Built together with Czechoslovakia, it studied the interactions between solar activity and the Van Allen belts. Intercosmos-4 had a diameter of 1.35m (4.4ft), a height of 1.5m (4.9ft) and a weight of 350kg (770lb). Built together with Czechoslovakia and East Germany, it carried out research on ultraviolet

rays and X-rays, and their effects on the Earth's ionosphere. Intercosmos-5 had a diameter of 1.2m (3.9ft), a height of 1.8m (5.9ft) and a weight of 400kg (880lb). Built in conjunction with Czechoslovakia, it studied the composition of the flow of charged particles and the influence of the Van Allen belts on the ionosphere.

Launching and orbital data - Intercosmos-1 was launched October 14, 1969 into an orbit with a perigee of 254km (158mi), an apogee of 626km (389mi) and an inclination of 48.38°.
Intercosmos-2 was launched December 25, 1969 into an orbit with a perigee of 200km (124mi), an apogee of 1,178km (732mi) and an inclination of 48.4°.
Intercosmos-3 was launched August 7, 1970 into an orbit with a perigee of 200km (124mi), an apogee of 1,295km (805mi) and an inclination of 48.41°.
Intercosmos-4 was launched October 14, 1970 into an orbit with a perigee of 255km (158mi), an apogee of 649km (403mi) and an inclination of 48.41°.
Intercosmos-5 was launched December 2, 1971 into an orbit with a perigee of 198km (123mi), an apogee of 1,181km (734mi) and an inclination of 48.42°.
All launchings took place from Kapustin Yar, using B-1 rockets.

DIAL/WIKA (WEST GERMANY/ FRANCE - 1970)

Satellite built in collaboration by France and West Germany for studying the belt of particles around the Earth, their distribution and the mechanics of excitation. The four onboard experiments dealt with intensity of Lyman-Alpha radiation, density of electrons, the energy spectrum of protons (5-40 MeV), electrons (>1.3 MeV) and Alpha particles (5-40 MeV), and variations of the magnetic field. Dial had an octagonal-based body with a diameter of 0.63m (2.1ft), a height of 1.01m (3.3ft) and a weight of 63kg (139lb).

Launching and orbital data - Dial was launched March 10, 1970 from French Guiana by a Diamant B rocket and placed in an orbit with a perigee of 318km (198mi), an apogee of 1,628km (1,011mi) and an inclination of 5.4°.

ARIEL-4/UK-4 (GREAT BRITAIN - 1971)

Radio astronomy satellite for measuring the intensity of radiogalactic sounds, emissions of radio noise at low and extremely low frequencies, and the temperature and density of electrons. In the shape of a cylinder, its diameter was 0,76m (2.5ft), its height 0.91m (3ft) and its weight 99.5kg (219lb).

Launching and orbital data - Ariel-4 was launched December 11, 1971 from Vanden-

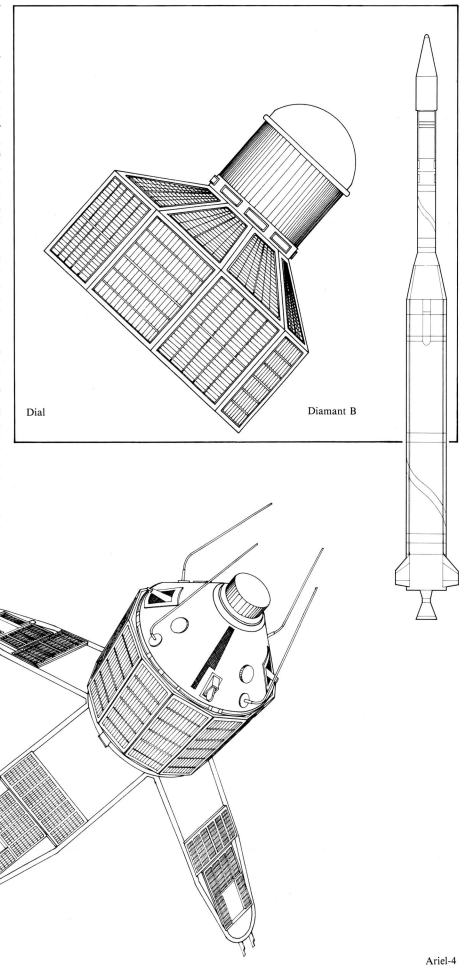

Dial

Diamant B

Ariel-4

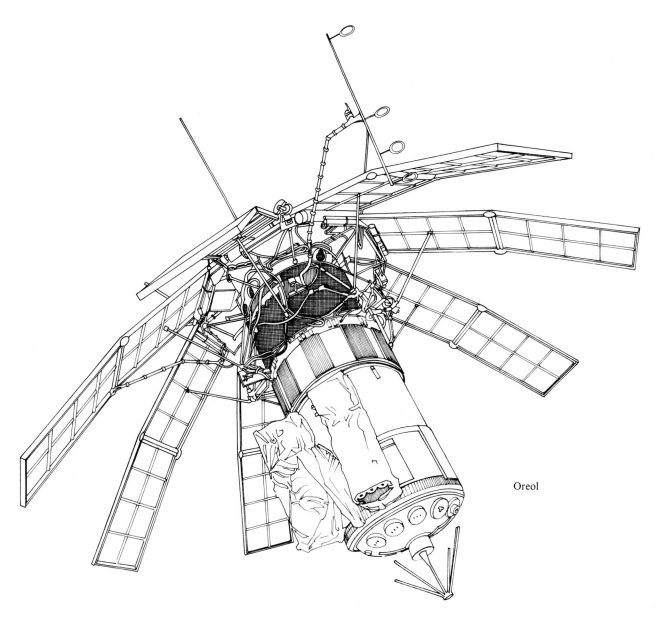

Oreol

berg by a Scout rocket and placed in an orbit with a perigee of 477km (296mi), an apogee of 593km (368mi) and an inclination of 82.99°.

OREOL/AUREOLE (USSR/FRANCE - 1971)

Soviet satellites, developed in conjunction with France, which studied Sun-Earth relations. About 1.8m (5.9ft) high, with a diameter of 1.5m (4.9ft), it weighed around 400kg (880 lb). On Aureole-1 France loaded an experiment to measure the energy spectrum of protons and electrons between 200 eV and 15 KeV of the solar wind. Aureole-2, weighing 500kg (1,100lb), continued studying the mechanism of energy transport from the Sun to the Earth, the correlation with phenomena in the magnetosphere, ionosphere and upper atmosphere, and the nature of the aurorae borealis.

Launching and orbital data - Aureole-1 was launched December 27, 1971 into an orbit with a perigee of 400km (248mi), an apogee of 2,477km (1,539mi) and an inclination of 73,98°. Aureole-2 was launched December 26, 1973, and sent into an orbit with a perigee of 400km (248mi), an apogee of 1,975km (1,227mi) and an inclination of 74°. Aureole-3 was launched September 22, 1981 into an orbit with a perigee of 402km (250mi), an apogee of 1,977km (1,228mi) and an inclination of 82.5°. The first two satellites were launched by Soviet C-1 rockets from the Plesetsk base, and the third, also from Plesetsk, by an A-2 rocket.

SHINSEI (JAPAN - 1971)

Satellite designed by the ISAS (Institute of Space and Aeronautical Science), in the shape of a 26-faceted polyhedron with a diameter of 0.75m (2.5ft), a height of 1.74m (5.7ft) and a weight of 66kg (145lb). Spin-stabilized; outside covered with 5,184 solar cells furnishing power of 30 watts. The two instruments on board were for measuring cosmic rays and, in the ionosphere, the density and temperature of electrons and the density of ions. A study was also carried out of high-frequency radio emissions from the Sun.

Launching and orbital data - Shinsei was launched September 28, 1971 from Kagoshima Space Center by a M-4S-3 rocket and sent into an orbit with a perigee of 870km (540mi), an apogee of 1,870km (1,162mi) and an inclination of 32°.

DENPA/REXS (JAPAN - 1972)

Satellite in shape of octagonal-based prism with a height of 0.68m (2.2ft) — 1.89m (6.2ft) including antennae — a width of 0.71m (2.3ft) and a weight of 75kg (165lb). Developed by the ISAS, it studied plasma waves and their density, the flow of electrons and the magnetic field in the Earth's vicinity. It investigated also the phenomena of radio waves propagation in the magnetosphere. The outside of the satellite was covered with 5,329 solar cells which provided power of 40 watts. The satellite was spin-stabilized. The prime contractor was the NEC (Nippon Electric Company.)

Launching and orbital data - Denpa was launched August 19, 1972 from Kagoshima Space Center by a M-4S-4 rocket and sent into an orbit with a perigee of 250km (155mi), an apogee of 6,570km (4,082mi) and an inclination of 31°.

INTERCOSMOS-6/-7/-8/-9/-10
(USSR - 1972)

Group of Soviet satellites built in conjunction with Eastern European countries. Intercosmos-6 had a diameter of 2.4m (7.9ft), a height of 5m (16.4ft) and a weight of 2,050kg (4,510lb). Participants were Hungary, Mongolia, Poland, Romania and Czechoslovakia. It studied the energy spectrum, the composition of cosmic waves, and micrometeorites. Intercosmos-7 had a diameter of 1.05m (3.4ft), a height of 2.5m (8.2ft) and a weight of 1,375kg (3,025lb). Participants were Czechoslovakia and East Germany. It studied solar X-rays and ultraviolet rays and their effects on the Earth's upper atmosphere. Intercosmos-8 had a diameter of 1.2m (3.9ft), a height of 1.8m (5.9ft) and a weight of 400kg (880lb). Participants were East Germany, Bulgaria and Czechoslovakia. It studied the concentration of electrons and positive ions in the ionosphere and measured the temperature of electrons. Intercosmos-9 had a diameter of 1.2m (3.9ft), a height of 1.8m (5.9ft) and a weight of 400kg (880lb). Participants were Poland and Czechoslovakia. It studied solar X-rays and ultraviolet rays and their effects on the Earth's upper atmosphere. Intercosmos-10 had a diameter of 1.2m (3.9ft), a height of 1.8m (5.9ft) and a weight of 400kg (880lb). Participants were East Germany and Czechoslovakia. It studied the existing relationships between the magnetosphere and the ionosphere.

Launching and orbital data - Intercosmos-6 was launched April 7, 1972 from Baikonur-Tyuratam by an A-1 rocket and went into a near-circular orbit at a height of 203-248km (126-154mi), inclined at 51.78°. Intercosmos-7 was launched June 30, 1972 from Kapustin Yar by a B-1 rocket and placed in an orbit with a perigee of 260km (162mi), an apogee of 551km (342mi) and an inclination of 48.41°. Intercosmos-8 was launched December 1, 1972 from Plesetsk by a B-1 rocket and sent into an orbit with a perigee of 204km (127mi), an apogee of 649km (403mi) and an inclination of 71.01°. Intercosmos-9 was launched April 19, 1973 from Kapustin Yar by a B-1 rocket into an orbit with a perigee of 199km (124mi), an apogee of 1,526km (948mi) and an inclination of 48.42°. Intercosmos-10 was launched October 30, 1973 from Plesetsk by a C-1 rocket and went into an orbit with a perigee of 260km (162mi), an apogee of 1,454km (903mi) and an inclination of 74.03°.

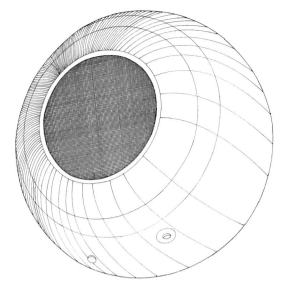

Intercosmos-6

INTERCOSMOS-11/-12/-13/-14
(USSR - 1974)

Soviet satellites built in collaboration with Eastern European countries.
Intercosmos-11 had a diameter of 1.2m (3.9ft), a height of 1.8m (5.9ft) and a weight of 400kg (880lb). Participants were East Germany and Czechoslovakia. It studied the effects of solar X-rays and ultraviolet rays on the Earth's upper atmosphere.
Intercosmos-12 had a diameter of 1.5m (4.9ft), a height of 1.8m (5.9ft) and a weight of 400kg (880lb). Participants were East Germany, Hungary, Romania and Czechoslovakia. It studied the atmosphere, the ionosphere and the flow of micrometeorites.
Intercosmos-13 had a diameter of 1.2m (3.9ft), a height of 1.8m (5.9ft) and a weight of 550kg (1,210lb). Czechoslovakia participated. It studied dynamic processes in the

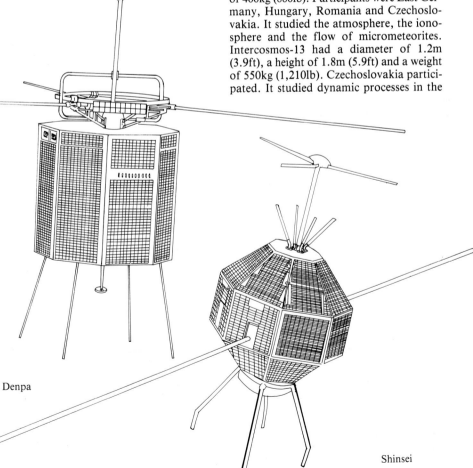

Denpa

Shinsei

magnetosphere and the polar ionosphere. Intercosmos-14 had a diameter of 1.5m (4.9ft), a height of 1.8m (5.9) and a weight of 550kg (1,210lb). Participants were Bulgaria, Hungary and Czechoslovakia. It studied the structure of the ionosphere and electromagnetic oscillations in the magnetosphere, and it measured the intensity of flow of micrometeorites.

Launching and orbital data - Intercosmos-11 was launched May 17, 1974 and its orbit had a perigee of 483km (300mi), an apogee of 511km (317mi) and an inclination of 50.64°. Intercosmos-12 was launched October 31, 1974 into an orbit with a perigee of 243km (151mi), an apogee of 707km (439mi) and an inclination of 74.02°.
Intercosmos-13 was launched March 27, 1975 and went into an orbit with a perigee of 284km (176mi), an apogee of 1,689km (1,049mi) and an inclination of 82.95°.
Intercosmos-14 was launched December 11, 1975 into an orbit with a perigee of 335km (208mi), an apogee of 1,684km (1,046mi) and an inclination of 73.99°.
All the satellites were launched from Plesetsk by C-1 rockets.

INTASAT (SPAIN - 1974)

First satellite launched by Spain to study certain aspects of space technology and to carry out experiments in the propagation acting as a relay of signals transmitted from high-altitude research balloons to receiving stations on the Earth. Experiments were also made in measuring the density of the ionosphere. Intasat was a 12-faceted cylinder with a diameter of 0.445m (1.5ft), a height of 0.45m (1.5ft) and a weight of 24.5kg (54lb). It was spin-stabilized, and the outside was covered with solar cells that furnished power of 2.77 watts. Technical life was two years. The satellite was built by the Spanish company Inta.

Launching and orbital data - Intasat was launched November 15, 1974 from Vandenberg by a Delta rocket and sent into a circular orbit at a height of 1,440-1,457km (895-905mi), inclined at 101°.

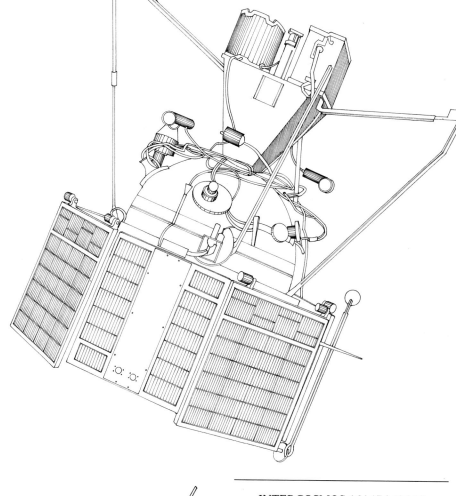

Intercosmos-12

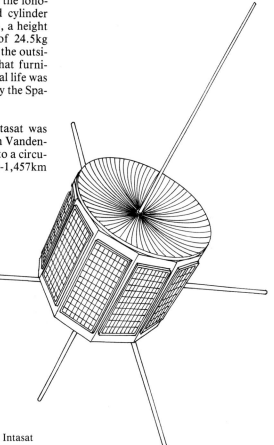

Intasat

INTERCOSMOS-16/-17/-18/-19 (USSR - 1976)

A group of Soviet satellites made in collaboration with Eastern European countries. Intercosmos-16, with East Germany, Sweden and Czechoslovakia participating, studied the effects of solar X-rays and ultraviolet rays on the Earth's upper atmosphere. Intercosmos-17 studied the energy of charged particles close to the Earth. Hungary, Romania and Czechoslovakia were participants. Intercosmos-18 carried out research into the magnetosphere and the ionosphere. Participants were East Germany, Hungary, Poland, Romania and Czechoslovakia. Similar research was done by Intercosmos-19 with the collaboration of Bulgaria, Hungary, Poland and Czechoslovakia. All these satellites had a diameter of 1.5m (4.9ft), a height of 1.8m (5.9ft) and a weight of 550kg (1,210lb).

Launching and orbital data - Intercosmos-16 was launched July 27, 1976 into a near-circular orbit at a height of 464-517km (288-321mi), inclined at 50.57°. Intercosmos-17 was launched September 24, 1977 into a near-circular orbit at a height of 466-514km (290-319mi), inclined at 82.96°. Intercosmos-18 was launched October 24, 1978 and its orbit had a perigee of 406km (252mi), an apogee of 764km (475mi) and an inclination of 82.97°. Intercosmos-19 was launched February 27, 1979 into an orbit with a perigee of 501km (311mi), an apogee of 991km (616mi) and an inclination of 73.98°. All launchings were from Kapustin Yar by C-1 rockets.

ISEE (USA/EUROPE - 1977)

Group of three satellites, two prepared by NASA (ISEE-1/-3) and one by the European Space Agency (ISEE-2) to be part of the research program known as the International Magnetosphere Study (IMS). The purpose of the two International Sun Earth Explorer satellites (ISEE-1 and -2), launched together into close orbits a variable distance apart, was to study the characteristics of space near to the Earth and its fluctuations. Among these was the fall in density of the magnetosphere in the zone called the "plasma-pause," the Earth's magnetosheath, the magnetopause where the Earth's magnetic field encounters the solar wind, the shock wave created by the wind when it meets the Earth, and other characteristics of the Earth's magnetic tail. ISEE-1 was a 16-faceted cylinder with a diameter of 1.73m (5.7ft), a height of 1.61m (5.3ft) and a weight of 340kg (748lb). There were 13 experiments on board. The satellite was designed and maintained in orbit by the Goddard Space Flight Center.
ISEE-2 was cylindrical, with a diameter of

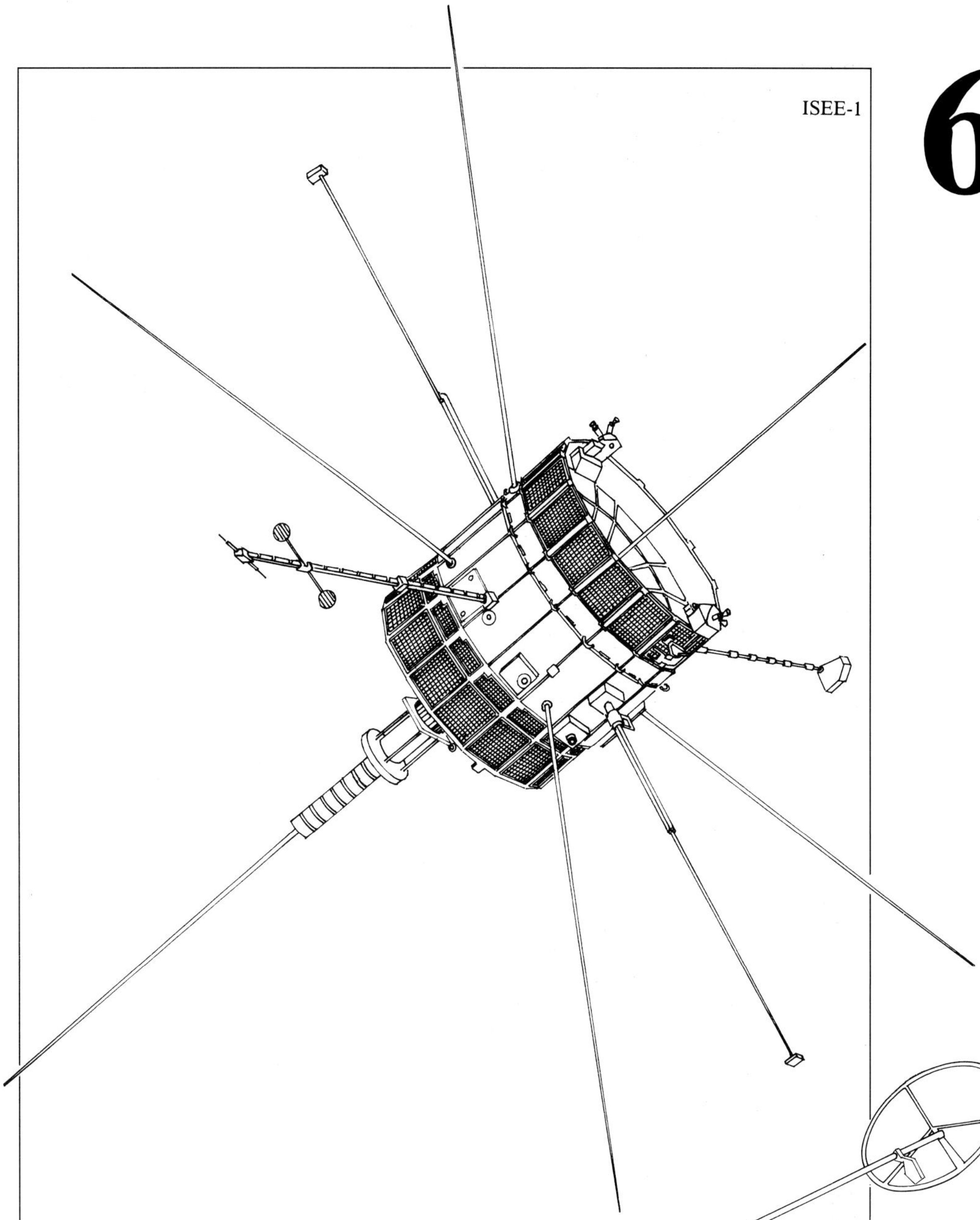

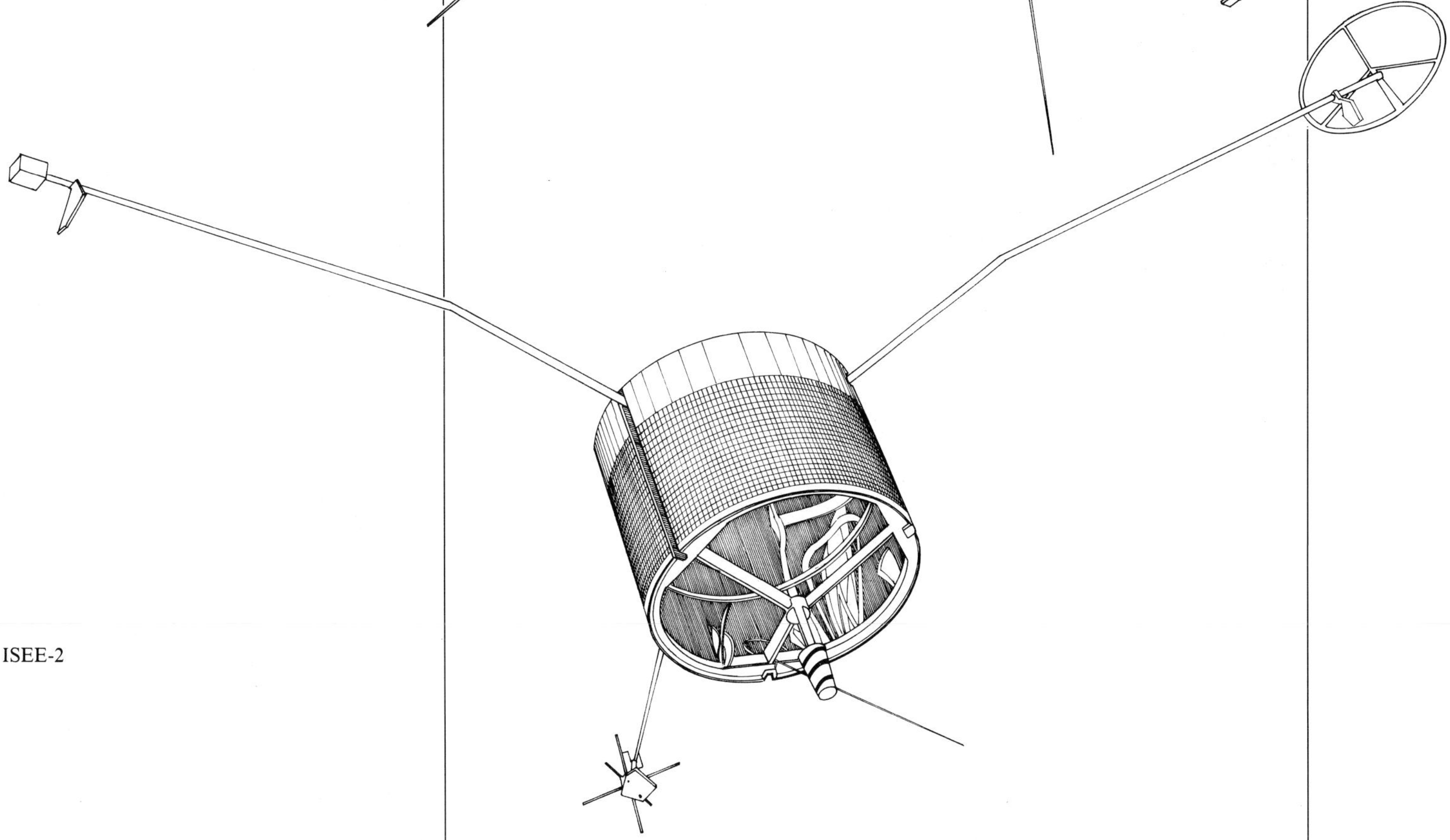

ISEE-2

1.27m (4.2ft), a height of 1.1m (3.6ft) and a launch weight of 157.3kg (346lb). The solar cells on the outside furnished power of 109 watts. On board were eight experiments. Design and management were by the ESTEC center of the ESA, and the satellite was built by the Star industrial consortium in which the German Dornier company was prime contractor. ISEE-3 was a 16-faceted cylinder with a diameter of 1.73m (5.7ft), a height of 1.61m (5.3ft) and a weight of 469kg (1,032lb). The spacecraft was designed by the Goddard Space Flight Center and was integrated and tested by the Fairchild Space & Electronics Co. There were 13 experiments on board.

Launching and orbital data - ISEE-1 and-2 were launched October 22, 1977. The orbit of ISEE-1 had a perigee of 337km (209mi), an apogee of 137,904km (85,680mi) and an inclination of 28.95°. ISEE-2 had a perigee of 341km (212mi), an apogee of 137,847km (85,644mi) and an inclination of 28.96°.

ISEE-3 was launched August 12, 1978 and put into a so-called "halo" orbit around a point situated between the Earth and the Sun, at a distance of 1,151,664km (715,529mi) from our planet. All launchings were from Cape Canaveral by Delta rockets.

GEOS-1/-2 (EUROPE - 1977)

Two satellites built by the European Space Agency (ESA) for studying the magnetosphere and carrying on board seven experiments: study of the magnetosphere in its magnetic and electric aspects; measurement of the flow of electrons and protons with energy of 0.5-500 eV; measurement of energy, angular distribution and composition of particles in geostationary orbit; measurement of spectra of energy and angular distribution of particles between 0.5-20 KeV; measurement of angular distribution and energy of electrons between 20 and 300 KeV, and energy of protons between 40 KeV and 2 MeV; deflection of a ray of electrons generated by the satellite; and study of magnetospheric storms. Prime contractor for the satellite, built by the European industrial consortium Star, was British Aerospace. The satellite was in the form of a cylinder with a diameter of 1.65m (5.4ft) and a height of 1m (3.3ft). Weight at launching was 575kg (1,265lb), of which 305kg (671lb) were taken up by the propellant for the apogee motor. Two-thirds of the outside surface of the satellite were covered with solar cells for providing power of 100 watts. Extending from the satellite were eight arms of varying lengths — maximum 20m (66ft) — supporting a number of instruments. Data was transmitted to the Earth at a maximum speed of 95.25 Kbit per second. The satellite was spin-stabilized and controlled from the ESOC center of the ESA at Darmstadt near Bonn. Geos-1 and Geos-2 had substantially the same characteristics.

Launching and orbital data - Geos-1 was launched April 20, 1977 from Cape Canaveral by a Delta rocket; but because of a malfunction of the rocket the satellite went into a wrong orbit with a perigee of 2,110km (1,311mi), an apogee of 38,357 km (23,831mi) and an inclination of 26.25°. Geos-2 was launched July 14, 1978 from Cape Canaveral by a Delta rocket and placed in a geostationary equatorial orbit in a position between longitudes 9° and 35°E.

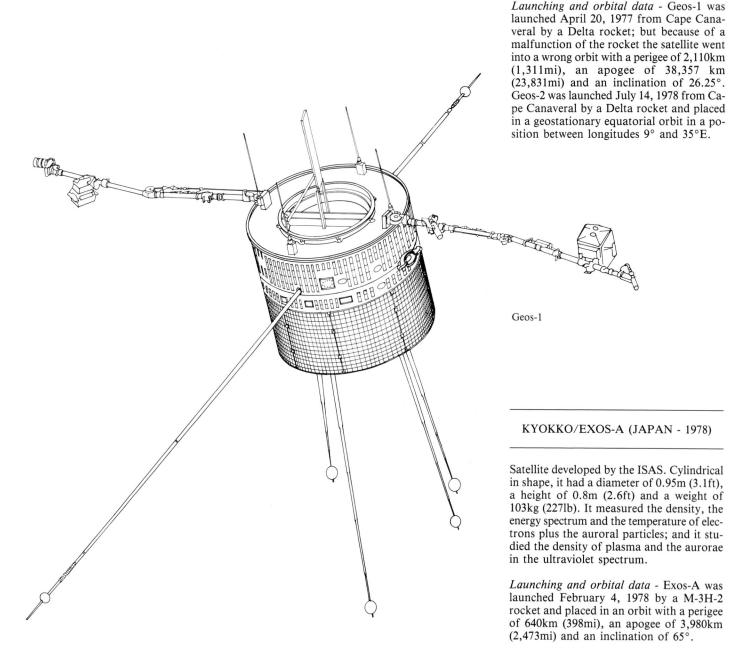

Geos-1

KYOKKO/EXOS-A (JAPAN - 1978)

Satellite developed by the ISAS. Cylindrical in shape, it had a diameter of 0.95m (3.1ft), a height of 0.8m (2.6ft) and a weight of 103kg (227lb). It measured the density, the energy spectrum and the temperature of electrons plus the auroral particles; and it studied the density of plasma and the aurorae in the ultraviolet spectrum.

Launching and orbital data - Exos-A was launched February 4, 1978 by a M-3H-2 rocket and placed in an orbit with a perigee of 640km (398mi), an apogee of 3,980km (2,473mi) and an inclination of 65°.

JIKIKEN/EXOS-B (JAPAN - 1978)

Satellite developed by the ISAS, in the form of a polyhedron, weighing 90kg (198lb). Its mission was to study phenomena of the magnetosphere such as plasma waves, electromagnetic fields, density of electrons and charged particles. Spin-stabilized, the prime contractor was the NEC company.

Launching and orbital data - Exos-B (Jikiken) was launched September 16, 1978 from Kagoshima Space Center and sent into an orbit with a perigee of 230km (143mi), an apogee of 30,050km (18,670mi) and an inclination of 31°.

DYNAMICS EXPLORER (USA - 1981)

Two satellites launched by the same rocket. They were 16-faceted prisms with a diameter of 1.34m (4.4ft) and a height of 1.14m (3.8ft). DE-1 weighed 402kg (893lb) and DE-2 414kg (911lb). Their task was to study the flow of radiations and particles from the Sun and their interaction with the Earth's magnetic field and with the upper atmosphere. The two satellites were built by RCA Astro Electronics.

Launching and orbital data - Dynamics Explorer-1 and -2 were launched August 3, 1981 from Vandenberg by a Delta rocket. DE-1 was sent into an orbit with a perigee of 559km (347mi) and an apogee of 23,295km (14,473mi). DE-2 had a perigee of 298km (185mi) and an apogee of 996km (619mi). Inclinations were 90°.

Kyokko

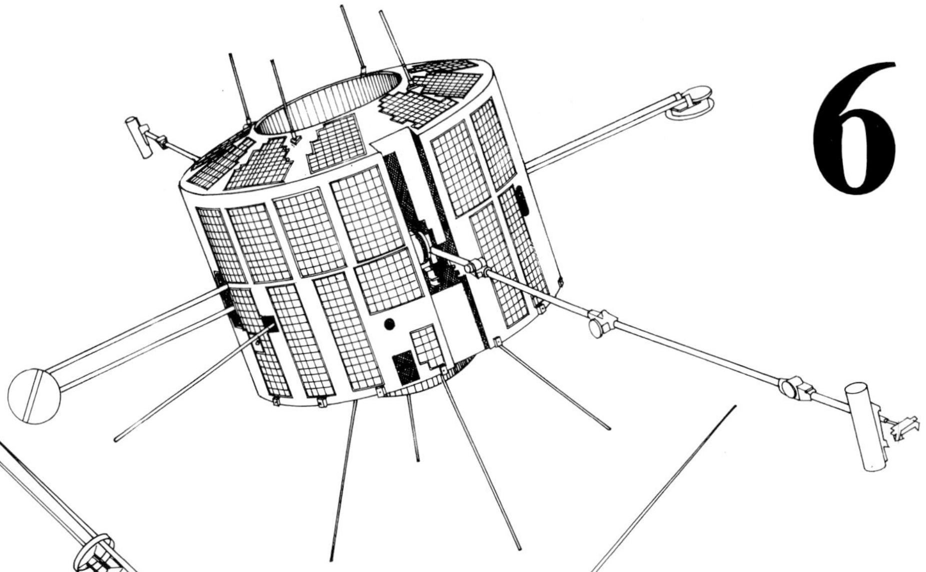

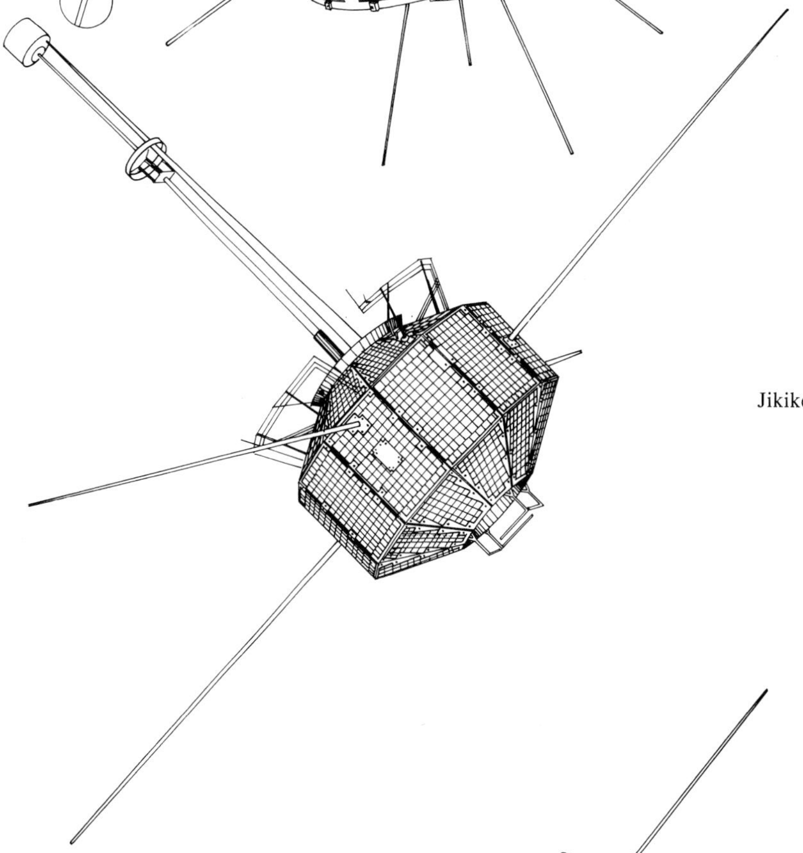

Jikiken

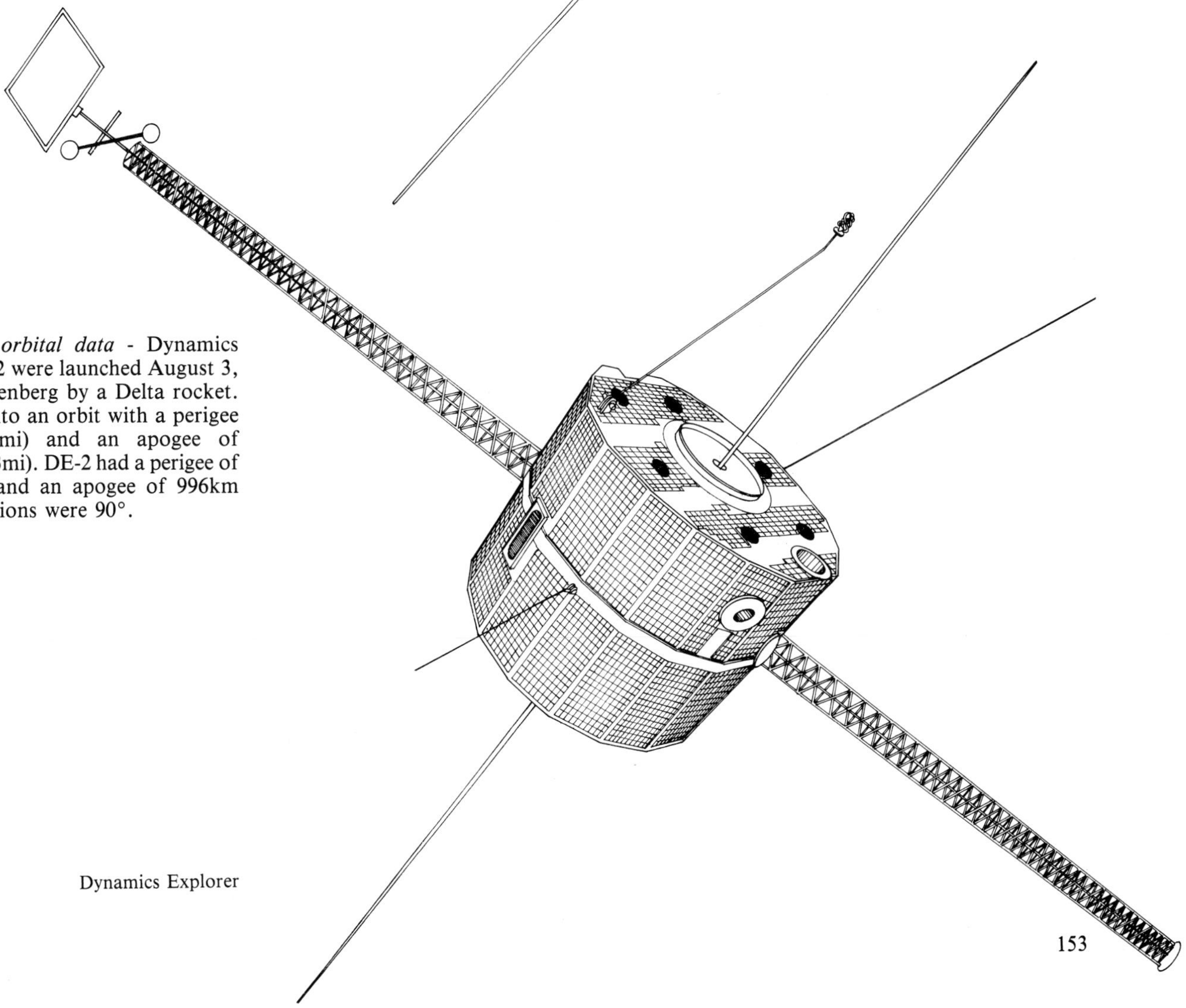

Dynamics Explorer

6

153

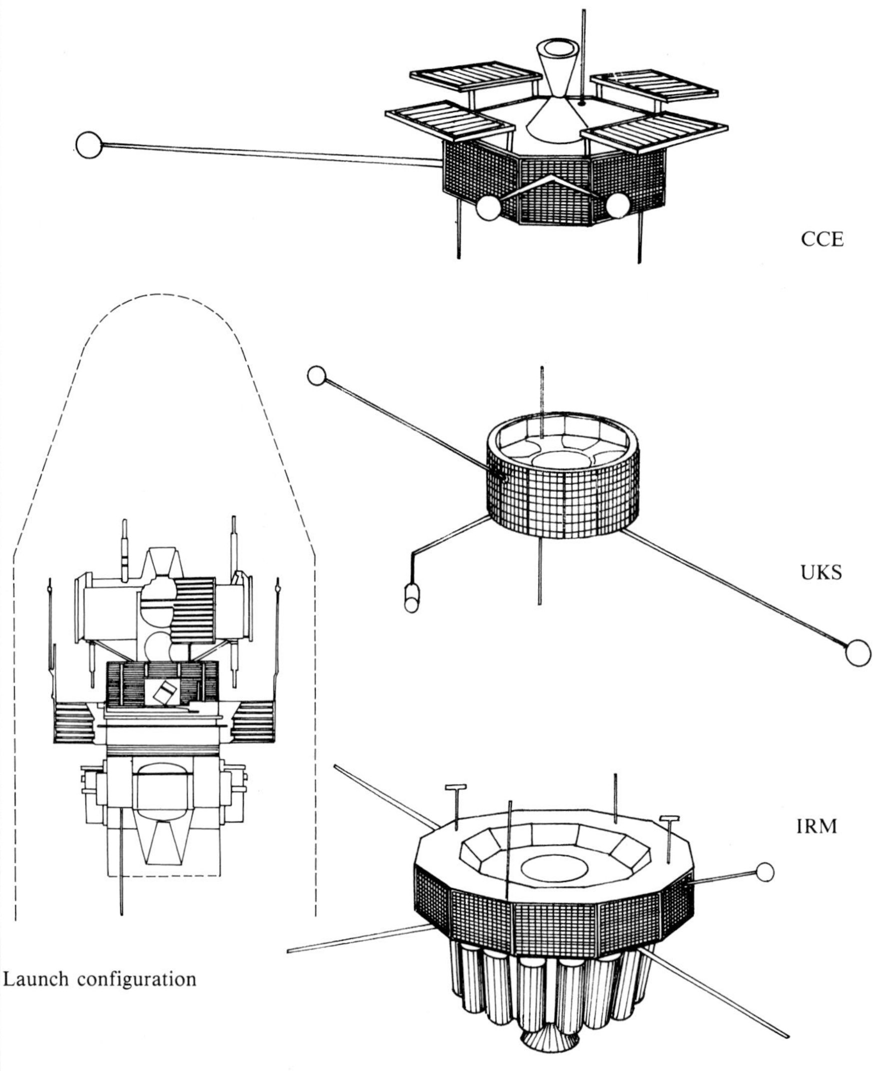

CCE

UKS

IRM

Launch configuration

The three AMPTE satellites

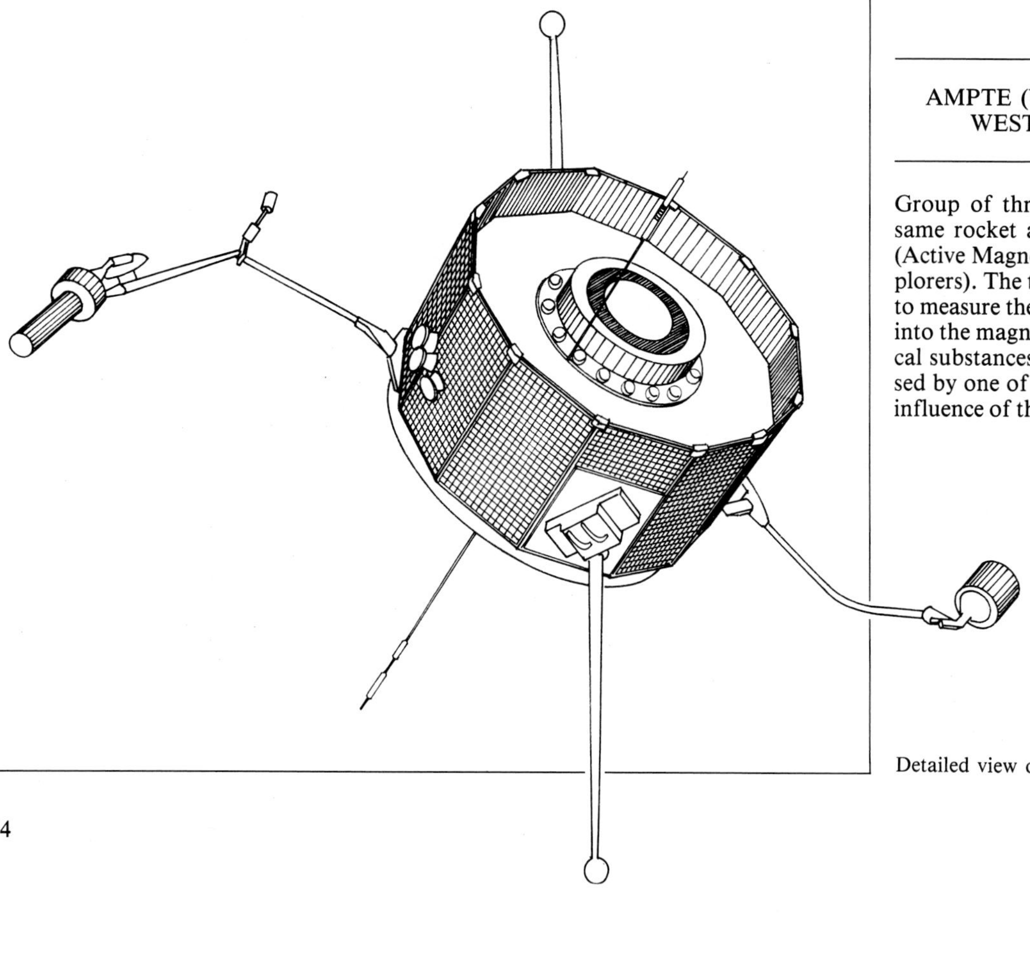

Detailed view of the UKS

CHINA-10/-11 (CHINA - 1981)

Two satellites launched in the course of a simultaneous launching of three satellites with a single rocket, designed for studying the Earth's upper atmosphere, the Earth's magnetic field, the ultraviolet and infrared radiations emitted by the Earth, and the X-rays and ultraviolet rays emitted by the Sun and their interactions with the Earth's atmosphere. China-10 had the form of two truncated cones, and it reentered the atmosphere on October 6, 1982. China-11 was in the shape of an octagonal-based prism 1.1m (3.6ft) high and 1.2m (3.9ft) across. Connected to one base of the satellite were four rectangular panels of solar cells which provided the necessary power. It reentered the atmosphere on August 17, 1982.

Launching and orbital data - China-10/-11 were launched September 19, 1981 by a B-1 rocket into an orbit with a perigee of 235km (146mi), an apogee of 1,610km (1,000mi) and an inclination of 59.6°.

HILAT (USA - 1983)

Hilat was an American scientific satellite derived from a modified Transit spacecraft. The instruments on board were finalized in the course of research on the ionosphere at high latitudes.

Launching and orbital data - Hilat was launched June 27, 1983 from Vandenberg by a Scout rocket and sent into a near-circular orbit at a height of 771-836km (479-519mi), inclined toward the equator at 82°.

AMPTE (USA/GREAT BRITAIN/ WEST GERMANY - 1984)

Group of three satellites launched by the same rocket and given the name AMPTE (Active Magnetospheric Particle Tracer Explorers). The three spacecraft were designed to measure the consequences of the emission into the magnetosphere of clouds of chemical substances (lithium and barium), released by one of the three satellites, under the influence of the solar wind. The behavior of the clouds will help to clarify the process that come about with the arrival of charged particles from the Sun. West Germany supplied the Ion Release Module (IRM) for the release of these substances, this satellite weighing 693kg (1,525lb); Great Britain provided the United Kingdom Subsatellite (UKS), weighing 77kg (169lb); and the United States the Charge Composition Explorer (CCE), weighing 242kg (532lb). The UKS was to carry out measurements close to the artificial clouds while the CCE studied the phenomenon from a lower orbit within the magnetosphere.

Launching and orbital data - The three satellites were launched August 16, 1984 from Cape Canaveral by a Delta rocket. The IRM and the UKS were placed in the same orbit with a perigee of 550km (342mi), an apogee of 112,886km (70,136mi) and an inclination of 28°. The CCE was placed in a lower orbit with a perigee of 966km (600mi), an apogee of 49,405km (30,695mi) and an inclination of 4°.

EXOS-C (JAPAN - 1984)

Satellite developed by the ISAS as a part of the Middle Atmospheric Program (MAP). The octagonal prism weighed 210kg (462lb). It was used to determine the structure and composition of the stratosphere and the mesosphere, and to analyze the interactions of the plasma and charged particles with the upper atmosphere. It also studied anomalies of the ionosphere above the area of the Earth's geomagnetic anomaly in Brazil. Prime contractor was the NEC company.

Launching and orbital data - Exos-C was launched February 14, 1984 from Kagoshima Space Center by a M-3S rocket and sent into an orbit with a perigee of 354km (220mi), an apogee of 884km (549mi) and an inclination of 74.6°.

PROGNOZ-10 (USSR - 1985)

Satellite launched as part of the Intercosmos program in collaboration with Czechoslovakia. Prognoz-10, which had the same dimensions as the preceding Prognoz, studied the shock wave generated by the solar wind when it encounters the Earth's magnetosphere.

Launching and orbital data - Prognoz-10 was launched April 26, 1985 from Baikonur-Tyuratam into an elliptical orbit with an apogee of 200,000km (124,260mi) and an inclination to the equator of 65°.

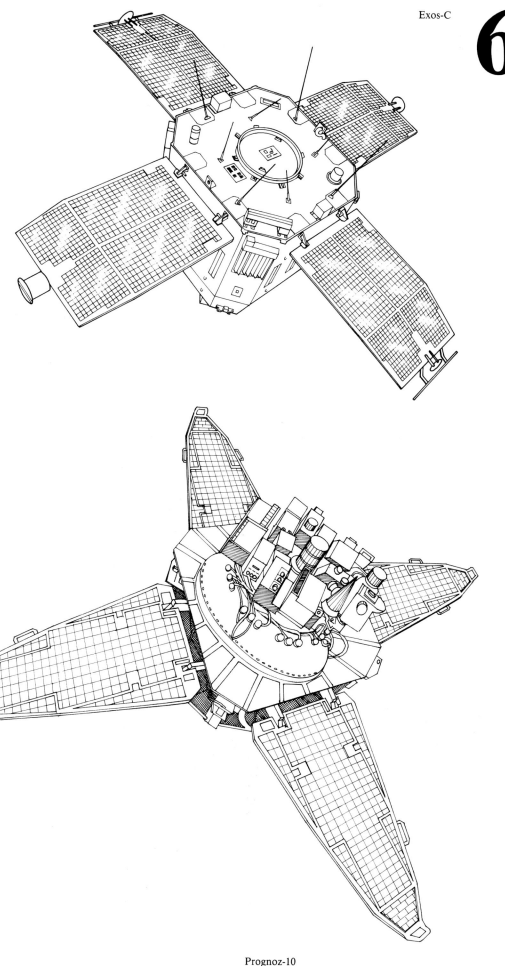

Prognoz-10

155

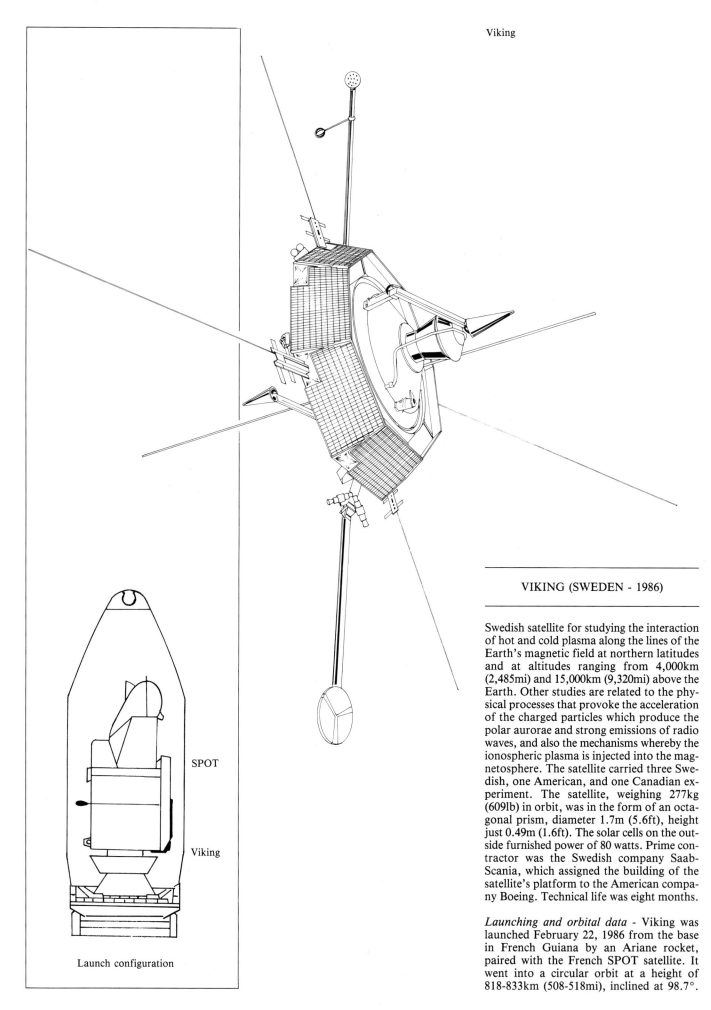

Launch configuration

SPOT

Viking

VIKING (SWEDEN - 1986)

Swedish satellite for studying the interaction of hot and cold plasma along the lines of the Earth's magnetic field at northern latitudes and at altitudes ranging from 4,000km (2,485mi) and 15,000km (9,320mi) above the Earth. Other studies are related to the physical processes that provoke the acceleration of the charged particles which produce the polar aurorae and strong emissions of radio waves, and also the mechanisms whereby the ionospheric plasma is injected into the magnetosphere. The satellite carried three Swedish, one American, and one Canadian experiment. The satellite, weighing 277kg (609lb) in orbit, was in the form of an octagonal prism, diameter 1.7m (5.6ft), height just 0.49m (1.6ft). The solar cells on the outside furnished power of 80 watts. Prime contractor was the Swedish company Saab-Scania, which assigned the building of the satellite's platform to the American company Boeing. Technical life was eight months.

Launching and orbital data - Viking was launched February 22, 1986 from the base in French Guiana by an Ariane rocket, paired with the French SPOT satellite. It went into a circular orbit at a height of 818-833km (508-518mi), inclined at 98.7°.

VANGUARD-3 (USA - 1959)

Magnesium sphere with a diameter of 0.508m (1.65ft), equipped with sensors for the detection of micrometeorites, a magnetometer attached to an external arm 0.66m (2.2ft) long, and an ionization camera for measuring X-rays. Spin-stabilized, orbital weight 45kg (99lb). The satellite was developed by the Naval Research Laboratory.

Launching and orbital data - Vanguard-3 was launched September 18, 1959 from Cape Canaveral by a rocket also named Vanguard and sent into an orbit with a perigee of 512km (318mi), an apogee of 3,744km (2,326mi) and an inclination of 33.35°.

EXPLORER-7/-11/-23/-30/-37/-38/-42/ -44/-48/-49/-53 (USA -1959)

The group of Explorer satellites was designed by NASA for astronomical studies. Explorer-7 had the shape of two conical sections joined at the base, diameter 0.76m (2.5ft), overall height 0.76m (2.5ft), weight 41.5kg (91.3lb). It studied X-rays emitted by the Sun and their influence on the Earth's ionosphere, it identified the heavy particles constituting cosmic rays, and it measured the heat emitted by the Earth. Explorer-11 was in the form of an octagonal-based prism 0.6m (2ft) high, with a diameter of 0.3m (1ft) and a weight of 37kg (81.4lb). It was the first satellite designed to detect high-energy gamma rays. The information gathered by the satellite led to the abandonment of the steady-state theory of the Universe which envisaged a continuous generation of matter and antimatter. Explorer-23 was cylindrical in shape with a diameter of 0.6m (2ft), a height of 2.3m (7.5ft) and a weight of 133kg (293lb), being designed for the detection of micrometeorites. Explorer-30/Solrad-1 took the form of a sphere 0.6m (2ft) in diameter and weighing 57kg (125lb). It was launched as part of the IQSY (International Year of the Quiet Sun) to measure solar X-rays. Explorer-37/Solrad-2 was in the shape of a dodecahedron 0.69m (2.3ft) high, with a diameter of 0.76m (2.5ft) and a weight of 90kg (198lb). It studied solar X-rays. Explorer-38/-49 (RAE-1/-2, Radio Astrono-

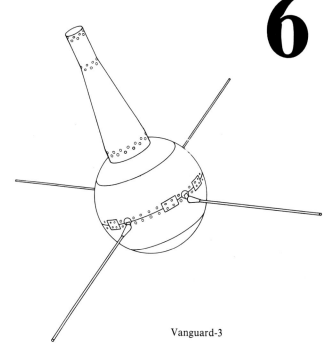

Vanguard-3

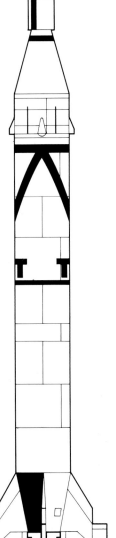

Juno II

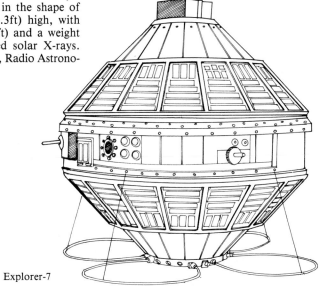

Explorer-7

my Explorer) were two satellites with a cylindrical central section 0.79m (2.6ft) high and 0.92m (3ft) wide. Four panels of solar cells 1.5m (5ft) long generated power of 38.5 watts. Weight in orbit was 200kg (440lb). The onboard equipment studied low-frequency radio emissions from the Sun, the planets (including Earth) and other cosmic sources. Explorer-42/-48/-53 (SAS-1/-2/-3) were three satellites built for the Goddard Space Flight Center, cylindrical in shape, with a maximum diameter of 0.55m (1.8ft), a height of 1.29m (4.2ft) and an orbital weight of 186kg (409lb). Four panels of solar cells protruded from the central section. SAS-1, also known as Uhuru (Freedom), compiled the first X-ray map of the sky, identifying 200 sources. SAS-2 detected the sources of gamma rays, and SAS-3 X-rays. Explorer-44/Solrad-3 was almost cylindrical, with twelve faces, diameter 0.76m (2.5ft), height 0.58m (1.9ft), orbital weight 118kg (260lb). Its function was to measure X-rays and ultraviolet rays emitted by the Sun.

Launching and orbital data - Explorer-7 was launched October 13, 1959 from Cape Canaveral by a Juno II rocket and sent into an orbit with a perigee of 556km (350mi), an apogee of 1,088km (666mi), and an inclination of 50.31°.

Explorer-11 was launched April 27, 1961 from Cape Canaveral by a Juno II rocket and sent into an orbit with a perigee of 487km (302mi), an apogee of 1,779km (1,105mi), and an inclination of 28.8°.

Explorer-23 was launched November 6, 1964 from Vandenberg by a Scout rocket and sent into an orbit with a perigee of 466km (290mi), an apogee of 977km (607mi), and an inclination of 51.95°.

Explorer-30 and Explorer-37 were launched November 19, 1965 and March 5, 1968 from Vandenberg by Scout rockets.

Explorer-38 was launched July 4, 1968 from Vandenberg by a Delta rocket. Explorer-49 was launched June 10, 1973 from Cape Canaveral into an orbit around the Moon.

Explorer-42 was launched December 10, 1970 into a near-circular orbit 522-533km (324-331mi) high.

Explorer-48 was launched November 16, 1972 into an orbit with a perigee of 444km (275mi), an apogee of 632km (393mi) and an inclination of 1.9°. Explorer-53 was launched May 7, 1975 and its orbit was 499-508km (310-315mi) high with an inclination of 2.9°.

Explorer-42/-48/-53 were launched from the Italian San Marco base in the Indian Ocean by Scout rockets.

Explorer-44 was launched July 8, 1971 from Vandenberg by a Scout rocket into an orbit with a perigee of 433km (269mi), an apogee of 632km (393mi) and an inclination of 51°.

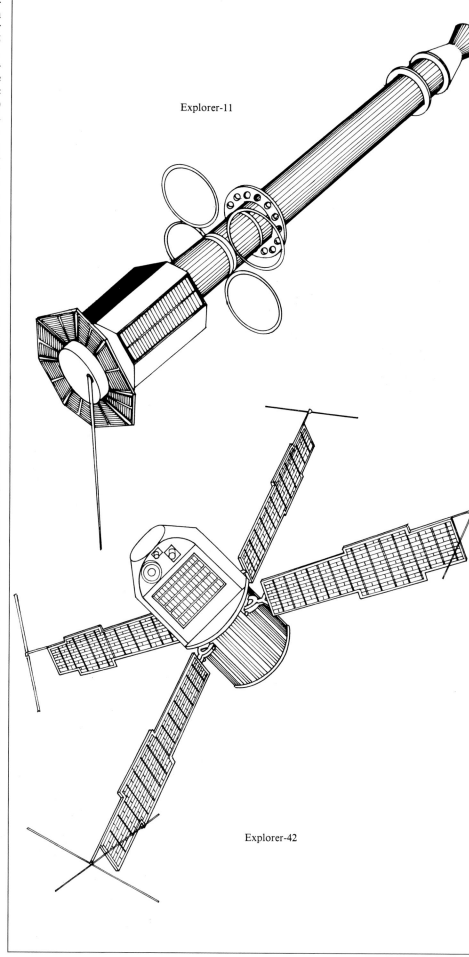

Explorer-11

Explorer-42

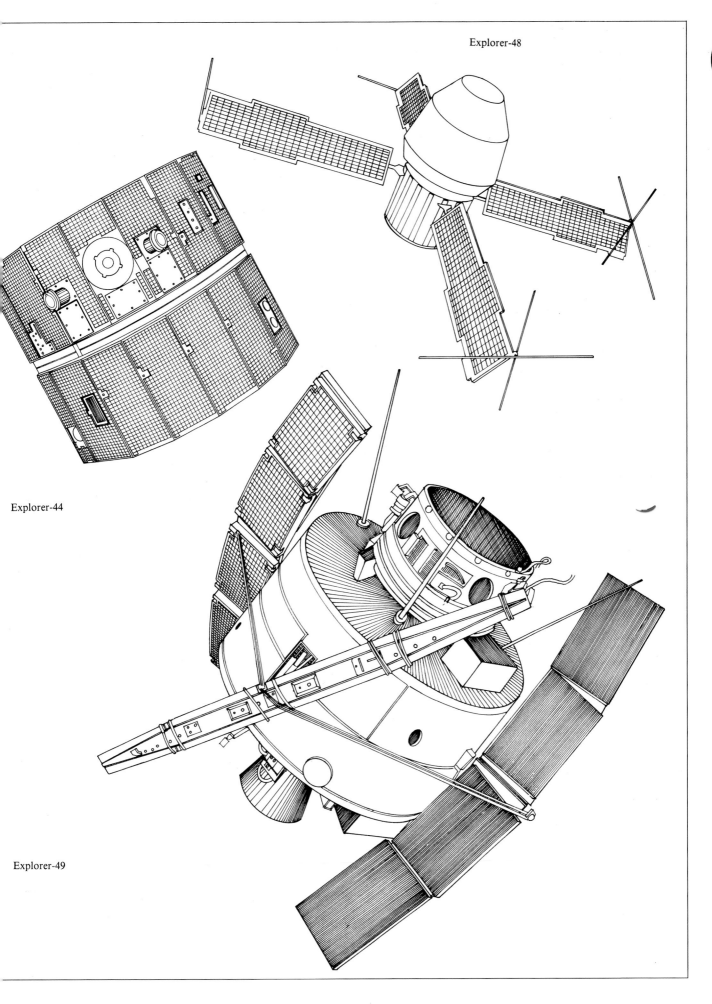

Explorer-48

Explorer-44

Explorer-49

6

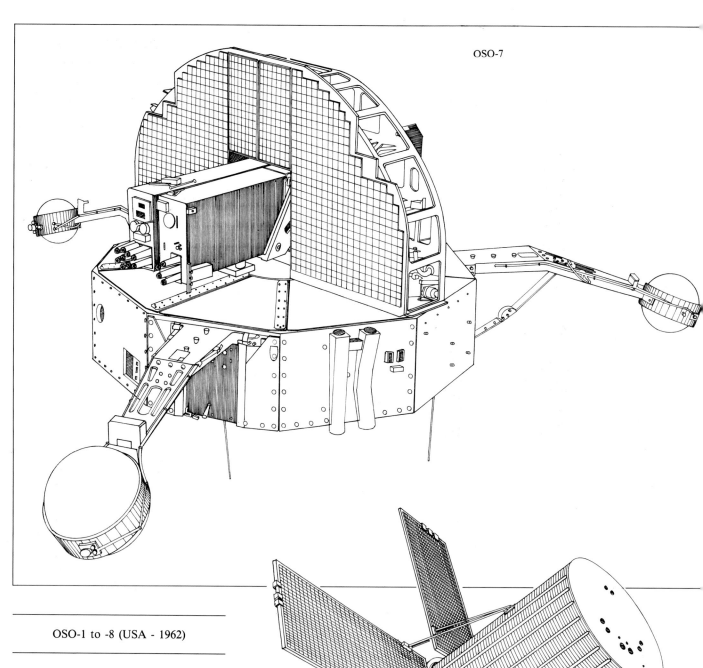

OSO-1 to -8 (USA - 1962)

Group of eight satellites built by Ball Aerospace for the Goddard Space Flight Center of NASA for the purpose of carrying out repeated observations of the Sun, for the study of solar physics and for the investigation of a broad spectrum of radiations emitted by the Sun. The first seven satellites were made up of two modules: the first was a nine-sided prism, diameter 1.12m (3.6ft), height 0.23m (0.75ft), and the second an almost semicircular panel of solar cells generating power of 38 watts, containing several instruments, and with a height of 0.71m (2.3ft). The total height of the satellite was 0.94m (3.1ft). The weight varied according to instruments carried from 207kg (455lb) for OSO-1, to 270kg (594lb) for OSO-4, and to 634kg (1,395lb) for OSO-7. The basic platform rotated so that the satellite was spin-stabilized, while the vertical panel remained fixed and pointed toward the Sun. OSO-8 was built along the same lines but its dimensions were different. The basic platform was cylindrical with a diameter of 1.52m (5ft) and a height of 0.72m (2.4ft).

OSO-1

160

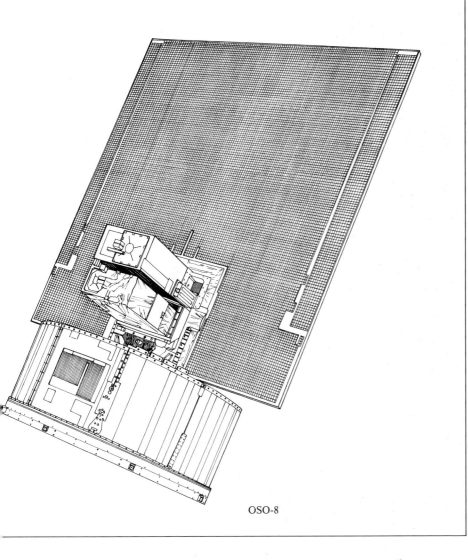

OSO-8

COSMOS (USSR-1962)

The Soviet Union launched numerous satellites under this name which carried instruments for astronomical observation. Among the first was Cosmos-7, cylindrical and spherical in shape, with a length of 4.3m (14.1ft) and a diameter of 2.4m (7.9ft). The weight was about 4,500kg (9,900lb). Other Cosmos satellites designed for astronomical research included numbers 8, 51, 163, 166, 208, 215, 230, 251, 262, 264, 461, 484, 490 and 561.

Launching and orbital data - Cosmos-7 was launched July 28, 1962 from Baikonur-Tyuratam by an A-1 rocket and sent into an orbit with a perigee of 197km (122mi), an apogee of 356km (221mi) and an inclination of 64.95°.

PEGASUS (USA - 1965)

Satellites derived from the second S-IVB stage of the Saturn-1 rocket to study the problem of meteoric impacts, with a view to taking these into account when designing the Apollo spacecraft for the journey to the Moon. The second stage had been furnished with two extensible wings each 15m (49.2ft) long and 4.6m (15.1ft) wide, which opened in orbit within 60 seconds. The central section of the vehicle was 29.2m (95.8ft) long and had a diameter of 4.3m (14.1ft). The two wings accommodated 208 panels formed of extremely thin sheets of aluminum, polyurethane, mylar and copper, which registered the impact of meteorites. Perforation by a meteorite caused a short-circuit. The system made it possible to determine the fall frequency and dimensions of meteorites ca-

The vertical panel of solar cells generating power of 110 watts was rectangular and measured 2.34m (7.7ft) in height and 2.09m (6.85ft) in width. The weight was 1,063kg (2,339lb). The onboard experiments were designed to study X-rays, gamma rays, ultraviolet rays and infrared rays emitted by the Sun and to observe certain regions of the sky within and without our galaxy.

Launching and orbital data - OSO-1 was launched March 7, 1962 and sent into a near-circular orbit 553-595km (344-370mi) high. OSO-2 was launched February 3, 1965 into an orbit 533-600km (331-373mi) high. OSO-3 was launched March 8, 1967 into an orbit 510-533km (317-331mi) high. OSO-4 was launched October 18, 1967 and its orbit was 525-557km (326-346mi) high. OSO-5 was launched January 22, 1969 into an orbit 530-550km (329-342mi) high. OSO-6 was launched August 9, 1969 into an orbit 489-551km (304-342mi) high. OSO-7 was launched September 29, 1971, its orbit being 327-564km (203-350mi) high; and OSO-8 on June 21, 1975 into an orbit 544-556km (338-345mi) high. All launchings were from Cape Canaveral by Delta rockets, and the orbital inclination to the equator was 33°.

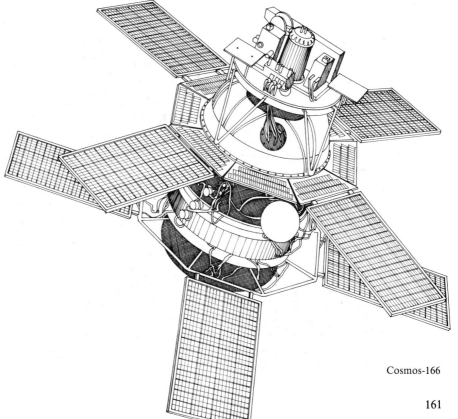

Cosmos-166

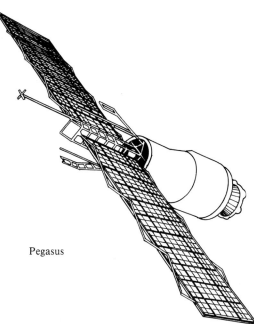

Pegasus

pable of damaging the spacecraft, the direction of fall and the strength of impact. Several panels of solar cells for providing the necessary power to the instruments were also attached to the two wings. The orbital weight of the whole vehicle was about 10.5 tonnes.

Launching and orbital data - Pegasus-1 was launched February 16, 1965 from Cape Canaveral and sent into an orbit with a perigee of 495km (308mi), an apogee of 733km (455mi) and an inclination of 31.73°. Pegasus-2 was launched May 25, 1965 into an orbit with a perigee of 502km (312mi), an apogee of 740km (460mi) and an inclination of 31.73°. Pegasus-3 was launched July 30, 1965, its near-circular orbit being 535-567km (332-352mi) and its inclination 28.8°.

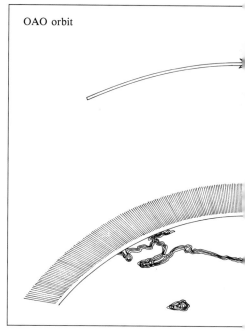

OAO orbit

OAO (USA - 1968)

NASA launched four Orbiting Astronomical Observatories (OAO), but only two functioned properly in orbit: OAO-2 and OAO-3 Copernicus. The two satellites had a central section in the shape of an octagonal prism 2.03m (6.6ft) wide and 3.05m (10ft) high, for OAO-2, and 5.92m (19.4ft) high for OAO-3. Weight in orbit was 2,012kg (4,426lb) and 2,223kg (4,891lb) respectively. The three-axis stabilized satellites had two panels of solar cells furnishing power of 1,600 watts. OAO-2 carried four photometers prepared by the University of Wisconsin and four telescopes of 0.31m (1ft) diameter prepared by the Smithsonian Astrophysical Observatory. The principal instrument carried by OAO-3, known as the Princeton Experiment Package, was an ultraviolet telescope 3m (9.8ft) long, with a mirror of 0.82m (2.7ft). On board were three additional small telescopes and a collimator for X-rays designed by University College, London. The two satellites, built by Grumman, studied interstellar gas, ultraviolet rays emitted by young and hot stars, and new sources of X-rays.

Launching and orbital data - OAO-2 was launched December 7, 1968 into a near-circular orbit 765-778km (475-483mi) high, inclined at 35°. OAO-3 was launched August 21, 1972 and placed in a near-circular orbit 736-744km (457-462mi) high, inclined at 35°. Both were launched from Cape Canaveral by Atlas Centaur rockets.

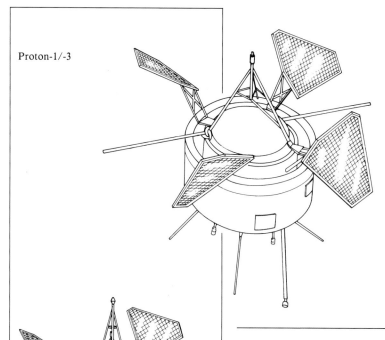

Proton-1/-3

Proton-4

PROTON (USSR - 1965)

Group of four Soviet satellites devoted to the study of high-energy cosmic rays, gamma rays and electrons of galactic origin. Cylindrical in shape, with a diameter of about 4m (13.1ft) and a height of 3m (9.8ft), it weighed 12.2 tonnes, of which 3.5 tonnes were scientific instruments. Proton-4 was the heaviest (17 tonnes), its scientific instruments weighing 12.5 tonnes.

Launching and orbital data - Proton-1 was launched July 16, 1965 from Baikonur-Tyuratam by a D rocket also known as Proton and sent into an orbit with a perigee of 183km (114mi), an apogee of 589km (366mi) and an inclination of 63.44°. The other launchings took place on November 2, 1965 (P-2), July 6, 1966 (P-3) and November 16, 1968 (P-4).

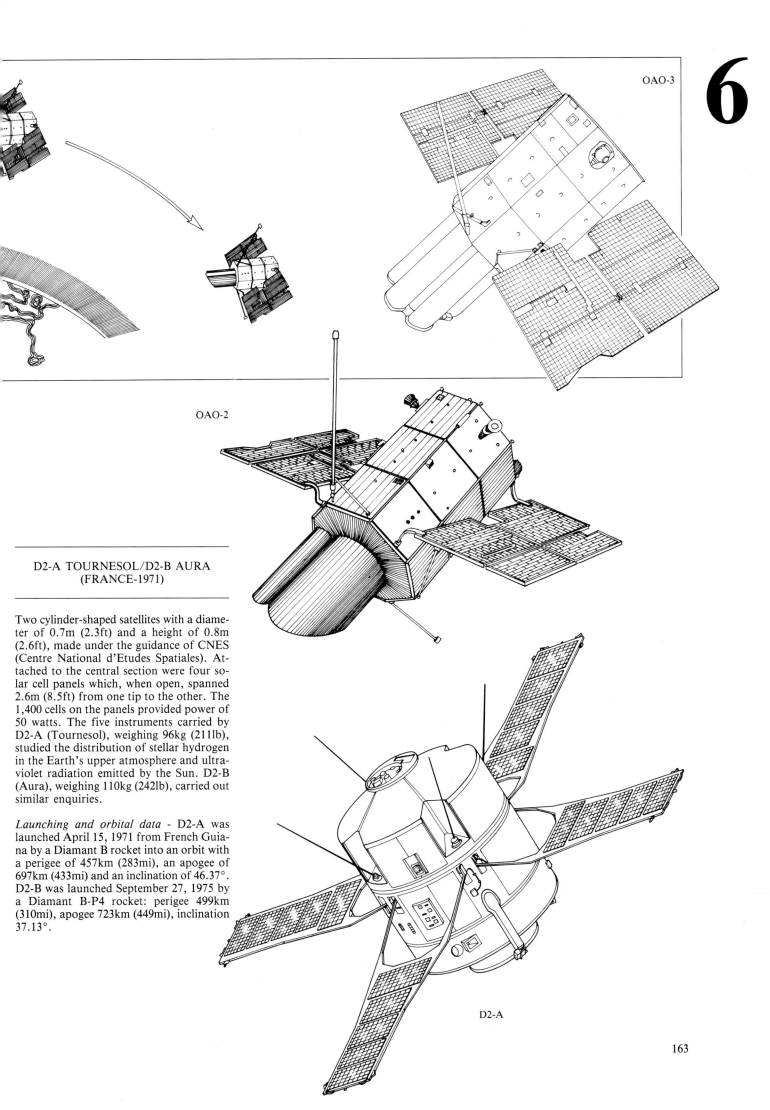

OAO-2

D2-A TOURNESOL/D2-B AURA
(FRANCE-1971)

Two cylinder-shaped satellites with a diameter of 0.7m (2.3ft) and a height of 0.8m (2.6ft), made under the guidance of CNES (Centre National d'Etudes Spatiales). Attached to the central section were four solar cell panels which, when open, spanned 2.6m (8.5ft) from one tip to the other. The 1,400 cells on the panels provided power of 50 watts. The five instruments carried by D2-A (Tournesol), weighing 96kg (211lb), studied the distribution of stellar hydrogen in the Earth's upper atmosphere and ultraviolet radiation emitted by the Sun. D2-B (Aura), weighing 110kg (242lb), carried out similar enquiries.

Launching and orbital data - D2-A was launched April 15, 1971 from French Guiana by a Diamant B rocket into an orbit with a perigee of 457km (283mi), an apogee of 697km (433mi) and an inclination of 46.37°. D2-B was launched September 27, 1975 by a Diamant B-P4 rocket: perigee 499km (310mi), apogee 723km (449mi), inclination 37.13°.

D2-A

TD-1A (EUROPE-1972)

The first ESRO's satellite. It was in the form of a square-based prism 1×0.9m (3.2×2.9ft), 2.16m (7ft) high. The three-axis stabilized satellite had two panels of solar cells at the sides which spanned 4.55m (14.9ft), furnishing power of 330 watts. Prime contractor was the French Matra. The seven instruments onboard carried out enquires on ultraviolet radiations, X-rays and gamma rays. TD-1A came to an end May 1974.

Launching and orbital data - TD-1A was launched March 12, 1972 from Vandenberg by a Delta rocket and sent into a near-circular orbit 533-545km (331-339mi) high and inclined at 97.6°.

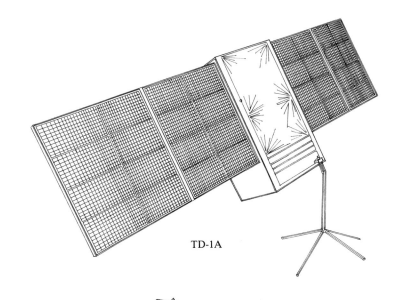

TD-1A

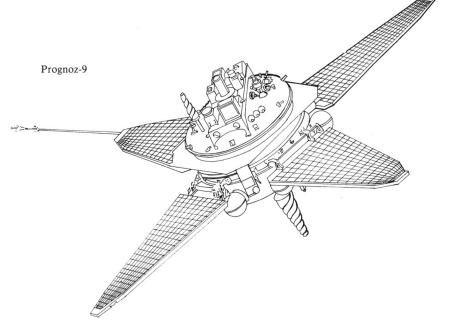

Prognoz-9

ANS (HOLLAND - 1974)

The Astronomical Netherlands Satellite (ANS) was built by a consortium of which the prime contractor was Phillips/Fokker VFW. The central box-shaped section measured 0.73x0.61m (2.4x2ft) at the base and was 1.23m (4ft) in height. Two panels of solar cells at the sides spanned 1.44m (4.7ft). The weight in orbit was 123kg (271lb), it was three-axis stabilized, and its technical life was six months. Instruments on board for carrying out three types of experiment were a detector of hard X-rays, supplied by the United States, a detector of soft X-rays, and a Cassengrain telescope for observing ultraviolet radiations from hot, young stars.

Launching and orbital data - ANS-1 was launched August 30, 1974 from the American base at Vandenberg by a Scout rocket. Because of a launcher failure, however, the

PROGNOZ-1 to -9 (USSR - 1972)

Series of Soviet satellites designed for studying the Sun. Prognoz-9, however, carried instruments for research on cosmic radiation in relation to microwaves. Among them was a small telescope for investigating the intensity of this radiation with a wavelength of 8 millimeters. The Prognoz satellites had a central section with a diameter of 1.8m (5.9ft) and a weight of 845kg (1,859lb).
Launching and orbital data - Prognoz-1 was launched April 14, 1972 from Baikonur-Tyuratam by an A-2 rocket and placed in an orbit with a perigee of 224km (139mi), an apogee of 446km (277mi) and an inclination of 64.92°. The other Prognoz satellites were launched as follows: February 15, 1973 (P-3); December 22, 1975 (P-4); November 25, 1976 (P-5); September 22, 1977 (P-6); October 30, 1978 (P-7); December 25, 1980 (P-8) and July 1, 1983 (P-9). Prognoz-9 was placed in an orbit with a perigee of 380km (236mi), an apogee of 720,000km (447,000mi) and an inclination of 65.5°.

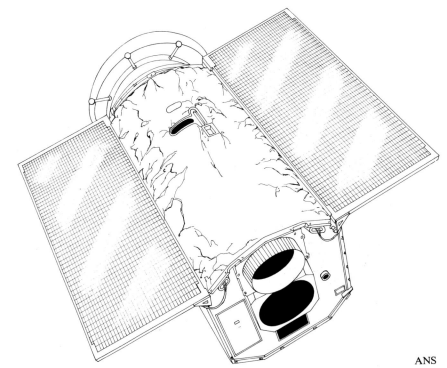

ANS

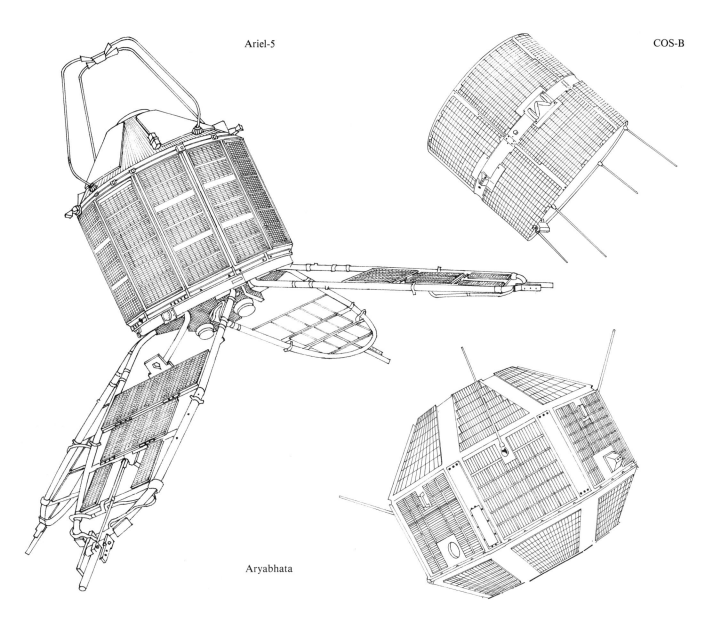

Aryabhata

satellite did not reach its programed orbit, but was placed in an elliptical orbit with a perigee of 258km (160mi), an apogee of 1,173km (729mi) and an inclination of 98.03°.

ARIEL-5/UK-5 (GREAT BRITAIN - 1974)

This satellite, also called UK-5, was almost cylindrical, with a diameter of 0.96m (3.15ft), a height of 0.86m (2.8ft) and an orbital weight of 134kg (295lb). Power was provided by solar cells on the outside of the satellite. There were six onboard experiments, two furnished by the United States, and all related to X-ray astronomy. Spin-stabilized, it fell out in the atmosphere in March 1980. The prime building contractor was the British company Marconi Space and Defense Systems Ltd.

Launching and orbital data - Ariel-5 was launched October 15, 1974 from the Italian base of San Marco in the Indian Ocean off the coast of Kenya by a Scout rocket, and

was placed in a near-circular equatorial orbit 504-549km (313-341mi) high, with an inclination of 2.88°.

ARYABHATA (INDIA - 1975)

The first Indian satellite was launched to test a series of technological procedures and also to conduct three experiments in the fields of X-ray astronomy, solar physics and aeronomics (high-altitude physical phenomena). The satellite was in the form of an almost spherical polyhedron with 26 faces, its diameter being 1.55m (5.1ft) and its height 1.19m (3.9ft). Its weight was 358kg (788lb) and the solar cells covering the outside provided power of 46 watts. The satellite's operations were controlled by the Indian Space Research Organization (ISRO). The three scientific experiments functioned only for one week although the satellite remained active until March 1981.

Launching and orbital data - Aryabhata was launched April 19, 1975 from the Soviet base

of Kapustin Yar by a C-1 rocket and was sent into a near-circular orbit at a height of 562-619km (349-385mi), inclined at 50.7°.

COS-B (EUROPE - 1975)

Scientific satellite of the European Space Agency which remained active for six years and eight months, carrying out observations on the sources of gamma rays. The only instrument carried on board was a telescope for surveying celestial gamma rays with energy superior to 20 MeV (millions of electron volts). The satellite was cylindrical in shape, 1.2m (3.9ft) high, with a diameter of 1.4m (4.6ft). The external solar cells furnished power of 135 watts. Spin-stabilized, it weighed 280kg (616lb). Prime contractor in its construction was the German MBB company, and the control center was the European Space Operation Center of the ESA at Darmstadt.

Launching and orbital data - COS-B was launched August 9, 1975 from Vandenberg

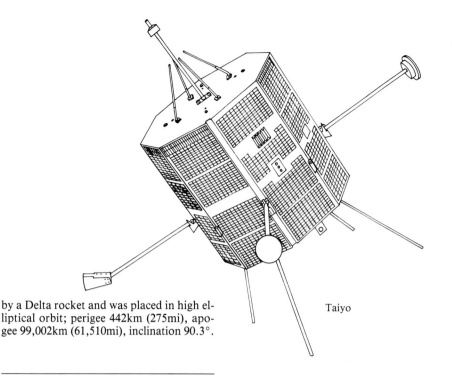

Taiyo

by a Delta rocket and was placed in high elliptical orbit; perigee 442km (275mi), apogee 99,002km (61,510mi), inclination 90.3°.

TAIYO/SRATS (JAPAN - 1975)

Satellite weighing 86kg (189lb) developed by the Institute of Space and Aeronautical Science (ISAS) of the University of Tokyo. In the shape of an octagonal prism, its diameter was 0.75m (2.5ft) and its height 0.7m (2.3ft). It was spin-stabilized. Prime building contractor was the NEC company. The satellite studied the interaction of solar radiation and its particles in the magnetosphere, thermosphere and mesosphere, it examined solar X-rays and solar radiation in the extreme ultraviolet range, and it measured the density and temperature of electrons and ions. SRATS (Solar Radiation and Thermospheric Structure Satellite) was covered on the outside with 5,200 solar cells which provided power of 30 watts.

Launching and orbital data - Taiyo (meaning Sun) was launched February 24, 1975 from Kagoshima Space Center by a M-3C-2 rocket and was placed in an orbit with a perigee of 260km (162mi), an apogee of 3,140km (1,951mi) and an inclination of 32°.

HEAO (USA - 1977)

Three satellites built by TRW as prime contractor and directed by the Marshall Space Flight Center. The three HEAO (High Energy Astronomical Observatories) were formed of a standard hexagonal prism-shaped module 2.4m (7.9ft) wide and 5.8m (19ft) high. Each satellite weighed 3,150kg (6,930lb), 1,350kg (2,970lb) of which were represented by experiments. HEAO-1 and -2, the latter called Einstein, studied the X-rays sources. HEAO-1 drew a map with 1,500 X-ray sources. HEAO-3 was concerned with the detection of gamma radiation and of cosmic rays.

Launching and orbital data - HEAO-1 was launched August 12, 1977 and placed in a near-circular orbit at a height of 428-447km (266-278mi), inclined at 22.76°. HEAO-2 was launched November 13, 1978 into a near-circular orbit at a height of 520-541km (323-336mi), inclined at 23.51°. HEAO-3 was launched September 20, 1979 and placed in a near-circular orbit at a height of 485-501km (301-311mi), inclined at 43.61°. All three satellites were launched by Atlas Centaur rockets from Cape Canaveral.

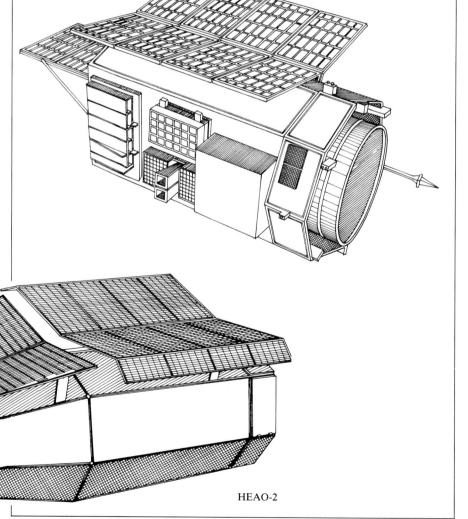

HEAO-1

HEAO-2

SIGNE-3 (FRANCE - 1977)

Satellite built as part of a collaboration with the Soviet Union for observations in the field of galactic and extragalactic X-rays and gamma rays. The body was cylindrical with a diameter of 0.7m (2.3ft) and a height of 0.8m (2.6ft). Weight in orbit was 102kg (224lb). Four panels of solar cells furnished power of 50 watts.

Launching and orbital data - Signe-3 was launched June 17, 1977 from Kapustin Yar site by a C-1 rocket and was placed in an orbit with a perigee of 459km (285mi), an apogee of 519km (322mi) and an inclination of 50.67°.

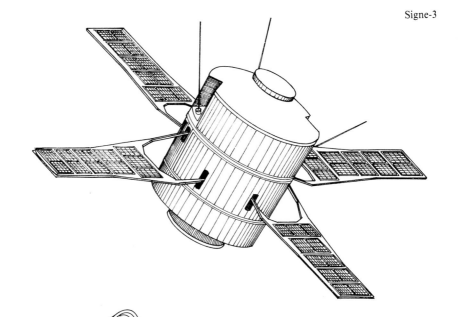

IUE

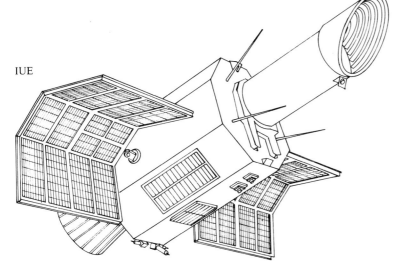

ARIEL-6/UK-6 (GREAT BRITAIN - 1979)

Satellite also called UK-6, shaped like a cylinder terminating in a hemisphere, with a diameter of 0.96m (3.15ft) and a height of 1.3m (4.3ft). Spin-stabilized, its orbital weight was 154kg (339lb). The four external panels of solar cells furnished power of 72 watts. On board were two experiments for X-rays and one for the study of cosmic rays built in collaboration with the United States.

Launching and orbital data - Ariel-6 was launched June 3, 1979 from Wallops Island by a Scout rocket and placed in a near-circular orbit at a height of 600-654km (373-406mi), inclined at 55.03°.

IUE (USA/EUROPE - 1978)

Satellite for ultraviolet astronomy built in collaboration by the European Space Agency and NASA. International Ultraviolet Explorer (IUE) weighed 382kg (840lb) in orbit and carried a Ritchey Chrétien telescope with an 0.45m (1.47ft) aperture, used exclusively for ultraviolet spectometry. The octagonal prism-shaped body was 1.3m (4.3ft) wide and the total height of the satellite was 4.3m (14.1ft). Two panels of solar cells furnished power of 150 watts. Prime contractor was the NASA's Goddard Space Flight Center.

Launching and orbital data - IUE was launched January 26, 1978 from Cape Canaveral by a Delta rocket and sent into an orbit 25,699km (15,951mi) at the perigee and 46,081km (28,630mi) at the apogee. The orbital inclination was 28.71°.

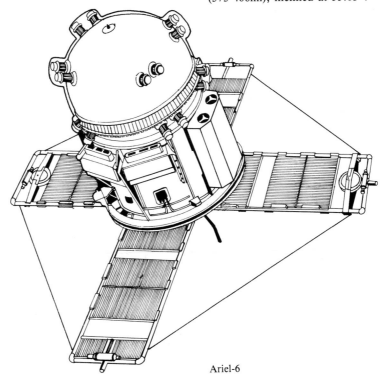

Ariel-6

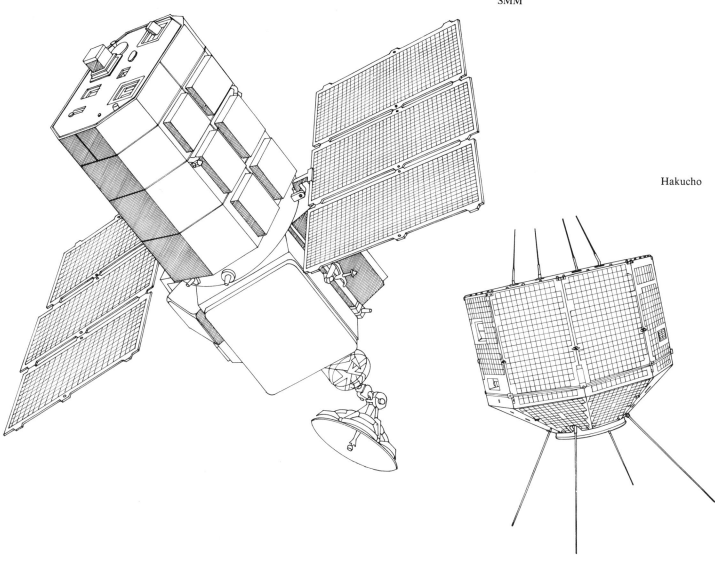

Hakucho

HAKUCHO/CORSA-B (JAPAN - 1979)

Satellite weighing 96kg (211lb) and designed by ISAS for studying X-rays from the stars and other points in the Universe. Corsa (Cosmic Radiation Satellite), spin-stabilized, was in the form of an octagonal prism 0.65m (2.1ft) high and 0.8m (2.6ft) in diameter. Prime contractor was the NEC company.

Launching and orbital data - Hakucho was launched February 21, 1979 from Kagoshima Space Center by a M-3C-4 rocket and placed in a near-circular orbit at a height of 550-580km (1,210-1,276mi), inclined at 30°.

SMM (USA - 1980)

The Solar Maximum Mission (SMM) was a NASA satellite carrying on board seven instruments for observing the Sun in different wavelengths: ultraviolet, infrared, X-ray and gamma ray. The satellite was 4m (13.1ft) high and 1.2m (3.9ft) wide. Two panels of solar cells provided power of 3,000 watts. The total weight was 2,315kg (5,093lb). SMM, managed in orbit by the Goddard Space Flight Center of NASA, developed a fault in the attitude control system in December 1980. A second fault affected a scientific instrument, the coronagraph-polarimeter. In April 1984, during the eleventh Shuttle mission of the spacecraft *Challenger*, the astronauts James von Hoften and George Nelson repaired both faults and enabled the satellite to resume functioning.

Launching and orbital data - SMM was launched February 14, 1980 from Cape Canaveral by a Delta rocket and placed in a high circular orbit at 566-569km (351-353mi), inclined at 28.5°.

HINOTORI/ASTRO-A (JAPAN - 1981)

Satellite designed by the Institute of Space and Astronautical Science (ISAS) for studying solar flares in the X-ray wavelengths, also taking pictures. During the life of the satellite 500 solar flares were inve-stigated. Hinotori was in the shape of an octagonal prism. It was spin-stabilized and weighed 188kg (414lb). Prime contractor was the NEC company.

Launching and orbital data - Hinotori was launched February 21, 1981 from Kagoshima Space Center by a M-3S-2 rocket and sent into a near-circular high orbit at 580-640km (360-398mi), with an inclination of 31°.

TENMA/ASTRO-B (JAPAN - 1983)

Tenma (also called Astro-B) was a satellite designed by the ISAS for studying X-rays emitted by the stars, galaxies and nebulae. The satellite weighed 216kg (475lb). Prime contractor was the NEC company.

Launching and orbital data - Tenma was launched February 20, 1983 from Kagoshima Space Center by a M-3S-3 rocket and sent into an orbit with a perigee of 450km (280mi), an apogee of 570km (354mi) and an inclination of 31.8°.

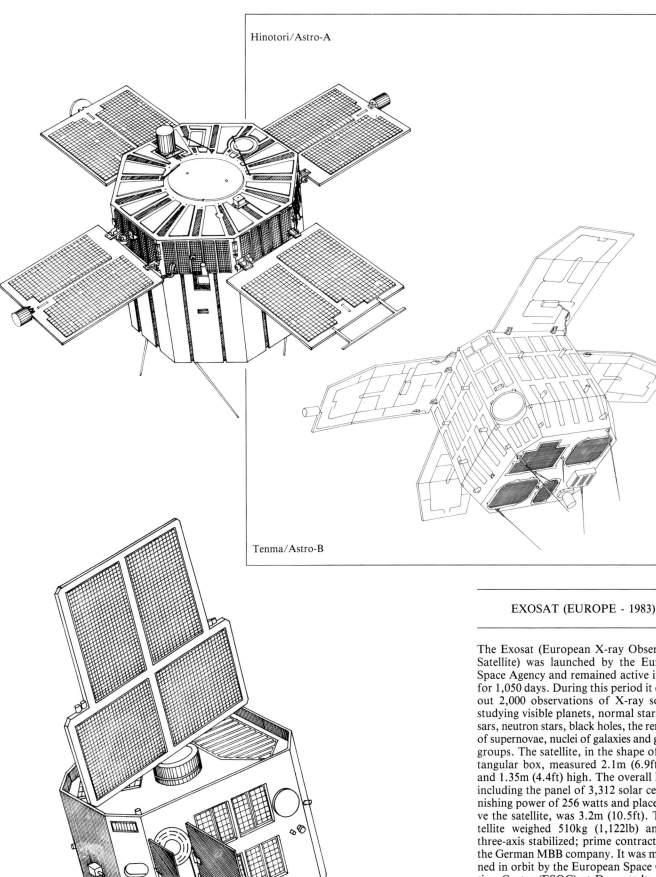

Hinotori/Astro-A

Tenma/Astro-B

Exosat

EXOSAT (EUROPE - 1983)

The Exosat (European X-ray Observatory Satellite) was launched by the European Space Agency and remained active in orbit for 1,050 days. During this period it carried out 2,000 observations of X-ray sources, studying visible planets, normal stars, quasars, neutron stars, black holes, the renmants of supernovae, nuclei of galaxies and galactic groups. The satellite, in the shape of a rectangular box, measured 2.1m (6.9ft) wide and 1.35m (4.4ft) high. The overall height, including the panel of 3,312 solar cells furnishing power of 256 watts and placed above the satellite, was 3.2m (10.5ft). The satellite weighed 510kg (1,122lb) and was three-axis stabilized; prime contractor was the German MBB company. It was maintained in orbit by the European Space Operation Center (ESOC) at Darmstadt.

Launching and orbital data - Exosat was launched May 26, 1983 from Vandenberg by a Delta 3914 rocket and placed in a markedly elliptical orbit with a perigee of 356km (221mi), an apogee of 191,581 km (119,030 mi), and an inclination of 72.5°.

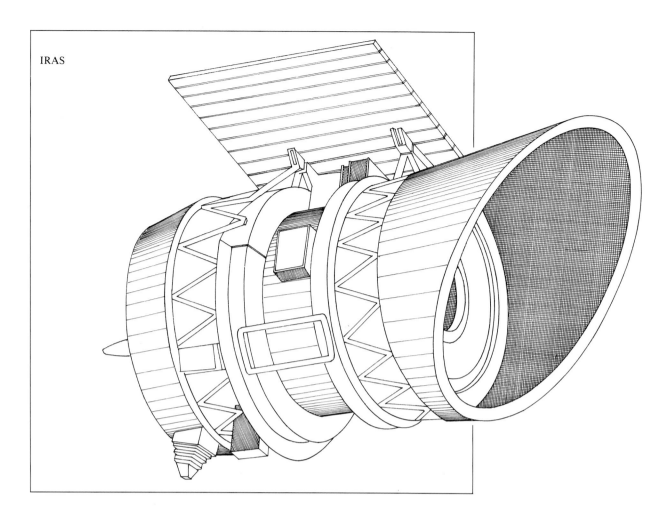

IRAS

IRAS (USA/HOLLAND/ GREAT BRITAIN - 1983)

Satellite developed jointly by NASA, the Netherlands Agency for Aerospace Programs and the British Science and Engineering Research Council. Infrared Astronomical Satellite (IRAS) was built by the Dutch industrial consortium Iciras and various American companies (Ball Aerospace, Perkin Elmer and Rockwell). IRAS was cylindrical, 3.6m (11.8ft) high, and the panels of 4,816 solar cells, furnishing power of 250 watts, measured 3.24m (10.6ft) when fully extended. The satellite carried a Ritchey-Chrétien telescope with an aperture of 0.57m (1.87ft) for studying sources of infrared radiation at wavelengths from 8 to 119 microns. The 62 infrared detectors were cooled by means of a store of 475 liters of liquid helium, which maintained the temperature of the equipment at 2° Kelvin (-270°C). The launch weight of the three-axis-stabilized satellite was 1,076kg (2,367lb). Other instruments were a low-resolution spectrometer and two additional infrared detectors at different wavelengths. IRAS remained operational for a year, detecting 250,000 sources of infrared radiation and discovering other things: unidentified cold objects, a ring of dust around the solar system, dust clouds (infrared cirrus) formed by graphite particles in interstellar space, five comets and also the existence of another solar system in formation around the star Vega.

Launching and orbital data - IRAS was launched January 26, 1983 from Vandenberg by a Delta rocket and placed in a near-circular orbit 896-913 km (557-567mi) high, inclined at 99.1°.

ASTRON (USSR - 1983)

Satellite equipped with a telescope (developed with French collaboration) designed to observe galactic and extragalactic radiations in the ultraviolet (0.1-0.35 microns) wavelength range, and an X-rays spectrometer-telescope SKR-02M (with photon energy of 2-25 KeV). The basic module of the satellite, weighing 3,250kg (7,150lb), was that of the Venus probe.

Launching and orbital data - Astron was launched March 23, 1983 from Baikonur-Tyuratam by a D-1-e rocket and placed in an orbit with a perigee of 2,000km (1,243mi), an apogee of 200,000km (124,260mi), inclined at 51.5°.

GAMMA-1 (USSR - 1987)

Satellite designed in collaboration with French and Polish scientists for studying the sources of gamma radiations. It uses a vehicle of the Progress type derived from the

Soyuz manned spacecraft. On board is a telescope for detecting gamma rays, and above this is an optical television Telezvezda telescope. The overall weight of the equipment is 1,500kg (3,300lb).

Launching and orbital data - The launch of Gamma-1 is scheduled for 1987.

SPACE TELESCOPE "HUBBLE" (USA/EUROPE - 1988)

Large orbital telescope designed by NASA together with the ESA (European Space Agency). With a cylindrical dome 4.26m (14ft) in diameter and 13.1m (43ft) long, the orbital weight is 11 tonnes. The Ritchey-Chrétien telescope has a primary mirror with a diameter of 2.4m (7.9ft) and a secondary mirror of 0.3m (1ft). There are six scientific instruments on board: Wide Field/Planetary Camera, Faint Object Spectrograph, High Resolution Spectrograph, High Speed Photometer/Polarimeter, Faint Object Camera, and Fine Guide Sensor. The European Space Agency is building the Faint Object Camera and the two panels of solar cells which will furnish power on board. The telescope provides an angular resolution of 0.1 seconds of arc (ten times greater than that obtainable by groundbased telescopes), operating in the spectral wavelengths ranging from 115 nanometers (extreme ultraviolet)

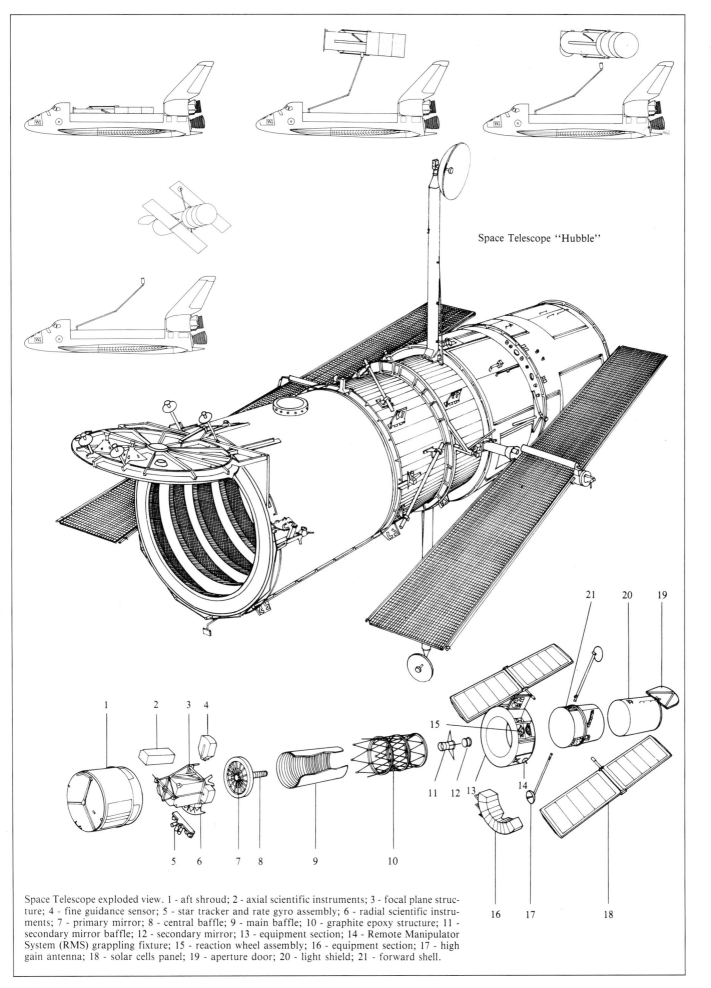

Space Telescope "Hubble"

Space Telescope exploded view. 1 - aft shroud; 2 - axial scientific instruments; 3 - focal plane structure; 4 - fine guidance sensor; 5 - star tracker and rate gyro assembly; 6 - radial scientific instruments; 7 - primary mirror; 8 - central baffle; 9 - main baffle; 10 - graphite epoxy structure; 11 - secondary mirror baffle; 12 - secondary mirror; 13 - equipment section; 14 - Remote Manipulator System (RMS) grappling fixture; 15 - reaction wheel assembly; 16 - equipment section; 17 - high gain antenna; 18 - solar cells panel; 19 - aperture door; 20 - light shield; 21 - forward shell.

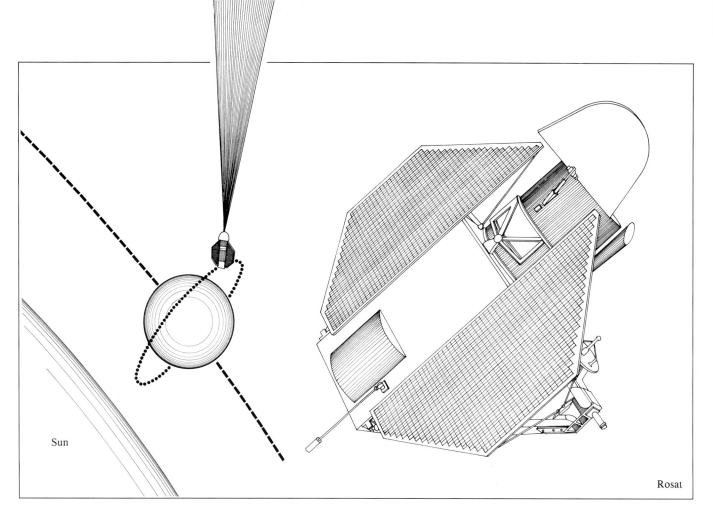

Rosat

to 1 millimeter (infrared). The optical system is being built by Perkin Elmer, and the integration of the satellite will be effected by the Lockheed Missile and Space Company. The telescope is capable of detecting objects 50 times fainter than those observed from the Earth-based telescopes and will make it possible to study celestial objects 14 billion light years from the Earth. The minimum operational life is 15 years but the telescope will be able to remain in space even longer with guaranteed maintenance by Space Shuttle astronauts.

Launching and orbital data - The Space Telescope will be carried into orbit by the American Shuttle and placed in a circular orbit 500km (310mi) high, at an inclination of 28.8°. The launch is scheduled for 1988.

ROSAT (WEST GERMANY - 1988)

Rosat (Röntgensatellit) is a German satellite designed to be carried into orbit by the American Space Shuttle. The vehicle, including the telescope, is 4.75m (15.6ft) long, 2.25m (7.4ft) wide and 4.38m (14.4ft) high. Three panels of solar cells on one side will furnish power of 1,020 watts. The total weight is 2,570kg (5,654lb). The instrument payload consists of an X-ray telescope with a focal length of 2.4m (7.9ft) and a diameter of 0.835m (2.7ft), and a Wide Field Camera with a focal length of 0.53m (1.7ft) and a diameter of 0.58m (1.9ft), designed in Britain and to be managed by the British Scien-

tific and Engineering Research Council. The satellite will carry out general reconnaissance of faint X-rays emissions in a band of the spectrum between 6 and 120 Angstrom, and will then analyze individual sources. Prime contractor is the German Dornier company.

Launching and orbital data - Rosat is to be launched with the NASA Shuttle in 1988 and will be placed in a circular orbit at a height of 475km (295mi), inclined at 57°.

HIPPARCOS (EUROPE - 1988)

Astrometric satellite of the European Space Agency (ESA). It will weigh 1,095kg (2,409lb) at launching, 210kg (462lb) of this being taken up by scientific instruments. Hipparcos (High Precision Parallax Collecting Satellite) is being built by the industrial consortium MESH, of which the French company Matra is prime contractor. The satellite in orbit will take measurements with its Schmidt telescope of five astrometric parameters of around 100,000 stars with a precision of 2 milliseconds of arc. A second experiment called Tycho will independently handle the data of the "star mapper" associated with the telescope and will be able to catalog 400,000 stars with a precision of 0.03 seconds of arc. The primary mirror of the telescope has a diameter of 0.29m (0.95ft) and a focal length of 1.4m (4.6ft). Three panels of solar cells will provide power of 350 watts. The satellite will have a technical life of two and a half years and will relay data

to the Earth at the speed of 24 Kbit per second.

Launching and orbital data - Launching of Hipparcos is scheduled for 1988 by an European Ariane rocket. Its final position will be in geostationary equatorial orbit at longitude 12° W.

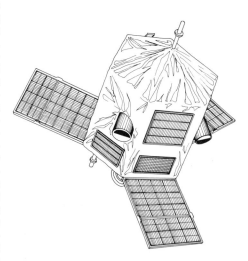

Hipparcos

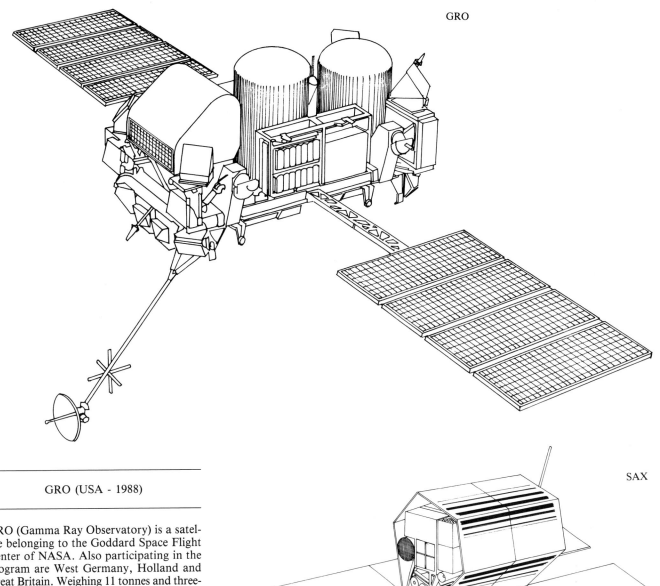

GRO (USA - 1988)

GRO (Gamma Ray Observatory) is a satellite belonging to the Goddard Space Flight Center of NASA. Also participating in the program are West Germany, Holland and Great Britain. Weighing 11 tonnes and three-axis stabilized, it will carry five instruments for surveying the sources of gamma radiation in space. The satellite is 7.6m (24.9ft) long and 3.8m (12.5ft) in diameter. The predicted operational life is two years. Prime contractor is the TRW company.

Launching and orbital data - GRO is to be launched with the Shuttle in 1988 and placed in a high circular orbit of 500km (310mi).

EUVE (USA - 1988)

EUVE (Extreme Ultraviolet Explorer) is being built to compile a map of the sky with the sources of radiation in the extreme ultraviolet range. The project is the work of the JPL company of Pasadena, and the instruments will be supplied by the University of California in Berkeley. EUVE will use four ultraviolet telescopes 0.4m (1.3ft) in diameter, and one spectrometer. The overall payload will weigh 498kg (1,095lb).

Launching and orbital data - EUVE will be carried into space with Shuttle and will be placed in a circular orbit at a height of 544km (338mi).

SAX (ITALY - 1989)

Italian satellite for studying hard X-rays in the 0.1-200 KeV wavelength emanating from within and from outside our galaxy. SAX (Satellite for X-ray Astronomy) will have the shape of a hexagonal prism 1.9m (6.2ft) wide and 2.2m (7.2ft) high. Weight at launching will be 900kg (1,980lb), 320kg (704lb) of which constitute the instruments. Two panels of solar cells each 6.6m (21.6ft) in length will provide the necessary power. Prime contractor is the Aeritalia company. Holland is also participating in the program.

Launching and orbital data - SAX will be taken into orbit by the American Shuttle in

1989 and then boosted into an elliptical orbit with an apogee of 600km (373mi), inclined at 11° to the equator, by means of the Iris upper stage. The apogee motor will subsequently send the vehicle into circular orbit.

ISO (EUROPE - 1992)

The ISO (Infrared Space Observatory) is an European Space Agency satellite for observing the sky in the distant infrared (0.8-200 microns), and designed to carry out a spectroscopic survey of galactic and extragalactic sources. The satellite's principal instrument is a telescope of 0.6m (1.97ft) diameter, criogenically cooled with helium and liquid hydrogen. The satellite is intended to

ISO

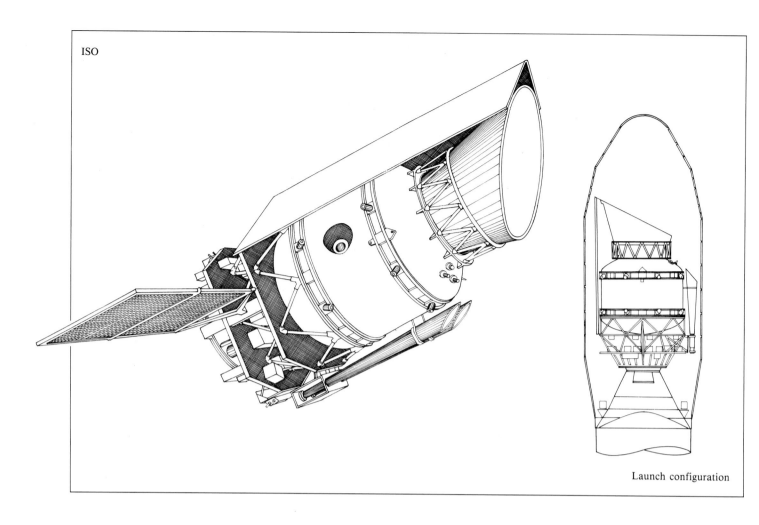

Launch configuration

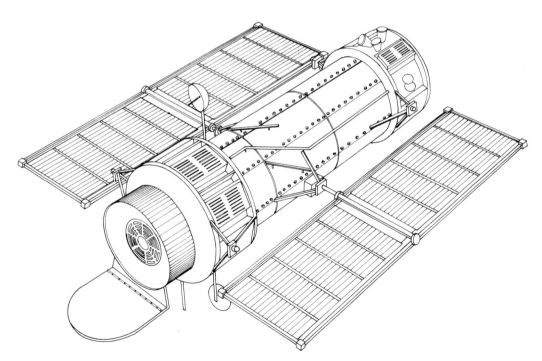

AXAF

174

function in orbit for about one and a half to two years. The instruments situated in the focal plane will operate at a temperature of 8° Kelvin. ISO, cylindrical in form, will be three-axis stabilized and will weigh 2,022 kg (4,448lb).

Launching and orbital data - ISO will be launched in 1992 from the test site in French Guiana by an Ariane rocket, and sent into an elliptical orbit with a perigee of 2.000km (1,243mi), an apogee of 39,000km (24,230mi), inclined at 5° to the equator.

AXAF (USA - 1993)

AXAF (Advanced X-ray Astrophysics Facility) will study sources of X-rays inside and outside our galaxy. The AXAF telescope will have an aperture of 1.2m (3.9ft) and a focal length of 10m (32.8ft). The resolution will be around 0.5 seconds of arc, and it will be possible to detect sources with energy of 0.1-9 KeV. AXAF will be cylindrical in shape, with a length of 14m (45.9ft) and a diameter of 4.2m (13.8ft). The weight will be 10 tonnes.

Launching and orbital data - AXAF will be carried into orbit by the NASA Shuttle in 1993 and will be placed in a circular orbit at a height of 520km (323mi), and with an inclination of 28.5°.

AUTOMATIC PLATFORMS

The orbital platforms, namely structures having onboard instruments for scientific and technological researches, were made possible after the Space Shuttle's advent.

Equipped with attitude control and telecommunications systems, they are conveyed and put into orbit by the Shuttle for as many months as necessary to perform their activity, then collected and brought back by the Shuttle during its next mission. Later on they can be conveyed again to space equipped with different instruments.

The first platform was constructed by West Germany and tested in orbit in 1983.

SPAS-01 (WEST GERMANY - 1983)

SPAS (Shuttle Pallet Satellite) was the first reusable automatic platform carried into space and then recovered by the American Shuttle. The platform was made of tubes of carbon fiber connected to titanium elements, and was designed and built by the German

MBB company. It weighed 1,500kg (932lb), 900kg (559lb) of which were taken up by the payload of scientific instruments; the length was 4.8m (15.7ft), the width 1.5m (4.9ft) and the height 4.4m (14.4ft). Three-axis stabilized, it was equipped with a propellant system for cold gas (nitrogen) attitude control. Working power was furnished by silver-zinc batteries. During the first mission there were experiments in microgravity, remote

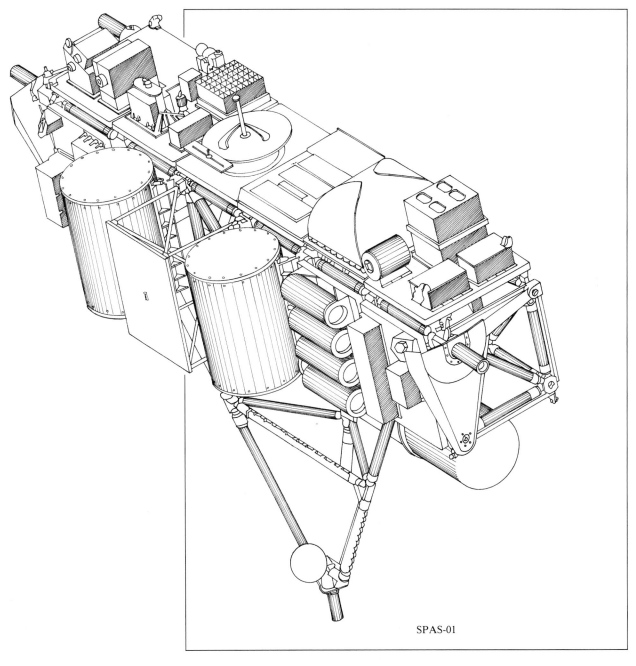

SPAS-01

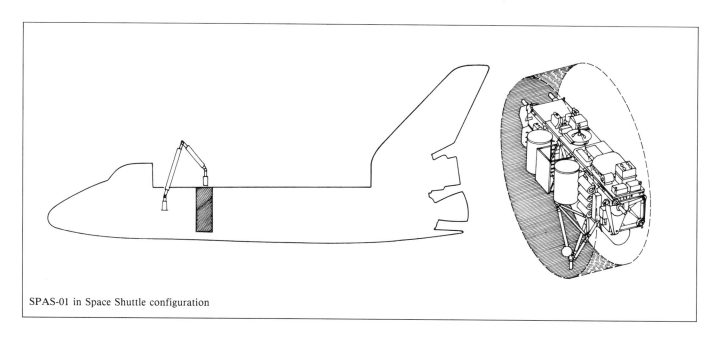

SPAS-01 in Space Shuttle configuration

sensing and the control of environmental pollution with eight types of instrument. The platform can be released in space for different lengths of time according to need, and then brought back to Earth to be prepared for another mission.

Launching and orbital data - SPAS-01 carried out its first free flight of nine and a half hours during the seventh Shuttle mission with the orbiter *Challenger* which began on June 18, 1983. The orbit was 297km (185mi), inclination 28°.

LDEF-1 (USA-1984)

LDEF (Long Duration Exposure Facility) was a passive-type platform carried into orbit by the Shuttle, released in space for a period of about one year and then brought back again to Earth by the Shuttle itself. It was a 12-faceted aluminum cylinder 9.14m (30ft) long and 4.27m (14ft) in diameter. The weight, when empty, was 3,360kg (7,392lb). It could carry experiments which required

long exposure in space. Developed by the Langley Research Center, and gravity-stabilized in orbit, LDEF-1 weighed 9,695kg (6,023mi) and carried 57 experiments on board.

Launching and orbital data - LDEF-1 was carried into space by the spacecraft Challenger during the STS 41-C mission begun on April 6, 1984. Its circular orbit was at a height of 460km (286mi), inclined at 28.5°.

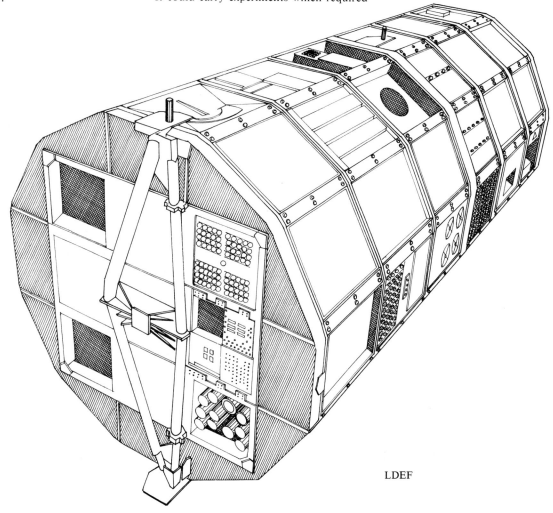

LDEF

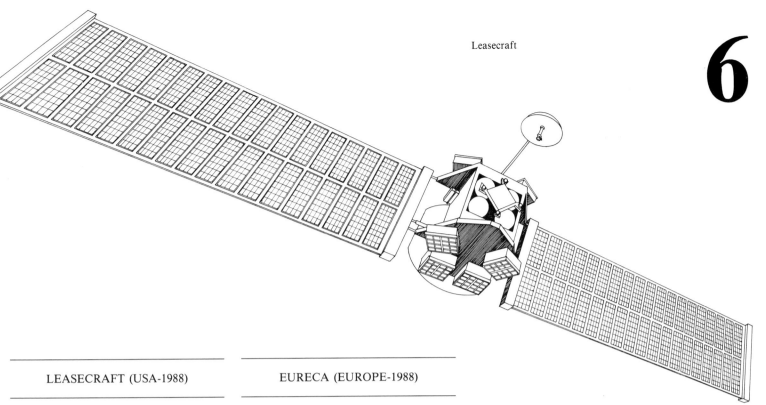

Leasecraft

LEASECRAFT (USA-1988)

Reusable automatic platform built by Fairchild Industries following an agreement with NASA (Joint Endeavor Agreement). The platform is 4.6m (15.1ft) long, 2,9m (9.5ft) wide and 4.6m (15.1ft) high; and it will be equipped with systems of power, propulsion, attitude control, communications, data handling and others necessary for carrying out its research functions, among its payload of instruments. Its work can be extended for ten years. Support during the missions of Leasecraft, carried into space by the Shuttle, will come from the Goddard Space Flight Center of NASA. Every six months the Shuttle will recover from the platform the materials produced.

EURECA (EUROPE-1988)

Automatic reusable platform made by the European Space Agency (ESA), weighing 4,000kg (8,800lb), of which 1,000kg (2,200lb) is taken up by the payload of instruments. The platform is 2.45m (8ft) wide, 4m (13.1ft) long. Two panels of solar cells with an area of 90 m² (968.7sq ft), furnish power of 5.4 kilowatts. The weight is 3.5 tonnes, of which 1t is taken up by the payload. The main group of experiments to be carried out in the first mission concerns the making of materials, and life science in conditions of microgravity. Prime contractor is the German MBB/Erno company.

Launching and orbital data - Eureca's first

mission is planned for 1988. It will be carried into space with the American Shuttle and from that height will go into its work orbit at an altitude of 500km (311mi), inclined at 28°, by means of its own system of propulsion. After a six months' stay in space it will be brought back to Earth by the Shuttle.

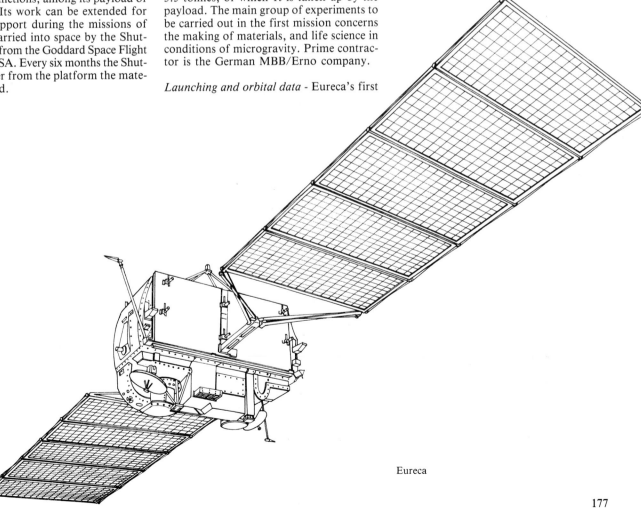

Eureca

Technological satellites

Group of satellites launched by many nations for testing new forms of space technology which can then be applied to satellites operating in various sectors. Some of them carry secondary instruments for scientific experiments. In this group are also the two American Sert spacecraft which have carried out tests on ionic propellants.

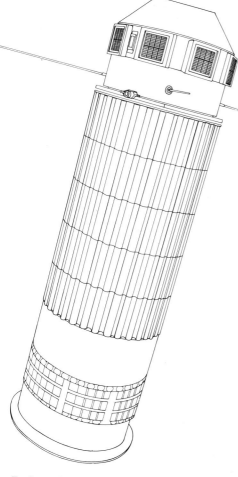

Explorer-13

Satellite	First launch	Perigee × apogee/inclination degree km (mi)	Nation
Explorer-13	8/25/1961	125x1,164 (78x723)/37°	USA
TRS	9/17/1962	204x668 (127x415)/81°	USA
Explorer-16	12/16/1962	750x1,181 (466x734)/52°	USA
Sert-1	7/1964	sub-orbital flight	USA
A-1/Asterix	11/26/1965	527x1,808 (327x1,123)/34°	France
Wresat	11/29/1967	193x1,259 (120x782)/83°	Australia
TTS	12/13/1967	287x490 (178x304)/32°	USA
Sert-2	2/4/1970	997x1,003 (620x623)/99°	USA
Ohsumi	2/11/1970	350x5,140 (217x3,194)/31°	Japan
China-1	4/24/1970	441x2,386 (274x1,483)/68°	China
Tansei-1	2/16/1971	990x1,110 (615x690)/30°	Japan

Satellite	First launch	Perigee × apogee/inclination degree km (mi)	Nation
X-4 Prospero	10/28/1971	547x1,582 (340x983)/82°	GB
SRET-1	4/4/1972	458x39,250 (285x24,390)/65°	USA
Explorer-46	8/13/1972	492x811 (306x504)/37°	USA
Tansei-2	2/16/1974	290x3,240 (180x2,013)/31°	Japan
X-3 Miranda	3/9/1974	704x916 (437x569)/97°	GB
SRET-2	6/5/1975	513x40,825 (319x25,369)/62°	USA
ETS-1/Kiku	9/9/1975	980x1,100 (609x684)/47°	Japan
Intercosmos-15	6/19/1976	484x518 (301x322)/74°	USSR
Tansei-3	2/19/1977	790x3,810 (491x2,368)/66°	Japan
Scatha	1/30/1979	185x43,905 (115x27,283)/27°	USA
Tansei-4	2/17/1980	520x610 (323x379)/39°	Japan
Rohini/RS-D1	7/18/1980	305x919 (190x571)/82°	India

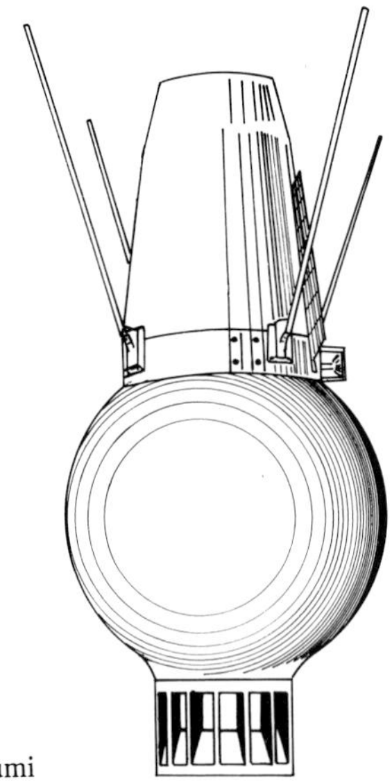

Ohsumi

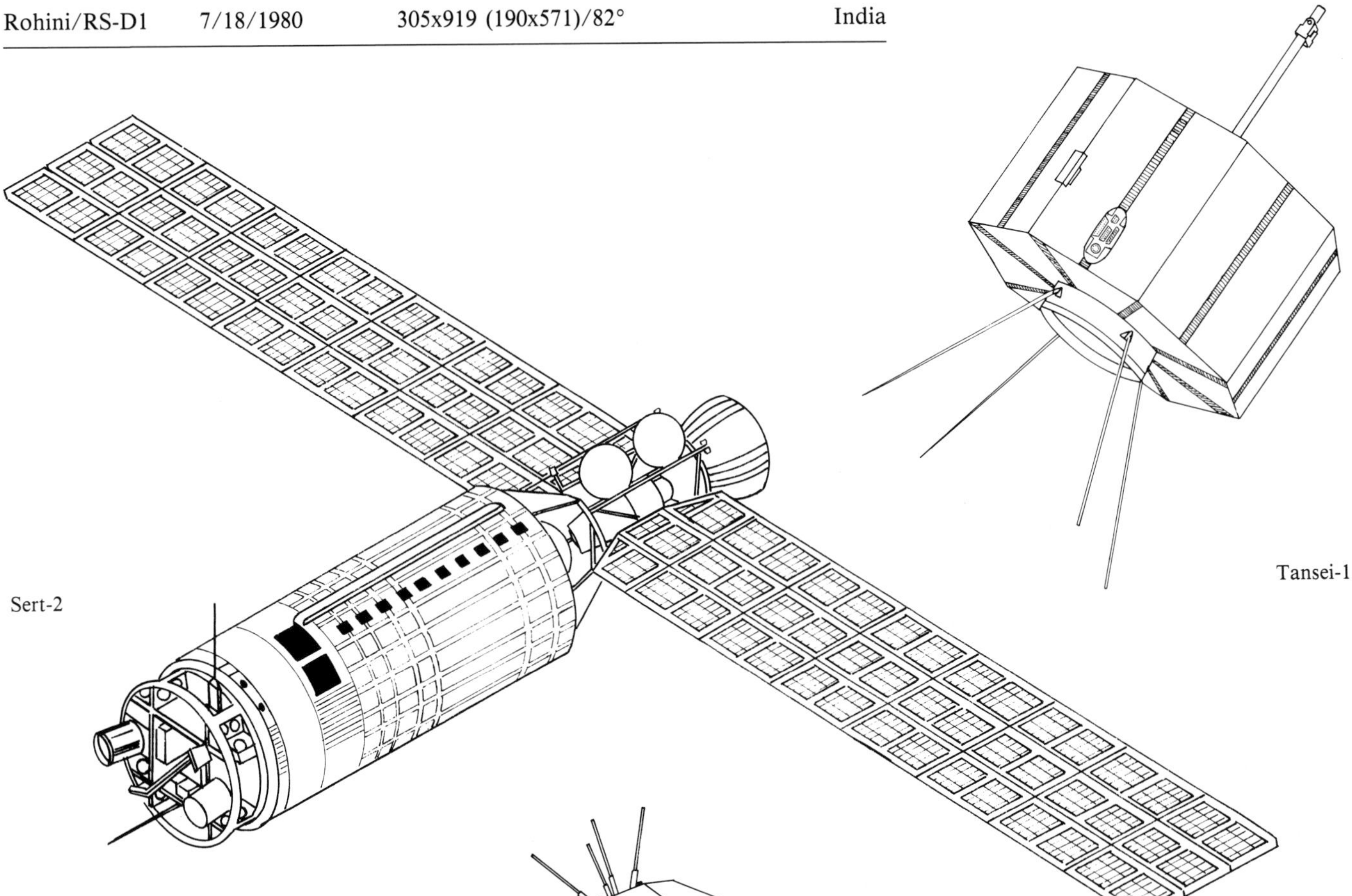

Tansei-1

Sert-2

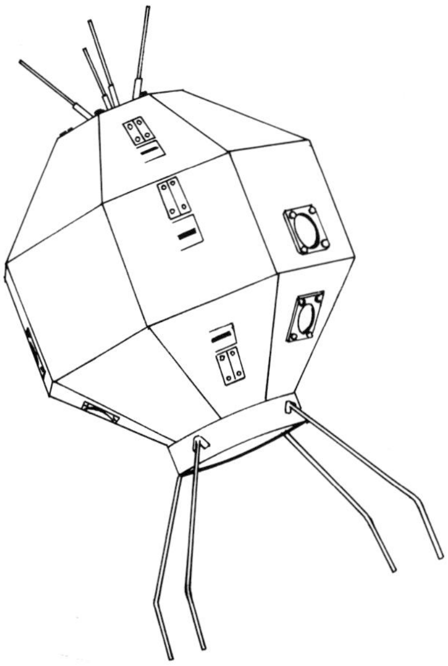

Tansei-2

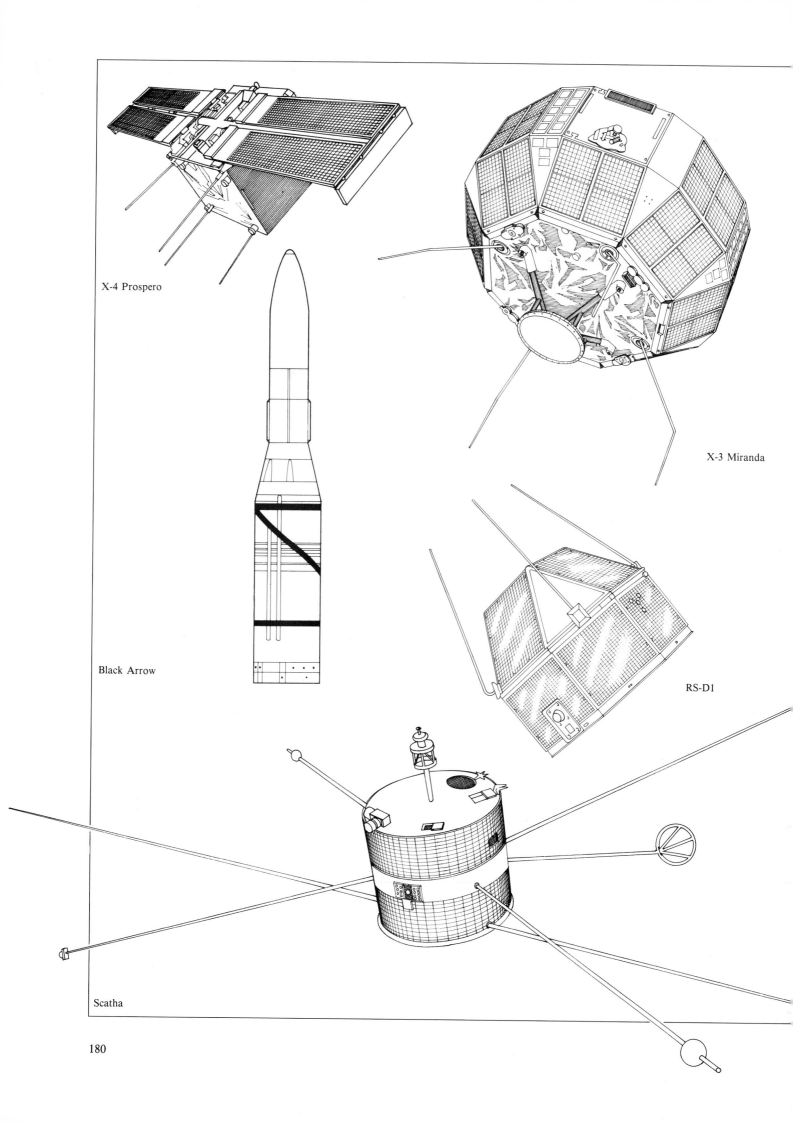

X-4 Prospero

X-3 Miranda

Black Arrow

RS-D1

Scatha

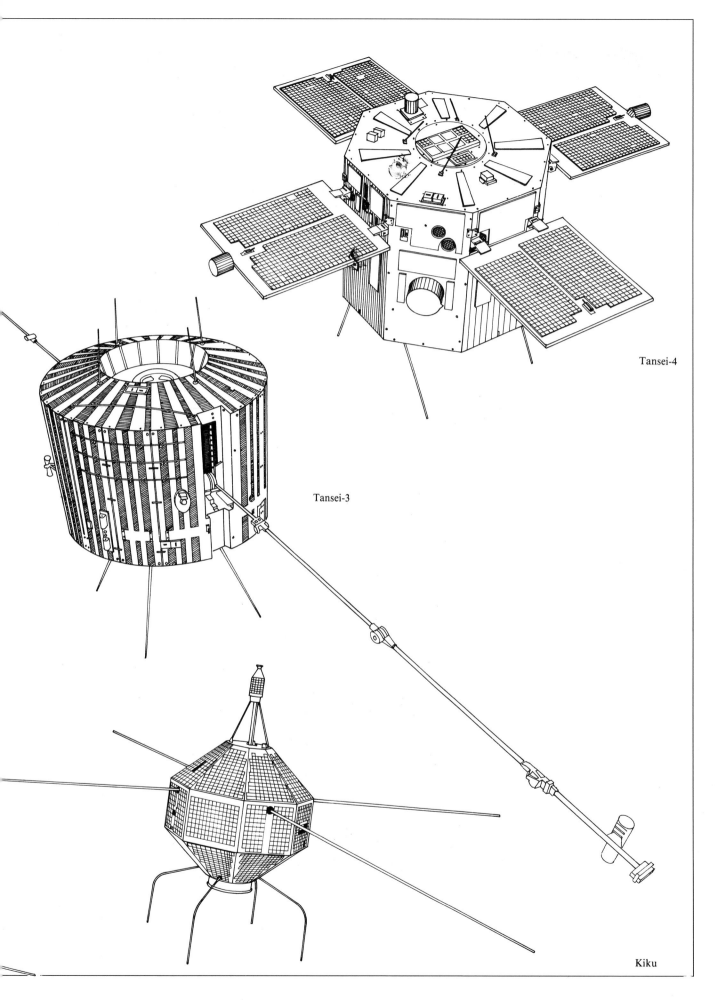

7

Tansei-4

Tansei-3

Kiku

PHOTOGRAPHIC
APPENDIX

EARTH RESOURCES SATELLITES

Above and below, the SPOT's HRV (High Resolution Visible) instrument. On the right, one image of the SPOT satellite. Below, right, Landsat-3 M SS. A technician examines the instrument's aperture. (Photo CNES; ESA; Matra)

Above, the American SMS-1, Synchronous Meteorological satellite.

Above, Meteosat in the launch configuration with the Indian Apple satellite.

Left, the "Fragment" system of the Soviet Meteor-Priroda satellite. (Photo Novosti)

Opposite. Above, Meteosat and Japanese GMS-2; below, Insat, the Indian domestic telecommunications and meteorological satellite. (Photo Selenia Spazio)

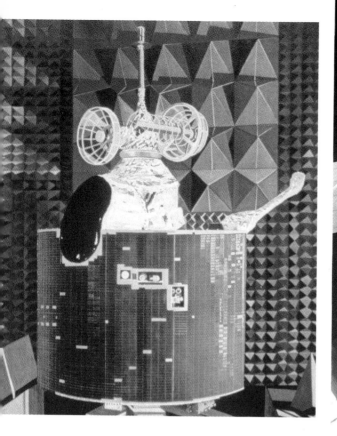

Above, the American GOES; right, the Soviet Meteor. (Photo Selenia Spazio; Novosti)

NAVIGATIONAL SATELLITES

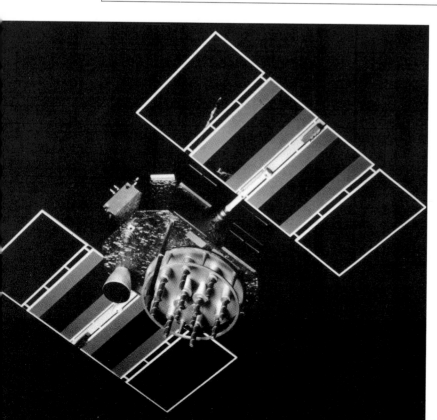

Left and above, the Navstar Block-2 satellite and the assembly line in Seal Beach, California. (Photo Rockwell International)

TELECOMMUNICATIONS SATELLITES

Above and right, Marecs-A and -B during tests in Toulouse, France. Below, TDF-1 in Aerospatiale's cleaned room in Cannes, France. (Photo ESA; Aerospatiale)

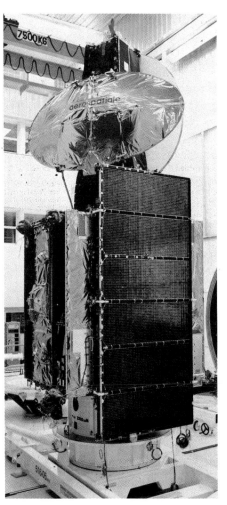

Left: SBS (above) and Anik (below); both satellites were loaded in the cargo bay (above) of the *Columbia* Space Shuttle. (Photo NASA)

China's STW-1, geosynchronous orbit communications satellite.

Opposite. The telecommunications payload (above) and the structure model of the Olympus satellite (below) during the antenna coupling tests. (Photo Selenia Spazio)

Above and right, the American TDRS-1. Below, RCA Satcom and the Japanese CS-2. (Photo NASA)

The Canadian Isis-2 satellite.

◄ Telecom-1 during preparation for launch at the Guiana Space Center in Kourou. (Photo ESA)

The Italian Sirio satellite.

The Dial satellite, a cooperation France-West Germany.

Above and right, the Soviet Molniya-1. (Photo Novosti)

Above, ATS-4 satellite. (Photo NASA). Right and below, Brasilsat undergoes final preparation for space simulation testing. (Department of Communications, Canada)

Opposite. Above, the second flight model of Arabsat in Aerospatiale's center. (Photo Aerospatiale). Below, OTS' antennae and Spacenet-1 satellite.

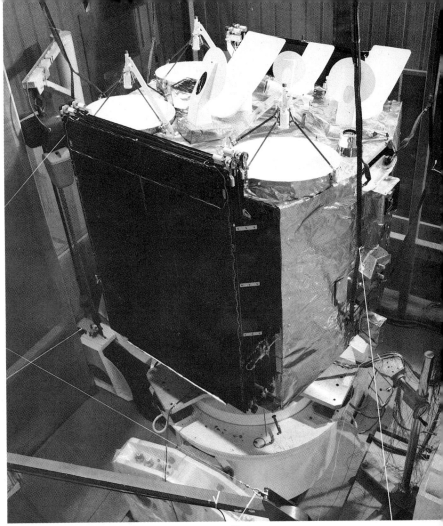

In this page. ECS (European Communications Satellite) during vibration (right) and solar array deployment (below) tests in Matra's integration chamber in Toulouse, France. Above, a particular of the antennae. (Photo ESA)

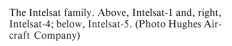

The Intelsat family. Above, Intelsat-1 and, right, Intelsat-4; below, Intelsat-5. (Photo Hughes Aircraft Company)

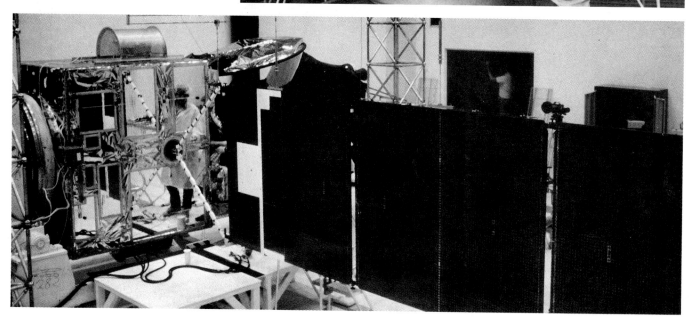

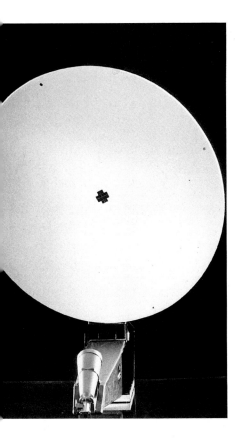

Above and below, the Intelsat-6 and Intelsat-5 antennae; right, Intelsat-5. (Photo Selenia Spazio; Ford Aerospace)

SCIENTIFIC
SATELLITES

Above, the Italian San Marco D/L; right, the British UK-3; below, the Soviet Cosmos-1514.

Above, Explorer-1 holded up by William H. Pickering, James van Allen and Wernher von Braun.

Left, Explorer-12 and, below, ISEE-2 in the vacuum chamber at ESTEC in Noordwijk.

Opposite. Esro-IV and TD-1A. (Photo ESA)

Above, left, IUE; above, right, COS-B. Right, Exosat in the vacuum chamber at ESTEC. (Photo ESA)

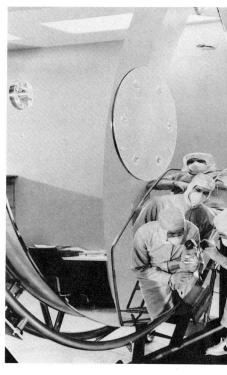

The Space Telescope (above, left), its Faint Object Camera (left, below), and mirror (above).

The Swedish Viking satellite during thermal balance tests.

INTO SPACE

The first repair operation in orbit. Astronaut George D. Nelson (right) prepares to dock with the malfunctioning Solar Maximum Mission satellite in April 1984. (Photo Martin Marietta) Below, right, James van Hoften uses his manned maneuvering unit to hover in the cargo bay after retrieval of the SMM satellite. (Photo Rockwell International)

Below, Bruce McCandless with the manned maneuvering unit used for the first time on mission 41-B. (Photo McDonnell Douglas)

The first space salvage mission. Above, astronauts Dale A. Gardner and Joseph P. Allen during the retrieval of the Westar-6 and Palapa-B2 satellites in Space Shuttle mission 51-A in November 1984 (Photo NASA). Right, Gardner turns his manned maneuvering unit into position to capture and stabilize the Westar-6 satellite. (Photo Martin Marietta)

Opposite. The launch sequency of the Anik-C2 satellite during Shuttle mission STS-7.

LAUNCH CENTERS

Opposite. Above, the French launch center of Kourou, in French Guiana; below, Cape Canaveral, in Florida.

Above, Kourou; right, the Japanese Tanegashima Space Center; below the Italian Santa Rita control platform, in the Indian Ocean.

Above, the transportation of a rocket-carrier to the launch site at Baikonur, in USSR.

Letf, Shuang Cheng Tse, in central China, 1,600 km West of Peking.

General index

Index by country

Bibliography

General
index

(Numbers in italics refer to illustrations)

210

41, 63, 64, 68, 109, 111, 112, 113, 114, 116,
118, 142, 146, 147, 150, 153, 158, 164, 169, 170
Vanguard, 108, *108*, 138, 157
— 1, 138, *138*
— 2, 108, *108*
— 3, 157, *157*
Van Hoften, James, *203*
VAS (Visible Infrared Spin-Scan Radiometer Atmospheric Sounder), 33
Vega, 170
VELA, 103, *103*
Venus, 170
Vertical Temperature Profile Radiometer (VTPR), 27
Very High Resolution Radiometer (VHRR), 27, 85
VHRR (Very High Resolution Radiometer), 27, 85
Viking, 16, 156, *156, 202*
Visible and Near-Infrared Radiometer (VNIR), 19
Visible and Thermal Infrared Radiometer (VTIR), 18
Visible Infrared Spin-Scan Radiometer (VISSR), 28, 30, 33
Visible Infrared Spin-Scan Radiometer Atmospheric Sounder (VAS), 33
VISSR (Visible Infrared Spin-Scan Radiometer), 28, 30, 33
VNIR (Visible and Near-Infrared Radiometer), 19
von Braun, Werner, 137, *199*
von Hoften, James, 168
VTIR (Visible and Thermal Infrared Radiometer), 18
VTPR (Vertical Temperature Profile Radiometer), 27

W

Wallops Island, 25, 28, 110, 112, 167
Weather Facsimile (WEFAX), 28, 30
WEFAX (Weather Facsimile), 28, 30
Westar, *83*
— 1, 69, *69*
— 2, 69
— 3, 69
— 4, 82, 83
— 5, 83
— 6, 83, *205*
Whitecloud (SSU), 106
Wide Field/Planetary Camera, 170, 172
Wika/Dial, 147, *147, 192*
WMO (World Meteorological Organization), 22, 23, 30
World Meteorological Centers, 22
World Meteorological Organization (WMO), 22, 23, 30
Wresat, 178

X

X-3 Miranda, 179, *180*
X-4 Prospero, 179, *180*
Xichang, 90

Y

Yuri
— /BS (Broadcasting Satellite), 88
— /BSE (Broadcasting Satellite Experiment), 78, *78*, 88
— 2A/BS-2A, 88, *88*

Z

Zimenski Observatory, 63

Index by country

(Numbers in italics refer to illustrations)

Arab Countries

— Arabsat (1985), 60, 91, 92, *93*, 94, *194*

Australia

— Aussat (1985), 94, *94*
— Wresat (1967), 178

Brazil

— Brasilsat-1 (1985), 91, *91*, 94, *193*

Canada

— Alouette-1 (1962), 64, *64*, 140
— CTS-Hermes (1976), 72, *72*, 73
— Isis-1/-2 (1969), 68, *68*, 146, *191*
— Radarsat (1991), *20*, 21
— Telesat/Anik (1972), 69, *69*, *188*
— Telesat-4/Anik-B (1978), 78, *78*, 79
— Telesat-5/Anik-D1 (1982), 83
— Telesat-6/Anik-C3 (1982), 83, 84

China

— China-1 (1970), 178
— China-2 (1971), 115
— China-3 (1975), 104
— China-9 (1981), 112
— China-10/11 (1981), 112, 154
— STW/China (1984), 90, *90*

Europe

— COS-B (1975), 165, *165*, 166, *201*
— ECS-1 (1983), *62*, 85, *85*, 86, *195*
— Esro (1968), 145, *145, 200*
— Eureca (1988), 177, *177*
— Exosat (1983), 169, *169*
— Geos-1/-2 (1977), 152, *152*
— HEOS (1968), 144, *144*
— Hipparcos (1988), 172, *172*
— ISO (1992), 173, 174, *174*
— Meteosat (1977), 29, *29*, 30, *30, 31*, 82, *184, 185*
— Olympus (1988), 97, *97*, 98, *189*
— OTS (1978), 76, *76*, 77, 85, *195*
— TD-1A (1972), 164, *164, 200*

ESA-Europe

— ERS-1 (1989), 18, *18*, 19, *19*

France

— A-1 Asterix (1965), 178
— D-1A Diapason (1966), 114, *114*, 115
— D-1C/-D Diademe (1967), 115
— D2-A Tournesol/D2-B Aura (1971), 163, *163*
— D-5A Pollux/D-5B Castor (1975), 116, *117*
— EOLE FR-2 (1971), 28, *28*
— FR-1 (1965), 144, *144*
— Peole (1970), 115, *115*
— Signe-3 (1977), 167, *167*
— SPOT-1 (1986), 16, *17*, 156, *156, 193*
— Starlette (1975), 115, *115*
— Telecom-1 (1984), 88, *191*

France/West Germany

— Dial/Wika (1970), 147, *147, 192*
— Symphonie (1974), 71, *71*
— TDF-1/TV-SAT-1 (1987), *94*, 95, 96, *187*

Great Britain

— Ariel-1/UK-1 (1962), 140, *140*
— Ariel-2 & -3/UK-2 & -3 (1964), 110, *110*, 111, *198*

218

Bibliography

Giovanni Caprara, *Il libro dei voli spaziali* - Vallardi, Milan 1984

U.S.Congress House. Committee on Science and Technology. *United States Civilian Space Programs 1958-1978* - Volume I - Washington, D.C.- U.S. Government Printing Office 1981

U.S.Congress House. Committee on Science and Technology. *United States Civilian Space Programs - Applications Satellites* - Volume II - Washington, D.C.-U.S. Government Printing Office 1983

U.S.Congress House. Committee on Science and Technology. *Space Activities of the United States, Soviet Union, and other Launching Countries/Organizations 1957-1981* - Washington, D.C.-U.S. Government Printing Office 1982

U.S.Congress House. Committee on Commerce, Science and Transportation. *Soviet Space Programs 1976-1980 - Manned Space Programs and Space Life Sciences* - Washington, D.C.-U.S. Government Printing Office 1984

U.S.Congress House. Committee on Aeronautical and Space Science. *Soviet Space Programs 1971-75* - Washington, D.C. - U.S. Government Printing Office 1976

Royal Aircraft Establishment, Farnborough, England - *The R.A.E. Table of Earth Satellites 1957-1982* - Macmillan Reference Books

Bill Yenne, *U.S. Encyclopedia of U.S. Spacecraft* - Exeter Books, New York, 1985

Reginald Turnill, *Jane's Spaceflight Directory* - Jane's

V.P. Glouchko, *Encyclopédie soviétique de l'astronautique mondiale* - Editions Mir, Moscou 1971

Rebrov, Kozyrev, Denissenko, *URSS-France exploration de l'espace* - Editions du Progrès, Moscou 1983

C. Richard Whelan, *Guide to Military Space Programs* - Pasha Publications Inc. 1984

W.L. Pritchard, J.J. Harford, *China Space Report* - AIAA, New York, 1980

U.S.Congress, Office of Technology Assessment - *U.S.-Soviet Cooperations in Space* - U.S. Government Printing Office, Washington, 1985

J. Cornell, P. Gorenstein, *Astronomy from Space- Sputnik to Space Telescope* - The MIT Press, 1983

W.Tucker, *The Star Spitters* - NASA 1984

W.Tucker, R.Giacconi, *The X-Ray Universe* - Harvard University Press, 1985

B. French, S. Maran, *A Meeting with the Universe* - NASA, 1981

R.S. Lewis, *Space Exploration* - Salamander Books, London 1983

K. Gatland, *Space Technology* - Salamander Books, London 1981

D. Baker, *The Shape of Wars to Come* - Hamlyn Paperbacks, 1982

Luigi Napolitano, *Space 2000* - AIAA, New York 1982

TRW *Space Log,* 1957-1982/1982-1983/1984-1985

OCDE *The Space Industry* Paris, 1985

and besides: papers of NASA, ESA, ISAS, NASDA, IAF, NOVOSTI, ISRO, INTELSAT, COMSAT, EUTELSAT, EOS and papers of aerospace industries of all world